formula 1
racing

acknowledgments

I should like to express my gratitude to Gérard Crombac, Editor-in-Chief of Sport Auto. *I am full of admiration for his exemplary, precise, factual race reports, which have been of invaluable assistance to me. I am equally indebted to Ami Guichard, Director of the incomparable* Année Automobile. *He allowed me to make a thorough search of his photographic archives, to borrow extensively from them . . . and to leave them in a mess!*

J.R.

JOSÉ ROSINSKI

formula 1
racing

THE MODERN ERA

MADISON SQUARE PRESS ®

Grosset & Dunlap
Publishers
New York

A MADISON SQUARE PRESS BOOK®

First published in the United States in 1974
by Grosset & Dunlap, 51 Madison Avenue,
New York 10010

Originally published and © 1972 by
Editions Denoël, Paris, France

Translated from the original French by Maureen Argyle

Photographs chosen by J.P. Thibault

Published and © English Language edition 1973
by Guinness Superlatives Limited

Library of Congress catalog card no.: 73-20242

ISBN 0-448-11562-X

Printed by Pollina, France

contents

introduction

the world of Formula 1   10

what is Formula 1 ?   12

modern Formula 1   18

English-style racing   20

the turning-point: 1959—60   23

the advent of Cooper-Climax and Jack Brabham 1959   24

1960   31

the 1500 Formula: 1961—65   40

Ferrari versus... Stirling Moss 1961   42

B.R.M. at last... one Hill succeeds another 1962   55

the coronation of Jim Clark 1963   64

a cliff-hanger championship 1964   72

Clark and Lotus unbeatable 1965   85

the 3-litre Formula: the return to power   100

Brabham's return to success 1966   102

enter Ford—but Brabham's success continues 1967   116

the death of Clark. But, with Graham Hill,

Ford and Lotus triumph 1968   138

Stewart and Matra-Ford: new wave victories 1969   165

the tragic success of Jochen Rindt 1970   193

Stewart in the style of Clark 1971   216

the rise of Emerson Fittipaldi 1972   240

Stewart's final triumph 1973   241

epilogue   242

introduction

the w

Formula 1 is the purest, the most exciting and the highest form of modern motor racing, but is it really the most suitable mode of expression for all that is best in the sport? This is a question that needs to be asked. After all, the very word "formula" implies a limitation of some sort, yet freedom is essential if a creative activity like design or an artistic pursuit like driving is to come to full flower. Once you put a rigid framework round the spirit of genius, you confine and restrict it and force it to materialize as something less than it might be: the possibility of perfection recedes.

There are those who advocate a free formula—a silly expression but part of the sporting technical jargon —whereby everyone could design and build the fastest possible four-wheeled device without any terms of reference at all so that, depending on his prejudices and financial and technical resources, every constructor would be at liberty to produce what he considered to be the ideal car—light and agile or heavy and powerful. Theoretically this is possible and it is reasonable in practical terms because a good racing car involves a number of design conflicts which must be reconciled so that the final result is a more or less successful compromise between them. In the course of a Grand Prix season the cars perform on a series of very different circuits ranging from the tight and twisting corners at Monaco which favor maneuvrability, through all the intermediate stages to the straight,

orld of formula 1

open stretches at Monza where speed is the overriding consideration. So, for example, a car with a very large capacity engine of necessity bulkier and heavier than a smaller-engined car, if only because of the extra fuel it has to carry, would probably be unbeatable on the Italian circuit but extremely vulnerable at Monaco. Because of situations like this a free formula would lead to an entirely open competition, a variety of technical approaches, remarkable performances and extraordinary reversals of fortune.

This is undeniable. However, it would also deprive racing of any coherence and diminish the impact of the driver's efforts. It would also lead to less close competition between the drivers and therefore to less spectacular racing than is possible with a capacity-based formula like Formula 1. At this level, motor sport is a matter of such complexity that a compromise between its twin poles, its two active partners—the man and the machine—is essential; there must be a balance between them so that the one cannot upstage the other and spoil the play. Ideally, any result they achieve together should always be the sum of two exactly equal performances. Here, as elsewhere, the path of history is clearly marked. In the early days the public reserved their greatest enthusiasm for the machinery, and regarded races as competitions between cars in which men played relatively minor roles. Then the time came when interest in Grands

Prix was stimulated as much by the competition between the drivers as by the rivalry between the marques. Now there are strong indications that the future will see today's sporting spectacle reduced to a mere spectacle and the car to being simply the champion's means of self-expression—this has already happened in the relationship between the motorcyclist and his machine.

Obviously such a development could be thwarted if we were to abandon the formula based on engine capacity, but equally obviously this formula provides what the paying public want, and without their support motor racing at this highly technical (or in other words, expensive) level would cease to exist. Freedom in this sphere would in effect lead straight back to machine-dominated racing. Thus the sport would be forced into an unpopular channel and the spectators deprived of those elbow-to-elbow struggles between drivers at the wheel of cars which, from the strictly technical point of view, are too uniform in appearance and performance but which, because they are so well matched, make for exciting racing. Close competition is a must and nothing is more conducive to this than putting the drivers on an equal—or nearly equal—mechanical footing.

Moreover, the fact that the constructors also have equality thrust upon them in the shape of a very closely defined formula, a formula which nevertheless leaves enough scope for the exercise of superior individual talent, makes

sound sense from the economic point of view. Freedom is a risky business: a serious miscalculation could involve the sort of financial catastrophe that would overwhelm most of the specialist constructors in whose hands the fate of motor racing rests at the moment.

For all these reasons the principle of a formula based on engine capacity is a valuable compromise even if it is not the complete answer—whether the outcome is interesting or dull depends to a great extent on the chosen capacity limit. There have been three distinct periods in the life of modern Formula 1 (from 1959 to the present day) corresponding to the three capacity limits which have been in force during this time and they have all been declared more or less successful.

This book does not pretend to be a detailed history of thirteen seasons of Formula 1 racing. It is merely an account of them. Perhaps it will not appeal to the purists because it is too general, too non-technical, while for the hero-worshippers there are too many facts and not enough tales of heroism. The enthusiasts will be irritated by repetition and the newcomers frustrated by gaps. In short, the critics will swoop down from all sides. So, why write the book and for whom? Well, for all those who love motor racing and can derive pleasure from a perhaps superficial but sincere and, I hope, lively picture of a fascinating world: the world of Formula 1.

what is formula 1?

A Formula 1 car is fundamentally a single-seater intended to run in Grands Prix, and Formula 1 itself is a relatively recent creation, being instituted in 1950 by the Commission Sportive Internationale (C.S.I.), the committee which controls motor sport on behalf of the Fédération Internationale de l'Automobile (F.I.A.). The F.I.A. is the central organization which brings together national motor clubs and federations from all over the world.

Grands Prix are speed events and, like the single-seater cars that run in them, have existed much longer than Formula 1. Broadly speaking there have always been two types of racing: one devoted to speed above all and the other also demanding qualities of endurance from both man and machine. Speed and stamina were undoubtedly essential for the inter-city road races which were held in the early days, events like the Paris–Bordeaux–Paris, the Paris–Vienna and the Paris–Madrid, but the exploration of speed pure and simple was conducted at that time by means of record attempts. These were once very popular, but now they have fallen out of favor probably because the realm of speed has moved from the ground to the air where the values are absolute and the effects far more spectacular. After all, even a commercial aeroplane has now broken the sound barrier while the car has still to approach this limit.

As far as the car is concerned, speed has assumed a much more complex significance. The circuits on which the racing car performs embody various ordinary road conditions so that braking, cornering and acceleration are just as important as the ability to reach the highest possible speed in a straight line. As traffic on the open road increased so open-road racing tended to disappear and closed-circuit racing began to take over. These circuits, though different in layout, are designed on the whole to simulate over a limited course the features that were once encountered in a road race.

The need for specialization grew with the development of motor sport. Right up to the Second World War it was not uncommon to see the same car take part in a Grand Prix and then in a long-distance race; all that was required for the latter was a set of mud-guards and some lights. A much more rigid classification replaced such methods, and over the years this classification had been more closely defined and split up into various categories with the result that there are now three international classes for single-seaters—Formulas 1, 2 and 3—all intended for high-speed racing. In fact these cars are not allowed to compete in long-distance events which are the province of two-seater machines called variously "sports" or "prototypes" depending on the period and the current regulations.

The World Championship of Drivers came into being at the same time as Formula 1 and is contested by drivers racing Formula 1 machines. It is an annual championship fought out over a variable number of Grands Prix which feature on a list drawn up by the C.S.I. In principle every organizing country has the right to submit one event annually for inclusion in this calendar which usually means that there are about a dozen Grands Prix counting towards the Championship, all restricted to Formula 1. After each event a certain number of points are awarded to the drivers depending on their final position—the winner gets 9 points, the second man 6, third 4, fourth 3, fifth 2 and sixth 1. At the end of the season the drivers are allowed to retain their best scores, the number retained being based on the number of Grands Prix held, and the one with the highest total is crowned World Champion. For a long time an extra point was awarded to the driver achieving the fastest lap in each race, but this system was abandoned because of the protests and doubts which arose about the accuracy of the timing equipment.

Although the C.S.I. is a world-wide organization and provides for American representation, Formula 1 is an essentially European creation with an essentially European viability. Since its inception only two American marques—Scarab and Eagle—have made serious attempts at it and the existence of Formula 1 is acknowledged only once a year in the United States —on the occasion of the U.S. Grand Prix.

American drivers, however, are less indifferent; one of their number, Phil Hill, took the World Championship of Drivers in 1961 and others, notably Harry Schell, Dan Gurney, Richie Ginther and Mario Andretti, have either won Grands Prix or played a major part in them. The international aspect of Formula 1 was evident from the start when a number of great South American drivers—Fangio, Mieres, Marimon—began to appear on the scene; as they disappeared their place was taken by Australians and New Zealanders like Brabham, Hulme, McLaren and Amon. Over the years Italy's contribution in terms of drivers has steadily declined while the British contingent has increased to the point where it is preponderant; the French are only now re-emerging after an almost total eclipse. Belgium, Switzerland, Sweden, Germany and Spain have all provided individual stars, but so far the countries of the East, of Africa and of the Far East have never been represented.

the anatomy of a grand prix

The circus usually arrives in town on a Thursday. There is, however, no question of a tent and only the utterly fanciful would see any similarity between a traveller's caravan and a racing transporter, that huge, flamboyant, ultramodern machine which houses not only the precious single-seaters but also their spare parts, a work-bench, welding equipment, and a battery charger. A team's plans for the season are drawn up in great detail months in advance—in fact the organization gets under way as soon as the calendar is drawn up and approved by the C.S.I.: one set of letters is sent off to reserve the necessary hotel rooms while another set goes out to book the required space in a well-equipped garage. Then the team manager and Grand Prix organizers negotiate the financial terms on which the team will compete. For many years the financial arrangements were settled once and for all at a meeting held in the close season between the two associations representing the Grand Prix organizers and the Formula 1 constructors. Until 1970 the usual method of payment was based on starting money: a competitor was signed up for a greater or smaller sum depending on his reputation and this sum was due to him from the very moment he started the race; where he finished, or indeed whether he finished, was entirely irrelevant. The organizers met each year to settle the rates to be offered to the teams. These were affected by variable factors which included the driver's reputation, whether or not he had been World Champion and whether he was on the list of graded drivers—this list is drawn up by the C.S.I. and includes the names of leading drivers according to their previous positions in the World Championship table. The team's recent successes were also taken into account.

This is a system which allocates most of the budget in advance and which consequently leaves the race badly endowed with prize-money and as a result it was frequently criticized. The first objection that comes to mind is that it tends to reduce racing to a mere for-mality because it provides no incentive to the drivers for whom, once their entry has been accepted, there is little difference financially speaking between retiring early, fighting for a good position or even winning. In fact this objection is easily answered in that the amount of starting money a driver receives is directly related to his past performance, which is as it should be. What is more, his other sources of income also depend to a great extent on where he stands in the World Championship table when he comes to sign his contracts with the constructor, the component firms and, in some cases, with the non-sporting concerns which provide sponsorship. Such considerations obviously encourage him to do his best at all times.

On the other hand, the great advantage of starting money is that it allows the constructors to work out a provisional budget before the season starts. Thus small firms engaged in this highly expensive and not necessarily profitable activity acquire some stability and are able to withstand a barren season without risking ruin or financial catastrophe. Undoubtedly, without the starting money system, a number of teams would never have been able to survive even a single bad season and would have found themselves undeservedly forced to quit. Ken Tyrrell, manager of Matra-International, who ran the Matra-Fords in 1968 and 1969, reckoned that he needed to win at least three Grands Prix, that is a quarter of the events in the calendar, to cover his expenses for one season. And yet he was organized in the cheapest way possible. In effect his chassis were on loan to him and were main-tained and repaired by Matra free of charge so that his expenditure was limited to buying and maintaining his Ford engines (about £10,000 each) and Hewland gear-boxes and paying a very small team of mechanics. He certainly was not faced with development and construction costs which are colossal.

This gives some idea of the difficulties which beset constructors like Ferrari and B.R.M. who are respon-sible for the complete operation, from the design, development and construction of their cars to the organization of their team. Obviously they have to find a source of income other than racing. For years Ferrari have provided revenue for their racing department by including a small "tax" in the sale price of their production cars, thus obliging every customer to make his contribution. B.R.M. however, have no such commercial outlets. They were founded by a syndicate composed of various big component manufacturers who paid their subscription in the hope that a successful 100 per cent British racing car would promote the sale of British production machines incorporating their products. Then, when this syndicate broke up, B.R.M., in spite of an often lacklustre career, found a Maecenas in Sir Alfred Owen, boss of Rubery Owen, the largest manufacturer of car components in Britain. Now, as far as money is concerned, Ferrari have become a satellite of the all-powerful Fiat while B.R.M.'s budget is balanced largely by the contributions of non-sporting concerns.

There have been four different sorts of teams competing in post-war Grands Prix. First, those from very large factories seeking to promote the image of their production models by direct participation on the racetrack. The firms prepared to stake their reputations in this way have been very few: Alfa Romeo (1948, 1950–51), Lancia and Mercedes (1954–55) and Honda (1964–68). Then there are the teams fielded by the smaller manufacturers; these are usually sports car specialists—Ferrari, of course, Maserati, Aston Martin, Talbot, Porsche, Matra. B.R.M. and Vanwall can be included in this category because their circumstances, even though different, are fairly comparable. Next there is the group which has become the most important in Formula 1, the "special builders" who generally confine themselves to designing and building chassis. The triumphs of Cooper, Lotus (now a specialist sports car constructor but originally a special builder), Brabham, McLaren, Lola, etc., have followed from the small beginnings of such people as Connaught and H.W.M. These teams derive their income from racing, and without the starting-money system their numbers would probably have been drastically reduced. Since the start of the 1960s they have been the backbone of Formula 1 and but for their support it is highly likely that this Formula, which only just managed to pull through the crisis of 1952–53 when it was virtually superseded by the less costly and more profitable Formula 2, would not have survived the attack of galloping financial consumption from which it was suffering.

Finally there are the private teams. These are few and far between and not easily competitive in the ultraperfectionist world of Formula 1. A complete list of those that have taken the field, often gallantly and sometimes quixotically, during these thirteen years would make tedious reading. Deservedly the most famous of them all was the Rob Walker team (Walker as in whisky). They contested every World Championship between 1959 and 1970 and, with their most distinguished driver Stirling Moss, nearly took the title on more than one occasion.

The special builders can only go on racing while they can obtain engines whose design and manufacturing costs are borne by someone else. This is a growing tendency. Coventry-Climax, Repco and Maserati have all been engine suppliers, but since 1968 this part has been played solely by Ford and their subcontractor, the extraordinary small English firm Cosworth—made up from the names of its founders, Mike Costin and Keith Duckworth. In 1970, out of a total of twenty-three cars lined up for the start of the South African Grand Prix, seventeen were fitted with Cosworth-Ford V8s. At the 1962 German Grand Prix, twenty-six cars came under starter's orders of which eleven had Coventry-Climax engines (either V8 or four-cylinder units). Before 1960 starting grids were much more evenly divided among Maserati, Ferrari, Vanwall, Mercedes and B.R.M., all of whom ran cars which were completely their own. In other words, Formula 1, more popular and apparently more prosperous than ever, depends in fact more and more on the policy of a single supplier, in this case Ford. If this policy were to change, the glorious circus would run the risk of being scattered to the four winds; in this respect contemporary Formula 1 is a colossus with feet of clay.

However, before the opening of the 1970 season, the starting-money system was abandoned. At a meeting in Geneva organizers and entrants signed an agreement instituting a more "egalitarian" method of payment which had the advantage of putting an end to haggling. In short, the agreement, which is negotiable annually, stipulates that the organisers shall undertake to collect a minimum sum of money to be distributed as follows: one part, a fairly small one, to be set aside to defray the competitors' travelling expenses; the rest, most of the budget, to be divided into three parts and paid out according to the running order at one-third distance, at two-thirds distance and at the end of the race. This system, which has the virtue of clarity, emerged from the consideration of a number of points and initially provoked howls of protest, but it has developed in a way that on the whole seems to satisfy most of the competitors. At this stage it is still too early to try and sort out what its consequences are likely to be in the long run.

However, to return to the circus. The cars arrive and, if it is a European Grand Prix, with them more often than not come the mechanics who travel in the huge cab of the transporter following the detailed route card drawn up for them by the team manager's office staff; this lists their stopping-places, useful names and addresses—accessory people, fuel people—and so on. The drivers, technical staff and pit crew also arrive on the Thursday, but they come their own separate ways. They all meet up at a team conference, often held on the Thursday evening, but if not they assemble for the first time, two hours before the opening practice session which is usually held on the Friday. From the technical point of view the cars are, in theory, ready to go. Immediately after the previous race the cars will have been completely stripped down, all their parts crack-tested, some replaced as a matter of course, others because of excessive wear or known weakness. Last year's race notes and any changes in the cars' specification—for example, percentage increase in power—will have been carefully considered to ensure that the theoretically most suitable final drive and gear ratios for the circuit are fitted, and the same care will have been taken over tyres and new brakes. The engines will most certainly have been overhauled and their power checked on the bench before being installed in the chassis. A team running two cars must have at their disposal at least five engines—two in the cars, two in the transporter and one back at the factory being overhauled.

Once on the track, the driver starts by checking that

these technical theories work in practice. With the growth of technology, chassis adjustments have become more and more numerous, delicate and decisive. In the 1950s most Formula 1 cars had rigid or de Dion rear axles which meant that their wheels were fixed in the vertical plane, but following the success of the mid-engined Coopers in 1959 four-wheel independent suspension became universal in Formula 1. With the advent of ultrawide tires in the middle 1960s, the tire companies themselves began to provide the data for the camber angle of the wheels: as soon as a car stops at its pit instant readings are taken of the inside, centre and outside tread temperatures and these reveal whether or not the tires are making maximum contact with the road and whether or not, therefore, they are providing maximum adhesion. To ensure stability and obtain the desired handling characteristics—oversteer, understeer or neutral— the engineers juggle with tire pressures, spring and shock-absorber settings, the diameter and adjustment of the anti-roll bars and even the castor angle, and aerodynamic features of the car. Front and rear braking distribution is carefully worked out and finally the result of all these operations is checked to make sure that it is not affected by the amount of fuel the car is carrying.

How the mechanics spend Friday night depends on what happened during practice; they may simply have to check everything over, they may have to change the gear ratios, sometimes they may have to fit another engine. . . . These are men who must be prepared to go without sleep from Friday morning to Sunday evening! The moment of truth for the drivers usually arrives during the last half-hour of the Saturday practice session when, at the wheel of a perfectly set-up car, they have to pull out all the stops to make sure of obtaining the best possible place on the starting grid. This great effort is very important for a number of reasons: tactically, starting from the front row involves less risk of being a victim of a bump in the opening stages of the race. This is always a dangerous period because all the cars are still tightly bunched together; it also means that there are fewer competitors to be overtaken later. Psychologically, a good time boosts morale and disconcerts the opposition. Drivers choose the last minutes of practice for their all-out attack because they hope the others will not have time to reply.

Although the term "race tactics" had some meaning in the 1950s, this is no longer the case. Then Grands Prix were longer—310 miles (500 km) against 186 miles (300 km) today—and sometimes it was necessary to stop for more fuel or new tires. Cutting the distance turned Formula 1 races into flat-out sprints where the only tactic possible is to drive as fast as you can, making the car perform to the limit from start to finish, except of course for the man in the lead who, provided he is far enough ahead, can dictate terms to his pursuers. Pre-race tactics remain, however, particularly when the weather is uncertain and the choice of tires is a gamble on how it will turn out. The most famous example of this is the case of Moss in the 1961 German Grand Prix. He decided to put rain tires on, his 1500 cc four-cylinder Lotus-Climax which suffered from a considerable power handicap compared with the V6 Ferraris. However, during the first part of the race Moss managed to keep the Italian cars at bay because the better grip of his softer tires gave him an advantage which his extraordinary skill could exploit. Nevertheless, if it had not rained he certainly would

not have been able to finish the race because his tire tread was wearing away too quickly. He was well aware of this but, unlike his opponents, he had chosen to stake his chance of winning on a change in the weather. When the heavens finally opened he was off, never to be caught. So, in the most unexpected manner, he won a race that on paper he could only lose.

On the other hand, the following incident, which occurred in 1957 on the same circuit—the Nurburgring—could not happen these days because there are no longer refuelling stops in Grands Prix. Fangio decided on this occasion that he would start with the tank of his Maserati 250F only half full and take advantage of the refuelling stop he was thus forcing on himself to have new rear tires fitted. Now practice had shown that if the cars were to go the distance on one tank of petrol and the same set of tyres, their drivers would have to proceed with restraint. This was the course chosen by Ferrari for Mike Hawthorn and Peter Collins while Maserati preferred to give Fangio the chance of building up a big lead in the early stages which could be utilised for a fuel stop and a change of tyres. Then at the end of the race the Argentinian could demand the maximum from his replenished motor-car and leave his starving rivals behind. It almost went according to plan, but Fangio's pit stop took longer than anticipated and when he set off for the last eleven laps of the daunting 14·17-mile (22·6 km) circuit instead of being 28 s in front he was 50 s behind the two leading Ferraris.

For three laps this gap remained and it seemed all over. Unfortunately for them, Collins and Hawthorn thought so too. At this point Fangio launched his attack, breaking and rebreaking the lap record, taking the Maserati to the limits of its ability and even beyond. The two Englishmen, handicapped and not at all sure that their cars could meet this massive challenge, saw their lead dissolve under the extraordinary pressure. Two laps from the end Collins was passed. On the penultimate lap, in spite of a final magnificent effort in which he forgot everything except the need to resist whatever the cost, Hawthorn was also overtaken. This was the last Grand Prix victory of Fangio's incomparable career and he owed it as much to his arms and his heart as to his brain. In a gripping final period of 3 h 30 min 38·3 s he had shown what normally inaccessible heights the art of a five-times world champion can reach; it was indeed a brilliant finale.

Since then Formula 1 Grands Prix have lost this epic quality; it has been replaced by a colder, logical, almost mathematical ritual. Nevertheless, it seems that a sorcerer, a miracle-maker will always appear to preserve the legend of Formula 1. After Fangio came Moss and he was followed by Jim Clark. Now Jackie Stewart and Emerson Fittipaldi have fallen heir to this role. These men could not be more different: what they have in common are the characteristics which make them great drivers: intense pride, cold determination, tremendous power of concentration, lightning quick reactions, physical strength, acute mechanical sympathy and competitive spirit. They also had or have something else besides: genius. Each one in his own particular way has expressed or expresses it behind the wheel. People have tried to list them in order, to compare their respective talents. A useless and empty exercise. It is enough to say that each in his turn was the best. Nothing more is needed.

modern formula 1

Why "modern" and why take the modern period as beginning in 1959? Surely Formula 1 cars, being what they are, are always modern, not to say futuristic, since the moment they appear they are by definition the most complete expression of automobile technology? This is an attractive idea but it fails to take into account a number of factors, notably economic, which often lead the constructors to indulge a tendency towards conservatism. Of course, whatever the period, it hardly ever happens that a team turns up at Grands Prix with the same type of car for more than one season, but the differences lie rather in model development than in radical change. The latter is only achieved when a very large company, not regularly competing in Formula 1, decide to join the battle. Owing to the fact that the technical prestige of their name is at stake before the eyes of the public and the press, the company are compelled to come up with something which is likely, on paper at least, to ensure that they start with the biggest possible advantage over the specialist constructors. Vast sums of money may be spent on research, development and expensive materials to get away from the beaten path. The last example of this sort was that of Mercedes when they returned to racing in 1954–55. About 50 engineers and some 200 technicians were set to work on the problem with the result that the Mercedes Formula 1 cars were much more sophisticated than their contemporary rivals, the strongest of whom were the Ferraris, Maseratis and Lancias. The Mercedes beat them all

hollow and gave Fangio two consecutive World Championship titles. The specification of the Mercedes W196 included some features that had not been used before in Formula 1: a properly constructed multi-tubular chassis, fuel injection and rear-wheel independent suspension. Later these were all to become standard throughout Formula 1, but until the Mercedes appeared there was not a single constructor anxious to try them out even though they embodied well-known and long-established principles. They were all quite satisfied with the well-tried system they had: a tubular chassis with weak or non-existent triangulation which was not very rigid but which gave easy access to the mechanical parts, carburetors (usually Webers) and de Dion rear suspension. In short, the cars differed in only one respect—the engine which, according to preference, could be either a four-cylinder (Ferrari), a straight six (Maserati) or a V8 (Lancia), and it is evident that a permutation of engines and chassis would have produced results very little different from those achieved by the original pairings, so similar were the chassis' characteristics.

Thus it takes a large manufacturer to introduce innovations to a formula which, because its terms of reference are fixed at the beginning of its five-year life-span, tends to produce cars with rather stereotyped specifications and encourage detail development while the basic concept remains unaltered. In this sense 1954 and 1955 (which were the first two years of the 2·5-litre Formula 1) were profitable from a tech-

◀ *Symbol of an era nearing its end: Fangio, five times World Champion, seen here at the wheel of a 2·5-litre Maserati 250F (Monaco G.P. 1957).*

Stirling Moss gives Cooper-Climax their first Grand Prix victory (Argentine 1958): the era of modern Formula 1 has started.

nical point of view, thanks to Mercedes. However, the occasions when a marque as powerful as Mercedes will put itself at risk in Formula 1 are very rare indeed, and if one had to quote a comparable case the nearest one could get would be Honda who competed between 1964 and 1968. After 1955 the specialist constructors found themselves alone again. They adopted some of the features of the W196, but in every case they were the ones most easily assimilated from the economic point of view. They would have stayed there for years had not two new factors joined together, almost completely by chance, to produce a real technical revolution of which the least that can be said is that it took everyone unawares and every constructor with more or less good grace found himself obliged to conform to its principles. To make a political comparison, Mercedes had come to power on a program of reform while Cooper's reign started with a *coup d'état* which completely overthrew the existing scale of values in the small society of Formula 1. The two stages were quite contradictory: the Mercedes reforms tended to lead to the perfection and sophistication, often at great cost, of established institutions; while the Cooper revolution virtually obliterated the forms of the past and replaced them with structures that were unheard of in Grands Prix—not the least of their characteristics was that they were based on and encouraged complete simplicity and therefore the cheapest cost price imaginable.

Nothing is modern for long, and these days Cooper no longer compete in Grands Prix; their original success was followed by a string of failures which were due to the fact that the revolutionary did not know how to develop. Nevertheless, the era that Cooper ushered in continues, an era that was officially recognised in 1959 when an Australian by the name of Jack Brabham became World Champion driver at the wheel of a Cooper-Climax.

The name of Cooper was only known to British enthusiasts when, just one year earlier, a Cooper had won the Argentine Grand Prix. It was driven by Stirling Moss for Rob Walker's private team, and had a 2-litre engine compared with the 2·5-litre units of the Ferraris and Maseratis. Then immediately afterwards, but on this occasion driven by Frenchman Maurice Trintignant, a Cooper won the Monaco Grand Prix, this time beating the Vanwall and the B.R.M.s as well. Most continental followers of motor racing just could not take these strange little devices seriously, they looked so much like scaled-down models beside the imposing 2·5-litre machines of the time. However, they very quickly made their presence felt and soon were even giving lessons: in 1961, the first year of the new 1500 cc Formula 1, all the single-seaters lined up for the opening Grand Prix of the season at Monaco were built to the pattern that in 1959 only Cooper were using!

english-style racing

When the Coopers, father and son—Charles (now dead) and John—decided to build their first racing car in 1946, they had no thoughts of Formula 1. In fact it was quite the reverse as their idea was to try and inject a little democracy into British motor racing by bringing it within the scope of small budgets, starting with their own which was remarkable only for its modesty.... Neither of them was a qualified engineer, but Charles, who was a good mechanic, had looked after several racing cars and therefore knew something about them; and John wanted to race. The two of them had a garage in the London suburbs.

The British competition regulations at that time included a class for racing single-seaters of 500 cc, but as there were no cars which answered to this description, the class existed only on paper. However, this was the class that attracted the Coopers who were looking for a cheap way to go motor racing. Of course, they could have made do like so many others by modifying a production car, but they wanted to go further than this and build something of their own. On the other hand they certainly could not go as far as building their own engine, gear-box or even suspension system. What they intended to do was fit cleverly adapted or modified proprietary components and parts to a chassis of their own design, a chassis which would be both simple, to keep production costs down, and light, to ensure competitiveness.

The first Cooper 500, driven by John Cooper and built in scarcely more than a month, had its competition baptism in the Prescott Hill Climb of 28th July 1946 where it aroused curiosity but unfortunately failed to get as far as the finishing line. The driver missed a gear change, the engine over-revved madly and a valve was ruined. The car was built up from the following parts: an air-cooled, push-rod, 497 cc, single-cylinder J.A.P. motorcycle engine installed behind the driver and giving 45 bhp at 6000 rev/min running on special fuel; chain-driven transmission; Triumph four-speed gearbox; half shafts with universal joints transmitting the power to the rear wheels; Fiat 500 Topolino independent suspension and transverse leaf spring and telescopic shock absorbers and Lockheed drum brakes. The chassis consisted of two box-channel sections joined together by welded cross-pieces, the body was made of aluminium and the whole thing weighed less than 660 lb (297 kg). This tiny single-seater, in spite of its low power, did a standing kilometre in under 36 s.

The car was an immediate success and by 1948 there were about ten of them on the race-tracks competing against one-off specials. It is worth recording that one of the first people to buy a Cooper 500 was a very young man called Stirling Moss who was just starting on a career that was to make him world famous. What is more, a whole new generation of great British drivers followed Moss's example: Peter Collins in 1949, then Lewis-Evans, Ivor Bueb future winner for Jaguar of the Le Mans 24-Hour race, and Roy Salvadori who did the same for Aston Martin. Harry Schell also made himself known at the wheel of a Cooper 500 in 1950 when the 500 class had become Formula 3 thanks to the C.S.I. who had just realized that this class was worthy of international status. Thus was created the first real steppingstone-to-success formula.

In 1952, the new Formula 3 Cooper, the Mk. 6, appeared with a multitubular chassis and it was decided to use this as the basis of a 2-litre Formula 2 car powered by the six-cylinder, push-rod 1971 cc Bristol engine which developed 127 bhp at 5000 rev/min. At this point, three other British concerns launched themselves into this formula which for two seasons virtually supplanted the moribund Formula 1 (4·5 litres or 1500 cc supercharged). These Formula 2 Coopers, driven by future World Champion Mike Hawthorn, Stirling Moss—of course, and even Juan Manuel Fangio among others, differed from the 500s in that they had their engine mounted classic style at the front. They were light and they held the road well, but they were outclassed in terms of power—the four-cylinder, double o.h.c. Ferrari, for example, gave 185 bhp, whereas the Bristol, even at the peak of its development never managed more than 150 bhp.

In 1954 the new Formula 1 (2·5 litres or 750 cc supercharged) came back into its own and because at the time no suitable British engine was available, Cooper's hopes of winning a Grand Prix were postponed until the Greek Calends. Therefore they concentrated their efforts on building a new small sports car with an 1100 cc Coventry-Climax engine installed again behind the driver. The following year, an Australian by the name of Jack Brabham, hoping to make a career for himself in Europe, went to see John Cooper and suggested that he should fit a good old Bristol engine, enlarged to 2·2 litres, in this chassis. This was soon done and the car was entered for the 1955 Formula 1 British Grand Prix at Aintree, where it by no means covered itself with glory and retired before the end.... Nevertheless on that day a partnership emerged, amid general indifference if not scorn, which only four years later was to crush the most distinguished opposition.

It was not long before there were more convincing signs of the success that lay ahead, notably the Formula 2 car conforming to the new regulations—1500 cc unsupercharged—which came out during the 1956 season. This very successful machine followed

John Cooper
(the one in the hat):
a mixture of shrewdness and flair.

the pattern that Cooper were to use right up to 1966: mid-engine (Coventry-Climax FWB four-cylinder, 1460 cc, single o.h.c., 100 bhp at 6000 rev/min; then, in 1957, Type FPF, double o.h.c., 141 bhp at 7000 rev/min), triangulated multitubular chassis, four-wheel independent suspension, compact and light—appreciably less than 880 lb (400 kg).

Although the Formula 2 Coopers were highly competitive in their own class, when they ran in Formula 1 in 2-litre form (the Climax bored out) they had 2·5-litre machines to contend with. Brabham was in third place when on the last circuit of the 100-lap race at Monaco in 1957 the oil pump on his car broke. All at once people began to take the small English car more seriously but they still thought—and rightly so because of the capacity handicap—that it was only likely to show up well among real Formula 1 cars on a twisty circuit like Monaco which demands agility rather than power.

It did not occur to anyone that, given more power, the mid-engined Cooper was a potential Grand Prix winner. Everyone was still totally prejudiced against this layout, ever mindful of the failure of Dr. Ferdinand Porsche's pre-war Auto Unions. These fantastic cars (600 bhp) had a reputation for being difficult to drive and this was put down to the fact that the driver sat in front of the engine. Cooper did not take long to prove that this had been a superficial diagnosis and that if anything had been to blame it was not the general layout of the car but probably the deficiencies of its rear suspension.

They started to make their point by winning the first Formula 1 event of the 1958 season, the Argentine Grand Prix in which, amid general amazement, Stirling Moss drove a Rob Walker 2-litre Cooper-Climax to victory. Yet again the defenders of the classic layout found excuses for this unexpected success.

As it happened, the C.S.I. had just made important changes to the regulations which had hitherto governed Formula 1. First, in order to accommodate the interests of the fuel companies who supported racing and therefore deserved the benefit of any publicity to be derived from it, they forbade special fuels in favor of aviation-type fuel which was much closer to the product sold to the general public. This caused serious tuning problems for Vanwall, B.R.M. and Maserati which were still unsolved when the 1958 season started.

Secondly, they decided to reduce the length of Grands Prix from 310 miles (500 km) to 186 miles (300 km), or from three hours' duration to two, in order to give them more spectator appeal.

The total effects of these two provisions were to completely alter ideas about Formula 1 cars. The aviation fuel cut fuel consumption almost by half, and because the races were shorter, the amount of fuel that had to be carried in the car, already lessened by the fall in fuel consumption, was reduced still further. This inevitably led to the construction of much lighter cars as they now had less weight to support. Furthermore their components could be of less generous proportions as they did not have to last so long.

Obviously the new regulations miraculously favored the little Coopers and their first victories were attributed to the new rules. Although there is some truth in this, it is far from being the whole story.

In fact other constructors reacted fairly quickly: Ferrari who installed a 2·5-litre engine in a smaller Formula 2 chassis and newcomer Lotus who built an extremely light and delicate single-seater fitted with the same 2-litre Climax as the Coopers. However, both these cars had their engines at the front, a layout which was soon to become completely outdated.

So, even if Cooper were the beneficiaries of a fortunate set of circumstances, it is none the less clear that they owed their success primarily to their faith in the concept of a mid-engined car. They were the only constructor to believe in this layout and they deserve to have the fact acknowledged.

Charles and John Cooper were often teased for being untechnical and their success was attributed to sheer luck when really it was due to their flair which enabled them to get the better of engineers of greater subtlety, engineers who were completely engrossed in an accepted theory until they were forced to pay "that old fox, Charles" and "good old John", of whom they spoke with such condescension, the most un-witting and greatest of compliments: imitation.

the turning point:
1959·60

Start of the Monaco Grand Prix 1959:
Behra: Ferrari (No. 46) leads Moss and
Brabham (No. 24) on Cooper-Climax.

1959

the advent of cooper~climax and jack brabham

When the effects of the Cooper revolution began to be felt, the 2·5-litre Formula 1 still had two years to run and the long domination of this Formula by Italian-built cars had just been broken by Vanwall who, in 1958, had carried off the first Constructors' Cup awarded by the C.S.I. Ever since the resumption of racing after the war this Italian supremacy had been successfully challenged only once—by Mercedes in 1954–55.

The Vanwall decision to rest on their laurels for the 1959 season seemed to leave the doorway to success wide open for Ferrari who had only lost to the British team by a hairsbreadth. However, this situation was to be altered by a new development: Coventry-Climax, the accredited supplier of engines to Cooper and Lotus, brought out a new four-cylinder, double o.h.c. 2·5-litre engine which for the first time would put Cooper on an equal footing with their rivals in terms of capacity . . . although they would still be down on power. Against the 220 bhp of the Climax Ferrari could muster 280–290 from their 65° V6s. Still, the British engine had a very flat power curve and high torque at low revs, while the Italian unit had a much more peaky output.

The Cooper works team for 1959 consisted of Brabham, who was their number one driver, and the American Masten Gregory who had a reputation for boldness. During the course of the season he was to lose his place to a young New Zealander by the name of Bruce McLaren. While on the subject of Brabham and McLaren, it is interesting to note that both of them were in their turn to become famous constructors, a job for which they were well prepared by their days with Cooper. The cars they drove were in fact

the first Formula 1 machines on which the possibilities of chassis adjustment were systematically exploited by their drivers; they thus acquired a great deal of experience which they subsequently used to their own advantage.

Besides the works cars, two more Coopers were regularly entered by the Rob Walker team for Stirling Moss and Maurice Trintignant and these were also fitted with Climax engines. There was one exception—an unsuccessful experiment with a B.R.M. unit. This car, whose chassis had to be slightly modified by Alf Francis, chief mechanic to Stirling Moss, appeared in practice for the 1959 Monaco Grand Prix but was not used in the race. The works Coopers had a four-speed gearbox made in London by Knight (who started with a Citroën-Ersa gearbox casing) while the Walker cars had five-speed boxes built in Modena by Colotti. The latter should have given Moss and Trintignant an advantage, but in fact they proved to be their Achilles' heel. Apart from that, the other components—chassis, suspension (front: unequal length upper wishbones and coil springs; rear: lower wishbones and upper transverse leaf spring), Girling disc brakes, light alloy wheels—differed only in detail.

Enemy number one for the Coopers were the Ferraris. The Dino 256s were an entirely different sort of animal. They retained the classic arrangement of front engine and virtually non-triangulated tubular chassis and although they now had disc brakes (Dunlop in this case) like the British cars, they were considerably heavier than the Coopers which weighed scarcely more than 1100 lb (500 kg). On the other hand they were much more powerful: their V6 double o.h.c. 2470 cc engine developed 290 bhp at 8800 rev/min

Bonnier gives B.R.M. their first Grand Prix victory (Zandvoort 1959). Here he is followed by Moss.

against the 220 bhp at 6500 rev/min of the Climax.

B.R.M. and Lotus also remained faithful to the front engine, but their chassis were clearly more highly developed than Ferrari's. Lotus, however, had applied themselves rigorously to the problem of weight with the result that their cars were scarcely heavier than the Coopers. They, too, used the Climax engine in a chassis that was very rigid—a truly scientifically triangulated multitubular space frame. The lines of the body were extremely fine and for a front-engined car its frontal area was very low, though still higher than the Cooper's. The same applied to the B.R.M., whose dimensions were so compact that it had a shorter wheelbase than the Cooper though the Cooper seemed the smaller car. With its properly triangulated tubular chassis, its well-set-up independent suspension, four-cylinder twin overhead camshaft engine giving 270 bhp at 8000 rev/min and excellent torque, the B.R.M.'s only apparent handicap was its weight. Still, it was a large one—over 330 lb (150 kg) compared with the Cooper.

This time no one was surprised when Brabham won at Monaco because Trintignant had done as much the year before and it was now acknowledged that this tortuous round-the-houses circuit suited the characteristics of the cars from Surbiton very well. Moss returned the best time in practice (1 min 39·6 s) heading Behra (Ferrari) by 0·4 s, Brabham by 0·5 s and the other two Ferrari drivers, Tony Brooks and Phil Hill, by 1·4 s and 1·7 s respectively, while the fastest B.R.M. driven by Bonnier, was on the third row of the grid, 2·7 s behind. In the race, Behra shot into the lead and, although unable to shake off Moss and Brabham, he stayed there until his engine blew up on the twenty-third lap. Whereupon Moss took over and steadily drew away from the Australian whom he was leading by nearly one minute when, nineteen laps from home, his transmission broke. Brooks was only 20 s behind the leader, but had to ease up as fumes leaking from the exhaust into the cockpit of his car started to make him drowsy. Meanwhile Trintignant, in third place, two laps in arrears, was comfortably ahead of Phil Hill. The three B.R.M.s had retired as had Graham Hill's Lotus, so two more Coopers, McLaren's (2·2 Climax engine) and Salvadori's (Maserati engine), took fifth and sixth places and completed the triumph of the only mid-engined cars in the race.

Nevertheless, the next two Grands Prix of the 1959 season brought some hope back to the traditionalist camp. On the Zandvoort circuit in Holland B.R.M. and Bonnier won their first official Grand Prix, beating the Coopers of Brabham and Gregory, while on the very fast Reims circuit there was no answering the Ferraris' superior power. Brooks won from his teammate Phil Hill and by slipping his Cooper between the Ferraris of the American and Gendebien, Brabham came third. Stirling Moss, driving a B.R.M. on loan for the occasion, spun at Thillois when he was challenging Phil Hill and was unable to restart. Behra stalled on the line, but he made a splendid recovery and was lying third when his engine broke. At the end of this event the Drivers' Championship looked wide open and it seemed likely that it would be fought out between Brabham (19 points) and Brooks (14) particularly as the British Grand Prix was to be held at Aintree, a circuit which gave every car an equal chance whatever its characteristics.

Brooks, however, was to see most of his hopes

evaporate when Ferrari, beset by strikes, withdrew. Even so, this English driver lined up for the start, but at the wheel of a Vanwall. Vanwall, owned by the famous bearing manufacturer, Tony Vandervell, had retired at the end of 1958 and their attempt at a comeback was very disappointing: the Aintree car was a smaller, lighter development of the previous front-engined model, but it proved impossible to adjust its fuel-injection system properly and Brooks, seventeenth fastest in practice 6·6 s behind Brabham, had to retire the car on the thirteenth lap with valve troubles.

Alongside Brabham's Cooper on the starting grid and with an identical practice time was an Aston Martin DBR 4/250 driven by Roy Salvadori. This car had first appeared, unsuccessfully, at Zandvoort and seemed technically beaten from the start. From its external appearance it could have been mistaken for a 1957 Maserati 250F so similar were its shape and impressive dimensions. It had a de Dion rear axle and was very heavy. In short its only strong point was its powerful straight-six front-mounted engine derived from the 3-litre unit of the DBR 1/300 which that year won the Le Mans 24-Hour Race and the Sports Car Constructors' World Championship. Outclassed at Zandvoort and absent from Reims, the Aston Martins revealed their speed—for the first and last time—in practice at Aintree. They did not, however, figure in the race: when they realized they were drenched in fuel their drivers stopped at the pits. Salvadori rejoined the race and finished sixth, one lap behind the winner Brabham. Moss had again elected to drive the B.R.M. and came in 22 s after the Australian, beating McLaren to the line by only 0·2 s.

So Brabham went into the next round with an increased lead in the Championship which was fortunate since the race was to take place on a circuit where the Cooper would be at a disadvantage. For political/financial reasons the German Grand Prix had deserted the Nurburgring for the Avus ring in Berlin. Basically, this circuit consisted of two straight stretches of motorway joined by a hairpin bend at one end and by a very fast 45° banked turn made of brick at the other. Obviously Avus promised to provide some extremely high average speeds, but no interest whatsoever from the driving point of view. Also, because of anxiety about tires, the Grand Prix was divided into two heats, the final classification to be obtained by an addition of the times.

The Ferraris were the big favorites in spite of the violent row which had blown up between their team manager, Romolo Tavoni, and Jean Behra who stormed out of the team and was immediately replaced by newcomer, Dan Gurney, a big American ex-marine completely unknown in Europe. Behra was therefore out of the Grand Prix, but he had found a drive with Porsche in a curtain-raiser event which was held in pouring rain on the eve of the big race. In these conditions there was no grip at all on the brick north turn and, as happens at Indianapolis in such circumstances, the race should have been cancelled. Unfortunately it was not, and after the Porsches of d'Orey and de Beaufort had been involved in spectacular accidents which miraculously left their drivers unharmed, it was the turn of Behra's car to go out of control on the banking. It spun off, went over the top and smashed into a block of cement. Its fearless driver, Jean Behra, was thrown out; he hit a flagpole and died instantly.

There was a tense, even anxious feeling in the air when the cars lined up the following day for the start of the Grand Prix. Two Ferraris—of Brooks and Gurney—shared the front row with two Coopers—of Brabham and Moss—but the English four-cylinder cars proved incapable of standing the pace set by the Italian V6s. Brooks, Gurney and Phil Hill, in that order, made sure of the first three places and were the only drivers to finish on the same lap. Brooks, now only four points behind Brabham, was back in the running for the Championship.

After Avus came a real road race—the Portuguese Grand Prix held at Monsanto near Lisbon. The circuit involved a tour of the town, over tram-lines and a variety of surfaces, but nevertheless it was rather fast, permitting averages of about 100 mile/h (160 km/h). The Coopers were very much at home here and monopolized the front row of the grid; Moss was in dazzling form and at 2 min 2·89 s was more than 2 s faster than Brabham and more than 4 s faster than Gregory. . . . Bonnier's B.R.M. was the leading front-engined car, nearly 5 s behind, while the Ferraris were further back still. It was undeniable that a turning-point in history was reached at Monsanto and later this was to be confirmed in a totally convincing manner at Monza in the Italian Grand Prix where speed and power are of fundamental importance. What happened was that these two races were won, one after the other, by Stirling Moss and his Cooper. Brabham went off the road in Portugal, but his third place in Italy ensured that he was still top of the table when the Championship entered its final round. Brooks, however, had failed to add to his score and was overtaken by Moss.

The last event of the series was to be held in the United States on the Sebring circuit a full three months after the Italian Grand Prix. This was too long an interval and although calculation showed that there were still three drivers in the running for the title, which made for an exciting situation, interest wore a bit thin. The winner of the Constructors' Cup was declared after Monza: Cooper succeeded Vanwall—the revolution had prevailed. Furthermore, B.R.M. were not slow to proclaim their allegiance and they changed the position of their engine and turned up to practice at Monza with an experimental Formula 1 car built to the Cooper pattern.

At the end of Sebring practice, Moss, who was trying out a new rear suspension (upper wishbones and coil springs), was clearly ahead of the field with a lap in 3 min dead, beating Brabham by 3 s and Brooks by 5·9 s. Brooks, also parading a completely new rear independent suspension system, could only win the Championship provided his rivals scored no points at all and provided he won the race and recorded the fastest lap (for which a point was still awarded) as well. Moss, too, needed victory in the race if he were to take the title. Brabham on the other hand had only to finish second and the Championship was his unless, of course, Moss came in first and achieved the fastest lap as well, in which case he would win by a whisker—half a point to be precise. Moss seemed set to do just that. He led from the start and six laps later was already 9 s in front of Brabham when his Colotti gear-box called it a day. So Brabham went into the lead; no longer troubled by thoughts of Moss and

Jack Brabham and Cooper-Climax: the partnership that dominated the 1959 and 1960 seasons.

Brabham at Reims, between Brooks (No. 24) and Phil Hill (No. 26).

Sequence of Hans Herrmann's accident at Avus; miraculously, the driver escaped without serious injury.

Tony Brooks, the "flying dentist": a star performer, particularly in the rain.

*Stirling Moss
on the way to winning
the Italian Grand Prix . . . but he did not stop Brabham
winning the title in 1959 . . . in spite of a painful finish
in the U.S. Grand Prix.*

secure in the knowledge that Brooks had seen his chances disappear on the first lap when he was bumped by another Ferrari driver, von Trips, he relaxed and waited for his team-mate McLaren who was running 2 s behind. Brooks had rejoined the race but victory now seemed beyond his reach.

However, the last dramatic scene of an exciting season had yet to be played. Only a third of a lap from home, the engine of Brabham's car died for want of fuel, and the car, carried forward by its momentum, came to rest 500 yd (455 m) from the line. McLaren, disconcerted, slowed down but Trintignant, now up with the leaders, failed to exploit the situation and rob McLaren of victory, a victory that would have been his first in Grands Prix and one that never came his way again. As the new World Champion pushed his lifeless Cooper towards the finishing line, Tony Brooks deprived him of third place. However, it did not matter. When Brabham, sweating and panting, straightened his back, a huge smile lit up his face. He had raced to win this title, in a car and on foot, and now it was his.

There was little time for Brabham to retire to his winter quarters and bask in his unexpected glory or rest on his newly gathered laurels because the 1960 Championship series was due to start in less than two months' time with the Argentine Grand Prix.

The interval was also too short for most of the constructors who had to be content with sending their 1959 models to Buenos Aires. All except Lotus, who had realized which way the wind was blowing and turned up with their mid-engined Type 18, at that time the smallest and lightest Grand Prix car ever. It had an almost perfectly triangulated multitubular space-frame chassis, "wobbly web" light-alloy wheels and rather angular bodywork which although not particularly attractive fitted the chassis like a glove. The result was a single-seater which at its highest point stood only 26·5 in (67·3 cm) from the ground and had the lowest frontal area ever. Colin Chapman, its designer, had deliberately neglected the aerodynamics of the bodywork because he recognized that from the point of view of drag the wheels had much greater significance than the bullet-shaped body of a single-seater. In addition to these features, the Lotus 18 had a rear anti-roll bar, four-wheel coil-spring suspension and half shafts which acted as upper suspension arms. Compared with the Cooper, this car represented a step forward. What is more, scarcely finished and brand new, driven by Innes Ireland, it jumped into the lead in the race and stayed there until gear-box troubles caused it to spin two laps later. It finished in sixth place while Bruce McLaren won his second consecutive victory ahead of Allison (Ferrari) and Trintignant/Moss who had shared a Cooper. Brabham's new title was not fitting too well—his gearbox broke—while Bonnier, who had taken over the lead from Ireland, was forced to retire his B.R.M. with valve troubles.

For everyone but Lotus, this Grand Prix was just a left-over from the 1959 season. The 1960 season, which was the last of the 2·5-litre formula, did not really start until the Monaco Grand Prix in May when it was obvious that the constructors had made every effort to come up with something new even though it might have to be scrapped at the end of the year. On the whole, however, the new features related to the chassis.

On the principle of honor to him to whom honor is due, Cooper will be examined first. Their cars differed mainly in their rear suspension system which, as on Rob Walker's cars, now had coil springs instead of transverse leaf springs, and there was also a rear anti-roll bar. They had obviously made a big and successful effort to reduce the cross-sectional area, but the elegant, harmonious lines of the body remained. On the mechanical side, the 2·5-litre Climax

engine (also fitted to the Lotus 18) now developed 240 bhp at 6750 rev/min, 20 bhp more say than in 1959, and the torque was further improved. Finally, the Knight gearbox now housed a fifth gear.

B.R.M. had three new cars for their new team— Bonnier stayed with them and was joined by Graham Hill and Dan Gurney, deserters from Lotus and Ferrari respectively. The B.R.M. tubular chassis were mid-engined and the engines were the same as those used the previous year; this was also true of the dimensions, brakes and wheels, while the "new" rear suspension system was really only an adaptation of the old one. In this form the B.R.M.s were some 110 lb (50 kg) heavier, but they had the advantage of a lower frontal area.

From Maranello came three scarcely modified Sebring-type Ferraris accompanied by a fourth completely new mid-engined machine. Its large-section tubular chassis was similar to that of the Coopers and its independent suspension system was superimposed by unequal length wishbones and coil springs. The engine was a Dino 246: 60° V6, 2417 cc, double o.h.c., 250 bhp at 8000 rev/min.

As Aston Martin had retired there were no other works teams at Monaco apart from a new American equipe set up by young, rich Lance Reventlow. His cars were called Scarabs and were very well made and finished, but unfortunately they were front-engined and therefore out of date. Furthermore, their four-cylinder, fuel-injection engine with desmodromic valves developed only 230 bhp which was not enough to enable them to qualify.

Rob Walker's team had acquired a Lotus 18 for Stirling Moss who had been very impressed with the car in Argentina. The British Racing Partnership, in whose colors Moss had competed with a B.R.M. the year before—his father and associates held the shares —had become the Yeoman Credit team which took its name from the finance company which provided backing. This team bought Coopers for Tony Brooks and for Chris Bristow and Henry Taylor, two young British hopes. Olivier Gendebien also had a Cooper. Masten Gregory had left the Cooper team for Centro-Sud and his place was taken by Bruce McLaren. The world champion motorcyclist, John Surtees, along with two more young hopes, Jim Clark and Alan Stacey, went to join Innes Ireland at Lotus. Finally, Ferrari had Phil Hill, Wolfgang von Trips and Cliff Allison while their new mid-engined experimental car was entrusted to an unknown Californian driver recommended to the Commendatore by Dan Gurney: Richie Ginther.

The 1960 Monaco Grand Prix, which was run in the rain, ranks as a historic event: it was the first Grand Prix won by Lotus, the marque that was to dominate

Formula 1 racing for the next ten years. They owed their victory to Stirling Moss. For the first twenty-three laps he let Bonnier set the pace, then he took over the lead and kept it until the finish where he was followed across the line by McLaren, Phil Hill, Brooks, Bonnier and Ginther. Brabham was still dogged by trouble; this time he went off the road, fortunately without hurting himself. Unfortunately this was not true for Cliff Allison who injured himself badly during practice and never fully recovered from the effects of the damage.

The Australian's luck turned with the next event, the Dutch Grand Prix, which he won. What is more, he also won the four races that followed. This series of victories robbed the World Championship of all excitement because even before the last two Grands Prix were run it was known that Brabham had taken the title for the second consecutive year. Similarly, Cooper made off with the Constructors' Cup with six G.P. wins out of a possible nine, a score which tallied well with their 1959 result—five out of eight.

At Zandvoort Brabham had conceded 0·2 s to Moss in practice, but in the race he took the lead, his green Cooper closely shadowed by the dark blue Lotus. Suddenly a huge stone was thrown up by one of the rear wheels of Brabham's Cooper, it hit one of the Lotus's wheels and literally slashed the tire so that Moss was forced to stop to have the wheel changed.

His chance of victory disappeared. It was from this incident that Brabham acquired his reputation for meanness and his charming nickname "Black Jack". Absolutely furious, Moss rejoined the race and, breaking and rebreaking the lap record, worked his way through the field to take fourth place in an event he certainly had not deserved to lose in such a ridiculous way. Ireland and Graham Hill were second and third. The Ferraris were completely outclassed and even the fastest of them could get no higher than twelfth in practice. *Sic transit. . . .*

But there was worse in store for the hapless Stirling Moss. During practice for the Belgian Grand Prix at Spa a rear wheel came off his Lotus when he was travelling at more than 130 mile/h (208 km/h). He was thrown out against a bank and broke both his legs and his nose and although he dealt with his period of convalescence in fine style, he was kept away from the race-tracks until the Portuguese Grand Prix. Brabham, rid of his toughest opponent, led an extremely fast race from beginning to end, averaging 133·6 mile/h (213·7 km/h). McLaren and Gendebien made it total victory for the Coopers which, although still appreciably down on power compared with the Ferraris (the difference amounted to about 40–50 bhp), were now as unbeatable on high-speed circuits as they were on twisty circuits which demanded agility. They managed to overcome their power handicap largely

Richie Ginther
at the wheel of the mid-engined
Ferrari prototype
at Monaco . . .

because of their lower wind resistance, more efficient braking (due to their low weight), better roadholding and better acceleration, the last two due to their general design. As regards behavior on the road, they were rivalled only by the Lotus 18 but, with Moss temporarily out of action, there was no Lotus driver capable of challenging Brabham.

. . . where this picture of Moss and his Lotus 18 at work was also taken: first Grand Prix victory for Lotus.

Phil Hill at full

Top: Dan Gurney (B.R.M.) in trouble at Zandvoort.
Above: Graham Hill (B.R.M.).
Above right: Innes Ireland (Lotus-Climax).
Bottom: Von Trips (Ferrari) and Brabham (Cooper-Climax): triumph for the mid-engined car.

The race at Spa in 1960 was a melancholy event. By the time it was all over Moss had been injured and two young British drivers had been killed: Bristow after an incident with the Belgian Willy Mairesse who was competing in his first Formula 1 Grand Prix and Stacey who was hit by a bird when he was travelling at about 125 mile/h (200 km/h).

High speed was also a feature of the French Grand Prix at Reims. Brabham was the winner at an average speed of 131·8 mile/h (210·8 km/h), a figure that compares well with his achievement in the previous race. Reims, however, does not demand such good road behavior as Spa so the Ferraris of Phil Hill and von Trips were able to give the Cooper a run for its money before they both had to retire with transmission trouble. Once again the Cooper triumvirate led the pack home, but on this occasion they were in a different order—Gendebien was ahead of McLaren. This race saw the second and final come-back of the Grand Prix Vanwall but, with Brooks at the wheel, it

was rammed on the line by Lucien Bianchi's Cooper; at the same moment both Graham Hill's B.R.M. and Trintignant's Cooper were eliminated in a similar fashion.

It was Brabham again at Silverstone although on this occasion he undoubtedly met his match in the person of Graham Hill who got within seven laps of his first Grand Prix victory. From pole position Brabham shot away into the lead while Hill sat motionless with a stalled engine. Once he started he rushed off in pursuit of the leaders, caught them up and literally left them standing as, completely unresisted, he went for Brabham and passed him. He was in the lead after fifty-five laps of magnificent driving, during the course of which he set a new lap record, but on lap 71 he spun to a standstill while overtaking a back-marker. So Brabham won again, but this time he was followed home by Surtees and Ireland both in Lotuses. The Aston Martins, attempting a final come-back, retired and were never seen again except in races for historic machines.

Brabham's remarkable run of success was to be continued in Portugal. However, he did not always have things his own way. The B.R.M.s had been fitted with a better rear suspension system (upper wishbones) and had shed about 66 lb (30 kg) in weight and Gurney made full use of these improvements to take the lead and give a brilliant ten-lap solo performance before retiring. Surtees took over and seemed all set to win when on the thirty-sixth lap his front fuel tank began to leak on to his feet, making the soles of his shoes slippery. His foot slid off the brake pedal and he was out. Immediately the way was open again for Brabham who finished ahead of his faithful follower McLaren and the young Jim Clark whose Lotus still bore the scars of his practice flip. Moss, back after his accident, was disqualified for getting a push after a spin.

Thereupon a bitter dispute broke out between the British contingent and the organizers of the Italian Grand Prix at Monza. The latter were very well aware that the Italian crowd would not appreciate the failure of the Ferraris so they decided to run their event not on the road circuit as usual but on the combined road-banked track circuit which would give their powerful national cars a better chance of winning. The British reckoned that the banking was dangerous and said they would withdraw if the organizers would not reverse their decision. They refused so the entry was reduced to three front-engined Formula 1 Ferraris, one rear-engined Formula 2 Ferrari, two Formula 2 Porsches and various hybrids. Phil Hill won what was to be the last Grand Prix victory for a front-engined car. A page of racing history had definitely, if not gloriously, been turned.

The honor of winning the last race of the 2·5-litre Formula 1, which had been in force since 1954, fell appropriately to Stirling Moss, without doubt the most brilliant driver in racing since Fangio retired. On the Californian circuit at Riverside it was Brabham's turn to have trouble: he had been leading for five laps when fuel leaking from the tank burst into flames. He stopped and Moss shot ahead, never to be caught; he was followed at a distance by Ireland in another Lotus and the Cooper boys, McLaren and Brabham, in that order.

38

The start at Monza:
the last Grand Prix victory
for a front-engined car.

the 1500 formula: 1961-65

For a time, five seasons to be precise, the age of speed was over and in the world of motor racing moaning and groaning became the order of the day. The British were particularly unhappy and made it known that it was nothing to do with them... they did not even want to hear about the new 1500 Formula 1.... Opinions were freely offered: Grand Prix racing would become boring, commonplace and dull; drivers would be little more than some sort of jockey; more talented drivers would be prevented from exploiting their superior skill; the public would not be interested in events for midgets.... The British faction even went as far as introducing a parallel formula called Intercontinental for single-seaters of up to 3 litres.

As it happened, the Intercontinental formula was a flop while the 1500 cc Formula 1 did what it set out to do practically from the start, in spite of the almost total lack of preparation on the part of the British teams who did, after all, provide the main body of the forces in the field.

The new Formula 1, with a life-span of five years, had been conceived by the C.S.I. as an answer to the still urgent problems raised by the 1955 Le Mans accident and its tragic consequences. Taking as their text the notion that circuits could only develop slowly towards better protection for the public and that such protection would cost a lot of money and never be complete, the sporting powers that be, among them the very powerful and influential race organizers, came to the conclusion that it would be simpler to rebuild the cars. The then President of the C.S.I. M. Pérouse, sought advice from a body of small-engine specialists who naturally favored a reduction in the capacity limit. More than anything, the C.S.I. wanted to curb the speed of Formula 1 and it was with this in mind that they agreed to this suggestion and, despite the opposition of the majority of constructors, adopted the 1500 Formula.

The constructors—particularly the British—took exception to this formula because they realized that such a capacity limit promised to increase the cost of engines which would inevitably need more cylinders if they were to deliver the last decisive scrap of power. It was not expected that the old chassis and particularly the old tires would have much trouble transmitting the power and torque of the 1500 cc units to the road since they had managed somehow to cope with the demands of the 2·5-litre engines. In other words, although 20 or 30 bhp were neither here nor there in the old formula, as was proved by the results, it was predicted that even 10 bhp would be of great significance under the new rules where every bit of power would be both useful and usable. Also, while the chassis, obviously a cheaper component than the engine, had played the more important part in achieving results in the 1959 and 1960 seasons, it was reckoned that the reverse would be true from now on.

In fact it proved to be only partly true. Although it is beyond doubt that the construction of Formula 1 cars and their 1500 cc engines got more and more expensive as they were continually refined, the engine-chassis balance remained in favor of the latter.

The drivers' objections were based on the assumption that the anticipated reduction in power would call for less driving skill and therefore penalize the more talented. They also maintained that their safety was at stake because, they said, spare power is a safety factor and with the 1500 cc engines there would be no available reserves. Although these arguments were theoretically sound enough, in practice they were shown to be rather academic. As it happened, the 1500 Formula did produce a hierarchy and did permit outstanding talent to emerge. Jim Clark in particular, in spite of the relative lack of power, managed to establish a clear and constant superiority over his rivals, comparable to that which the 2·5-litre Formula had enabled first Fangio and then Moss to exercise. As for safety, the new formula was to prove no more dangerous than its predecessor. In the final analysis, perhaps only the public suffered as a result of the reduced capacity because the cars soon started to look unimpressive and above all they were so very much alike that they were the very opposite of spectacular. Nevertheless, the 1500 Formula produced some very exciting races, particularly on the fast circuits, where the outcome was in doubt right until the end, much to the enjoyment of the spectators.

Briefly then, the 1500 Formula, from the technical, sporting and spectator points of view, was more successful than expected and the objections that were raised—sometimes with justification—when it came into force were in fact swept away by the very people who had made them in the first place: the drivers and constructors. But the latent conflict between the latter and the organizers, which was to emerge and develop with increasing bitterness, can be dated from this period. In fact it was not long before two organizations were formed—the Formula 1 Constructors' Association and the Grand Prix Drivers' Association—with the aim of defending their interests against the bureaucrats of the C.S.I. and the circuit organizers. At that time the latter held the monopoly of power and legislated for the sport without worrying too much about the opinions of the active participants. Although the arguments are still going on, these two associations nevertheless managed to make their voices and then their demands heard above the ceaseless row that very nearly ended in secession in 1967 when a split was avoided only by a hairsbreadth.

Eleven makes competed in Formula 1 World Championship Grands Prix during the five seasons—1961–65—of the 1500 cc Formula, four of them from start to finish: Ferrari, Lotus, Cooper and B.R.M. Porsche contested only the first two while Brabham did not appear until the middle of 1962, the one season that saw the Lolas in Formula 1. There were three unsuccessful bids in 1963—A.T.S., Scirocco and B.R.P.—and in 1964 and 1965 Honda joined in.

On the whole the Lotus-Climax was the dominant machine of the period, winning 22 Grands Prix out of 47, the other 25 victories being shared among B.R.M. (11), Ferrari (9), Brabham-Climax (2), Honda, Porsche and Cooper-Climax (1 each).

Fifteen drivers won at least one Grand Prix for the seven makes. Jim Clark, who crossed the finishing line first on no fewer than 19 occasions, was obviously as outstanding as his car, but he managed to win the title only twice (1963 and 1965). He was followed by Graham Hill (10 of B.R.M.'s 11 victories and the title in 1962), John Surtees (3 wins for Ferrari and the title in 1964), Dan Gurney (3 wins, 1 for Porsche and 2 for Brabham), Phil Hill (2 wins for Ferrari and the title in 1961), von Trips (2 wins for Ferrari), Stirling Moss (2 wins for Lotus), Richie Ginther (1 win for Honda), Bruce McLaren (1 win for Cooper), Lorenzo Bandini and Giancarlo Baghetti (1 win each for Ferrari) and finally Jackie Stewart (1 win for B.R.M.). The total number of drivers who scored points in the five World Championship series between 1961 and 1965 was 42.

During this period a new wave of drivers came in to replace most of the stars of the previous formula. Fangio had already retired when the 1500 Formula 1 started and Moss, although he had never been formally crowned, succeeded him in the number one spot. Sadly, this great English driver had a serious accident at Goodwood at the beginning of 1962 and brought his brilliant career to a premature end. Although he achieved his two most extraordinary performances during the one season he raced under the new formula, he was only second in the Championship. Of the old hands, Brabham continued but was unable to win a race; Gurney, McLaren and Bonnier also remained, but von Trips (who was killed while racing) and Tony

Brooks had gone from the scene by the end of 1961. Trintignant and Salvadori retired in 1962 and Phil Hill a year later. Masten Gregory became only an occasional competitor.

The great shining star that emerged was Jim Clark and the lesser lights included Graham Hill, John Surtees, Richie Ginther, Lorenzo Bandini, Jackie Stewart, Innes Ireland, Mike Spence, Joseph Siffert, Peter Arundell, Trevor Taylor, Denis Hulme, Jochen Rindt, the Rodriguez brothers, Willy Mairesse, Chris Amon, Richard Attwood and Ludovico Scarfiotti. This list includes many of the drivers who were later to be prominent in 3-litre Formula 1 racing, the notable exceptions are the French contingent (Beltoise, Pescarolo, Servoz-Gavin and Cévert) and the Belgian Jacky Ickx. In other words, most of the great contemporary drivers were brought into the limelight by the 1500 Formula which is something to its credit.

And what of the new regulations? In addition to fixing the upper capacity limit (at 1500 cc), they stipulated a lower limit of not less than 1300 cc. The use of aviation-type fuel (130 grade) was forbidden in favor of the highest grade of fuel on sale in Europe (101·5 octane). This discouraged supercharging from the start, if it needed further discouragement—the equivalent capacity of 750 cc was retained by the C.S.I. The only attempt at a supercharged 750 was made by the French constructor D.B. who ran a supercharged two-cylinder Panhard-engined single-seater in a non-Championship event. It was not a success.

The other trouble-making point when the regulations were issued was the minimum weight which had been fixed at 1100 lb (500 kg) with oil and water but no fuel. The constructors had their way over this and the limit was dropped to 990 lb (450 kg). The regulations also stipulated that Formula 1 cars should be fitted with a self-starter, a dynamo and a circuit breaker. For safety reasons it was forbidden to take on oil during a race and a catch tank had to be fitted to the breather. A roll-over bar must be fitted to protect the driver should the car turn over and the cockpit must be so designed that the driver could get out without having to remove anything. A dual braking system was also compulsory. Finally, it was stipulated that all four wheels should be directly exposed to the air, thus it was forbidden to streamline them into the body of the car. There was no doubt about it, the legislators feared speed like the plague. . . .

ferrari
versus...
stirling moss

1961

The year 1961 was to be Ferrari's. They were the only team to have planned far enough ahead to be ready for the first race of the season. Porsche, who were taking the plunge into Formula 1 after several seasons in Formula 2, had also worked hard, but inevitably they encountered problems that Ferrari knew how to avoid. Lotus and Cooper had to wait until the summer before the Coventry-Climax V8 they were counting on materialized. The B.R.M. V8 took even longer to appear—in fact it failed to appear at all that year.

The experimental Formula 1 car that Ferrari ran at Monaco and their Formula 2 cars, built on the same lines but powered by 1500 cc units (exactly as required by the new Formula 1) taught them a great deal and they made good use of their experience. In 1961 this Italian marque competed in seven of the eight Grands Prix in the World Championship series and won five of them. They lost the other two, not to stronger mechanical opposition, but to a driver of genius at the height of his power. On paper this man was the arch-loser, but he would never admit defeat and managed to get more than anyone thought possible from a car that was notoriously down on power, if not completely outclassed. The 1961 season was to be Moss's last; it was also to be his greatest, the legendary performances he gave at Monaco and the Nurburgring made sure of that. It is undeniable that no other driver competing at that time could have accomplished what Moss, going off to fight the Ferraris like Don Quixote tilting at windmills, managed against all reason to achieve.

British cars had been successful in the past despite their appreciable lack of power in relation to the Ferraris, and in this respect there was nothing new about the situation that faced them in the first season of the new Formula 1. What was new was that Ferrari had learned something from their failures and had consequently modified the layout of their chassis. In this respect they were now on a near-equal footing with their British rivals. The latter believed that Ferrari would persist in using their front-engined cars. Unfortunately, it was a case of wishful thinking on the part of the British. Since they were no longer inherently inferior in terms of road behavior, the Ferraris could at last take full advantage of their extra power which hitherto had been used only to compensate for the deficiencies of their chassis.

At Monaco, the Ferrari drivers were the great favorites: Phil Hill, the German Count Wolfgang von Trips and the little Californian Richie Ginther. Their 65° or 120° V6 engines (190–200 bhp at 9500 rev/min) gave them an edge of at least 30–40 bhp compared with the opposition from Cooper, Lotus and B.R.M., all of whom were using the four-cylinder 1500 Climax Mk. 2 (150 bhp at 7500 rev/min).

In fact the Cooper works team had done no more than put a 1500 engine into their old 2·5-litre chassis. Consequently, neither Brabham, the reigning champion, nor McLaren made much impression on the 1961 season and Cooper went into a decline almost as soon as they reached their peak. Lotus, on the other hand, introduced a new model, still using a multi-tubular chassis but with more flowing lines and an even lower frontal area. It was known as the Type 21. It was this car that first brought to Formula 1 the type of rear suspension which was to be adopted gradually by all the constructors and which is still prevalent

today: lower wishbone, short transverse upper arm, and two long radius rods attached to the chassis in line with the rear cockpit member. The front suspension was no less original and was also widely copied: the streamlined upper wishbones acted on coil springs which were mounted inboard and no longer exposed to the air stream in order to reduce drag. In addition, the Lotus 21 was the only machine that did not weigh more than the minimum limit—990 lb (450 kg).

Before the season started it was thought that Porsche would be Ferrari's toughest opponent but the flat eight engine which should have been the German team's chief weapon did not appear at Monaco—in fact it was not seen at all in 1961. The Formula 1 Porsches with their four-cylinder engines were therefore just developments of the earlier Formula 2 cars fitted with a new classic-style front suspension—wishbones and coil springs—and a multitubular chassis widened at the rear to take the eight-cylinder engine that was still to come. The distinctive features of these cars were their Kugelfischer fuel-injection system and drum brakes.

The Monaco race was the first official act of the new play. Everyone waited for the results of practice with great curiosity, eager to know just how much slower than the 2·5-litre formula the new Formula 1 would be. The record stood at 1 min 36·2 s and it was Moss, driving his Lotus 18, who got nearest to it with 1 min 39·1 s, still a respectful distance away. Ginther (Ferrari 120°) was 0·2 s behind, Clark (Lotus 21) and Graham Hill (B.R.M.-Climax) 0·5 s.

The critics of the new formula grinned from ear to ear. . . . If the 1500s were already 3 per cent slower on the circuit best suited to their characteristics—lightness and agility—what on earth would they be like on the high-speed tracks? As it happened, this pessimistic outlook was to be modified during the race when Moss and Ginther, in the course of their epic duel, got down to 1 min 36·3 s.

For the more detached observer, the most interesting aspect of the practice results was their closeness: Moss and Brooks (B.R.M.-Climax), who was eighth fastest, were separated only by one second and, excluding Brabham who took part in just one practice session (he made a round trip to Indianapolis to qualify a Cooper for the 500-Mile Race), a mere 3·3 s stood between the first and next-to-last positions on the starting grid—the latter position was filled by Trintignant driving a Cooper-Maserati for the Centro-Sud team. The new formula was undoubtedly going to provide closer competition than ever and while the very small variations in performance would be enough to allow the better drivers to pull clear of the rest, they never had enough margin to take things easily. As a result there was a change in driving style: concentration, accuracy and consistency became more important than all the other required attributes, particularly physical strength.

The driving position imposed on Clark and Ireland by the new Lotus was quite a revelation. In order to drive this extremely slender car, the driver had practically to lie down, his hands on a tiny steering wheel, his arms almost straight and his shoulders pressed against the sides of the body. This position, in addition to permitting a lower frontal area, was more comfortable for the driver, but it was only feasible in a machine that could be driven without a lot of sweeping gestures, in other words, a car with precise, light and high-geared steering. Since the balance between power and handling had clearly moved towards the latter, the driver no longer needed the strength and space that Fangio had required for his popular technique of great power slides controlled by the accelerator and steered by armfuls of opposite lock. On the contrary, such things had to be avoided from now on in order not to waste even the tiniest scrap of power.

The characteristics of the new Formula 1 cars undoubtedly enabled less talented drivers to approach the times recorded by the stars because they made driving near the limit easier, but such drivers were no more capable of sustaining this level than they had ever been so there was nothing to stop the natural and logical emergence of an élite during the years of the 1500 cc Formula 1.

This point was proved in the very first Grand Prix of the new formula when victory went to the driver rather than to the car—in fact it was almost a case of the man versus the machine. On paper Stirling Moss had no hope of winning at Monaco where he was up against three Ferraris which weighed the same as the old Lotus he was using—a little more than 1100 lb (500 kg). They were, however, considerably more powerful. No doubt the British chassis, compared with the Italian one, was a partial compensation, but only partial. If the view was taken that the reduction in capacity made all drivers equal, it could not explain why drivers of the calibre of Phil Hill, von Trips and Ginther were beaten by Moss. This is what happened. After Ginther had led for the first fourteen laps, Moss, followed by Bonnier (Porsche) who eventually was unable to stand the pace, succeeded in overtaking him and went on to build up a lead of 10 s. What he lost in the long climb up to the Casino, this astonishing English driver recovered coming down in braking and overtaking the back-markers. After pottering for a lap Ginther let fly, came to grips with the situation and gradually whittled down the gap which, ten laps from the finish, was no more than 5 s. . . . It was too late, however, and Moss was still 3·6 s ahead at the end of the 100th lap of a fantastic pursuit race which had covered 195 miles (312 km).

So, the apparently unbeatable Ferraris had started the season badly, but they did take second, third (Phil Hill) and fourth (von Trips) places. In any case, it was not long before they had their revenge: seven days to be precise, the Dutch Grand Prix having been brought forward a week so that it could be run on Whit Monday, in spite of the F.I.A. ruling that there must be an interval of at least fourteen days between events counting towards an international championship. . . .

Once again practice produced very slight variations in times. Brabham, seventh fastest, was only 0·9 s away from Phil Hill and von Trips who, on this occasion, had recorded the best times. These two and the third Ferrari driver, Ginther, who was only 0·1 s behind, filled the front row of the grid.

The three Ferraris were now using 120° V6 engines with 190 bhp. Right from the start, the young German Count "Taffy" von Trips surged into the lead towards a victory that only his team-mate Phil Hill was capable of wresting from him, although for the first time in the history of Formula 1 Grands Prix all fifteen cars that started actually finished the race. As for Ginther, he was in trouble with a partly jammed throttle and a seat that had become detached from its mountings, and he had to give way first to Jim Clark,

who made magnificent use of the Lotus 21's cornering ability, and then to Stirling Moss who went past him on the inside of Tarzan corner on the last lap. In the Championship, Moss and von Trips now shared first place ahead of Hill, but Moss's position seemed very precarious since the next event was the Belgian Grand Prix on the very fast circuit at Spa.

Practice showed that it was indeed precarious. This time the variations in performance were considerable and Moss, eighth fastest, was 8·9 s behind Phil Hill. In addition to their usual trio, Ferrari had engaged Belgian champion, Olivier Gendebien, to drive a fourth 65° V6-engined car. The race was a real Ferrari procession in spite of the fact that, according to the Italian team management, the only order given to the drivers was "May the best man win. . . ." Phil Hill beat von Trips to the line followed by Ginther and Gendebien in that order: total victory for Ferrari. The leading non-Ferrariite was John Surtees who finished fifth nearly 1 min 30 s behind the winner in his Yeoman Credit Cooper-Climax. Moss was in eighth position, nearly a lap in arrears; in the Championship, Phil Hill and von Trips overtook him and Ginther caught him up.

The festival of speed was to continue on 2nd July with the French Grand Prix at Reims . . . and, it was thought, another Ferrari benefit. Once again, the Hill-von Trips-Ginther trio was given a reinforcement, the fourth musketeer on this occasion being the young Italian hope Giancarlo Baghetti with a 65° V6 car.

There were no surprises in practice which ended with the front row of the grid fully occupied by Ferraris—Hill, von Trips and Ginther. They lined up in that order and in that order finished the first lap with Moss right behind them leading the rest of the field. On the fourth lap Ginther spun at Thillois causing Moss to fall back; he no longer had a slipstream and the other two Ferraris disappeared into the distance. Meanwhile the unlucky Surtees had damaged his suspension while trying to avoid Ginther.

It seemed that the race was all over, the only vestige of interest left being whether Phil Hill would beat von Trips or whether von Trips would beat Phil Hill. Simple arithmetic said that it was von Trips's turn. But fate had other ideas. On the twentieth lap von Trips stopped at his pit with a boiling engine: thus ended the phenomenal reliability record of the Ferraris—ten cars had started in the last three Grand Prix and ten had finished. However, the cause of von Trips's retirement was hardly commonplace: his radiator had been blocked by bits of softened tar thrown up from the road by the wheels of Phil Hill's car.

But the sultry heat that hung over Reims that day was no kinder to Phil Hill than it had been to his team-mate and Championship rival. Out on his own in the lead, he lost concentration and spun at Thillois corner where the surface was breaking up and very slippery. The Ferrari was undamaged but the engine stalled and refused to restart on the starter. After a lot of effort, Hill pushed it into life but for him the race was over. . . .

Then there was Ginther. After his spin he had worked up to second place which he was holding securely when called upon to take over the torch from his fellow American. His hopes of winning his first Grand Prix lasted for one lap. He had scarcely realized

he was in the lead when he saw his oil pressure drop; he stopped at his pit. . . . The regulations forbade the taking on of oil so he went out again for half a lap . . . at the end of which, pressure gauge reading zero, he, too, was forced to give up.

These three dramatic events gave the race a new lease of life. Suddenly it was wide open. In fact, there were three drivers, who had fought wheel-to-wheel from the start, now in the victory stakes: Gurney and Bonnier driving Porsches and new boy Baghetti who was really considered too inexperienced to have much chance of outmaneuvering such veteran opposition. However, the unbelievable happened. Bonnier was the first to yield when his engine gave up the ghost two laps from the end. On the last lap the red Ferrari and the silver Porsche, still glued together in that order, appeared on the Soissons straight. At Thillois Baghetti braked early and Gurney outflanked him with ease and took the corner first. The young Italian, amazingly calm and astoundingly clear-sighted, had planned his move to perfection: immediately he tucked in behind Gurney and the trap closed on the over-confident American. A few hundred yards from the line, Baghetti pulled out, the Ferrari drew level with the Porsche and overtook just in time to take victory by a length. So Ferrari won again, but by the narrowest of margins—this Austerlitz had very nearly been a Waterloo. . . . Showered with praise and drowned in champagne, Baghetti the novice had performed with the coolness of an old hand to protect the Scuderia from such a fate.

Fifteen days later the sweltering sun of Reims gave way to the refreshing and typical British rain. However it did not merely rain at Aintree; just before the flag fell for the British Grand Prix it started to come down by the bucketful which was obviously a good thing for Moss, still in the running for the Championship as a result of the Ferrari failure at Reims. However, it was Phil Hill who got away first, ahead of von Trips and Ginther, but Moss was right behind them. The cars looked like canoes on the track streaming with water as Moss passed Ginther and von Trips relieved Phil Hill of the lead. Moss in his turn challenged the ex-leader and overtook him. He then closed on von Trips, but met with such fierce resistance that it was he, the great Moss, who was forced into

Moss at Aintree: the one who makes the mistake in a race for motorized canoes.

The young, unknown Giancarlo Baghetti triumphs at Reims, ahead of the experienced Gurney, and saves Ferrari from total defeat.

making the mistake: his Lotus went into an enormous spin which, thanks to his skill as a driver for all weathers, cost him only 10 s, but. . . .

However magnificent it had been, Moss's challenge was doomed to failure: his Lotus was forced out with brake trouble as it had been at Reims. In any case, the rain stopped half-way through the event, a strong wind dried the track and in these conditions even Moss could not have resisted the string of Ferraris which finished as expected: von Trips, Hill, Ginther. Apart from the weather conditions, the most notable feature of this Grand Prix was the appearance of the four-wheel-drive Formula 1 Ferguson. Moss drove this experimental car in practice when the track was damp and it turned out to be faster than anything else on the circuit, a fact that made his supporters regret that he did not choose to drive it in the race. They reckoned that if he had, he could have built up an early substantial lead during the downpour which the Ferrari drivers would have found difficult to cut down later. . . . However, Moss chose the Lotus and the Ferguson was driven by veteran Fairman who was not possessed of his extraordinary talent. Suddenly von Trips (27 points) and Phil Hill (25) were on their way to the title while Moss stayed where he was with 12.

However, the 1961 season of sensational productions was not yet over. After his masterly interpretation of the heroic "charge of the light brigade" at Monaco, Moss was now to present a fabulous production against the magnificent backcloth of the Nurburgring: his own personal motorized version of the story of the Teutonic Knights. However, the centre of attraction at the German Grand Prix was not Moss and his Lotus-Climax four-cylinder but Brabham and his slightly modified Cooper fitted with the first Coventry-Climax V8 which was ready at last. It was of classic layout with the cylinders set at an angle of 90°, each bank having its own cylinder head and double overhead camshaft. There were four double-choke downdraught Weber carburetors mounted on long inlet pipes, indicating that careful attention had been paid to middle-range power. The exhaust system was extraordinarily complicated: it consisted of eight pipes, two pairs per bank, each pair joining a pair from the other bank and ending in a megaphone. This viper's knot arrangement was necessary because of the firing order of the two-plane crankshaft V8. The Cooper was now heavier—1170 lb (530 kg)—but more powerful; with 170 bhp it was fairly comparable with the Ferraris which weighed very little less.

Brabham experienced a fair amount of trouble in practice, but eventually he recorded a lap time of 9 min 1·4 s which was bettered only by Phil Hill (8 min 55·2 s), the one driver to break the nine-minute barrier. Moss and his four-cylinder Climax were no more than 0·3 s behind Brabham, however. . . .

A short while before the start, a violent storm broke over the circuit and everyone rushed to fit the new Dunlop D12 rain tires. Everyone, except Brabham. He had been forced to use larger-diameter tires at the back to prevent his car bottoming, and the D12s were not available in the size he needed so he had to line up with rain tires at the front and dry-weather R5 Dunlops at the rear—a combination which made the car undrivable and caused him to shoot off the road on the first lap after he had been in the lead from the start. It was a convincing demonstration that with the new V8 the Cooper could out-accelerate the rest.

Ferrari V6.

Coventry-Climax V8.

*The Climax V8
installed in the modified
Cooper chassis.*

The injection B.R.M. V8.

To return to the start of the race. After the shower, the sun had come out again and the Ferraris—like the Porsches—were refitted with their dry-weather tires. In fact it was realized that while the D12s could be used to advantage during the early part of the race when the track was still damp, once it dried out they would wear away too quickly to last the distance. This was a valid and sensible reason for removing them but it did not appeal to Stirling Moss. He preferred to bluff it out with his rain tires, gambling on the return of the bad weather. This was how the scene was set when the flag dropped for what can be called a truly historic Grand Prix.

With Brabham out of the way, Moss exploited the extra grip of his tires to the utmost and after three laps Phil Hill was trailing by 10 s. However, as expected, the track dried out very quickly and von Trips, beating and rebeating the lap record, first caught up with Phil Hill and then passed him; Hill tucked in close behind. The two Ferraris then began to whittle down the time difference between them and Moss which soon fell to 7 s. It seemed inevitable that Moss would be beaten and there was even some doubt whether he would manage to finish the race without having to stop for a new set of tires. . . . At this point his luck turned, with the weather. The sky clouded over and Moss was rescued by the rain which bathed the circuit once more. His lead quickly grew to 20 s and von Trips and Phil Hill had to declare themselves beaten by Moss for the second time that season. Thanks to this win he was now right behind them in the Championship with the prospect of having the promising V8 Climax in his Lotus for the two Grands Prix still to be run. Was he at last to seize the crown that more than ever and more than any other drive he deserved?

The answer came with the following Grand Prix held on 10th September at Monza and it was negative. This race also determined which of the Ferrari drivers, von Trips or Phil Hill, would be the 1961 World Champion and did so as early as the second lap. Braking for the Parabolica, where tragedy lurked, von Trips's Ferrari and Jim Clark's Lotus touched. The Lotus spun off and came to rest on the inside of the track, leaving Jim Clark unhurt. The Ferrari veered towards the outside bank which it climbed before bouncing against the fence crowded with spectators, fourteen of whom were to die. Von Trips was flung out of the car and fell heavily on to the track. He was killed by the impact much to the distress of all those who had been lucky enough to know him, a great champion and a gentleman, not only by birth but by nature.

So Phil Hill won the Italian Grand Prix and with it the World Championship which had eluded Moss yet again. In the event, he had been forced to give up the idea of using the V8 Climax because of serious overheating problems. Instead he drove the works four-cylinder Lotus 21, sportingly lent to him by his friend Innes Ireland, so that he had something better than his old Lotus 18 with which to defend his position. Despite this sporting gesture, Stirling Moss, who fought furiously with Gurney for sixth place, had to retire, victim of a wheel-bearing failure.

The second British reply to the power of Ferrari was presented in practice for this dramatic Grand Prix: a new B.R.M., delicate and elegant in appearance and fitted with a 90° V8, built at Bourne, and quite different from the Climax V8. While the latter was just oversquare, $2·48 \times 2·36$ in $(63 \times 60$ mm$)$, the B.R.M. was much more so with a bore of $2·7$ in $(68·5$ mm$)$ and a stroke of 2 in $(50·8$ mm$)$. The four overhead camshafts were gear-driven (the Climax used a chain). Another notable difference was that the B.R.M. had a Lucas fuel-injection system; this system was fitted to the Climax the following year. Finally, the exhaust pipes did not cross from one bank of cylinders to the other, as on the Climax, but went directly into a long pipe underneath the car. Driven by Graham Hill, the V8 B.R.M. was fifth fastest in practice and was the only car to beat a Ferrari—there were five of them entered for the race. Unfortunately, Graham had to give up the idea of using the V8 in the race and the only British V8 that started was the Climax in Brabham's Cooper, but this soon developed overheating troubles and the Australian had to retire.

The spectators at this Grand Prix were called upon to witness two events, the shattering death of von

*Wolfgang von Trips,
archetypal gentleman-driver.*

Trips and the emergence of a new talent. This was the very young Mexican driver Ricardo Rodriguez who had been entrusted with a Ferrari. After recording the second-best time in practice, he was struggling for the same position in the race when his engine blew up. It seemed as though cruel fate wished to compensate for the loss of one great driver by the simultaneous revelation of a possible replacement in the same team.
. . .

After their bitter victory at Monza, Ferrari claimed the 1961 World Championship for Phil Hill, and the Constructors' Cup and left the German and British teams to fight among themselves for the last Grand Prix of the season, the U.S. Grand Prix held at Watkins Glen, not far from New York. Once again the only V8 in the race was in Brabham's car and once again it overheated, but he did at least have the satisfaction of leading for half the distance. After Brabham disappeared, Moss and his four-cylinder Climax found themselves in front, but the engine ran a bearing and in

the end Innes Ireland gave Team Lotus their very first Grand Prix victory, a victory which was also his first personal success in a World Championship event.

So ended the inaugural season of the new 1500 cc Formula 1; it had been marked by the notable superiority of the Ferraris which had been overcome on only two occasions. The Italian team owed their two defeats to the exceptional talent of one man, Stirling Moss. However, apart from his exploits and the amazing development of the French Grand Prix, it was a season lacking in suspense. Yet, the delayed and tentative appearance of the British V8s suggested that the following year might be much more exciting, since there would be time to sort out these new weapons during the winter that lay ahead.

*Four Ferraris on their own at Monza: symbol of a season
which, apart from the exploits of Moss, they dominated
outrageously.*

1962

b.r.m. at last...
one hill
succeeds another

As it turned out, the situation in 1962 was to be completely reversed. During the close season a crisis developed at Ferrari which resulted in the mass walk-out of engineers and technical staff, among them engineer Chiti—he went to Bologna to produce cars for A.T.S., a marque financed by Count Volpi and the industrialist Giorgio Billi—and team manager Romolo Tavoni. Because of this the Scuderia had to make do with slightly modified 1961 models for the 1962 season and while they had been almost unbeatable the previous year, this time they were to be completely outclassed by the new opposition from Britain and Germany.

Porsche had managed at last to sort out their flat eight air-cooled engine which they mounted in a new multitubular chassis; it was much slimmer in appearance and had disc brakes. Its suspension system had wishbones and torsion bars rather than the otherwise universal coil springs. Each bank of cylinders had a double overhead camshaft and two double-choke Weber carburetors; it developed about 185 bhp at 9200 rev/min. As in 1961, Gurney and Bonnier were engaged to drive the Porsches.

In spite of his recent victory at Watkins Glen, Innes Ireland was sacked from Lotus who brought in Trevor Taylor to back up Jim Clark, their great hope—he had collected some promising results in 1961. Colin Chapman had built a new multitubular chassis to take the Climax V8, the Type 24, but at the same time he was working on something entirely new and this was to be the sensation of the first Grand Prix of 1962—the Dutch at Zandvoort. It was the Type 25 which, just when the multitubular chassis had become universal in Formula 1, abandoned this type of structure for one which was to have a profound effect on the technique of chassis construction for years to come until everybody else had more or less followed suit, with the exception of . . . Brabham. He had left Cooper in order to build his own cars in association with another Australian, Ron Tauranac, an engineer. They were to continue with the multitubular space frame for another eight years—until 1970—and for several seasons they were the only, and not unsuccessful, supporters of this type of construction. However, at the beginning of 1962 the first Formula 1 Brabham was unfinished and Jack bought a Lotus 24, which he painted lime green, to start the season.

The so-called monocoque chassis of the Lotus 25 was in fact a sheet of aluminium alloy shaped into a U; it had longitudinal panels riveted along its sides which formed boxes containing the petrol tanks. In short, it was a kind of bathtub, completely open at the top which ended at the front ahead of the toe-board, with a steel structure carrying the suspension and steering; at the rear it was closed by a large square-section frame above the gear-box and in the centre were two frames carrying the dashboard and the fireproof bulkhead at the driver's back. The advantages of this type of construction, apart from its tremendous elegance and neatness which made a pleasant contrast to the usual forest of tubes, was firstly, increased rigidity. Here the gains were considerable compared with the multitubular space frame; the latter can theoretically produce results that are just as good in this respect, but in practice it is a necessarily imperfect structure because the cockpit cannot be sufficiently triangulated at the top and the rigidity of the whole is only equal to that of its weakest part. Second, reduced

weight—it scaled less than 88 lb (40 kg). Finally, improved safety: the driver no longer ran the risk of being injured by a bent or broken tube in the event of a collision.

The gear-box was a five-speed ZF and the engine the V8 Coventry-Climax which had been improved. The leaky cooling system, which had caused the overheating problems, had been corrected. For the 1962 season the FWMV/1A developed 187 bhp at 8500 rev/min. This engine not only powered the Lotuses, it was also fitted (with a Colotti gear-box) to the chassis of a marque making its debut in Formula 1: Lola. The Lola's designer, Eric Broadley, had made a name for himself as a constructor of excellent small sports cars and had been chosen by the Yeoman Credit team to build cars for Surtees and Salvadori. His design for the multitubular chassis was very classical but the suspension it carried was most original, as far as geometry went at least. At the front the upper wishbone consisted in effect of a transverse arm linked to a fore-and-aft radius arm attached to the top of the cockpit torsion member. The rear suspension was distinctive solely for the fact that the upper wishbone was inverted, i.e. the apex was attached to the chassis while its base was formed by the top of the hub carrier; the lower wishbone was replaced by a single transverse arm and the system completed by two radius rods.

The third Climax customer—before the Brabham appeared—was Cooper. Their cars, entrusted to Bruce McLaren and Formula Junior discovery Tony Maggs, differed in that they had a six-speed gear-box which allowed the best possible use to be made of the relatively narrow speed range of this engine.

Richie Ginther had replaced Tony Brooks at B.R.M. where he became number two to Graham Hill. Their cars were the ones that had appeared in practice at Monza in 1961; they had slightly more than 180 bhp at 11,000 rev/min, this very high speed being a consequence of the oversquare dimensions of the engine. The gear-box was a five-speed Colotti which was later to show a certain incompatibility with the strong vibrations from the B.R.M. V8. These Bourne-made cars had the same sort of power as the Lotus 25s and also held the road well, but they suffered from a weight handicap compared with Chapman's latest creation; this was principally due to the fact that they had to pay for their properly rigid tubular chassis and the price was a certain heaviness.

The final works team entered for the World Championship 1962 were Ferrari, where the Belgian Willy Mairesse took over from Ginther as test/racing driver alongside Phil Hill. Ricardo Rodriguez and the Italian hopes, Baghetti and Bandini, were also given drives by the Italian team during the 1962 season, a season which for Ferrari was to be as dismal as the 1961 season had been brilliant.

As for the private teams, Rob Walker had been deprived of the services of the irreplaceable Stirling Moss who had been seriously injured in a race at Goodwood at the beginning of the season and lost to motor sport. Formula 1 had lost its leader, its driver-standard against which the talents of all the others were measured. Maurice Trintignant took his place in the dark blue Lotus with its white band. The British team U.D.T.-Laystall signed up Masten Gregory and Innes Ireland to drive their V8 Climax- or B.R.M.-engined Lotus 24s.

The Championship opened among the dunes of

Zandvoort: for once, the Dutch Grand Prix preceded the Monaco event. All the new cars lined up for the start and Jim Clark took the lead ahead of Graham Hill and Gurney. Only these three looked like possible winners, but first the gear-lever of the Porsche's six-speed gear-box broke and then the Lotus 25's transmission failed, thus leaving Graham Hill to win his first Grand Prix and B.R.M. their second—their first since Bonnier's victory three years earlier on the same track. Trevor Taylor (Lotus 24) finished second while the reigning champion, Phil Hill, came in third with his Ferrari, which was more conspicuous for the wire wheels it still sported than for its performance. Apparently its 190 bhp V6 engine could not make up for the deficiencies of its chassis and suspension system.

At Monaco the duel between Graham Hill and Jim Clark continued until they were forced to retire one after the other, Hill because of low oil pressure and Clark because of another transmission failure, this time due to the clutch. It was Bruce McLaren who took the flag after a steady, intelligent performance which enabled him to fight off a last-minute attack from Phil Hill; his winning margin was only 2 s, but it was enough.

The two unlucky but brilliant exhibitions which Jim Clark had mounted at Zandvoort and Monaco established him as the leader of the New Wave of drivers. He drove the Lotus 25 with great precision and in his hands it seemed, if not the best prepared, at least the fastest of the Formula 1 cars around. Everybody was just waiting for him to win and this he did in the Belgian Grand Prix. However, at the beginning of the race, it was Willy Mairesse and Trevor Taylor who fought for the lead. Clark got himself badly placed at the start but, completely unopposed, he disposed of this handicap and shot off towards his first Grand Prix success. Behind him Mairesse and Taylor were engaged in a sparring match which ended in a collision; this seemed to have been provoked by the Belgian who later complained that Taylor had tried to box him in in order to protect his teammate's lead. With these two out of the way, Graham Hill found himself in second place in spite of a failing engine, and in the lead for the Championship stakes.

The French Grand Prix took place on the fast, difficult circuit at Rouen in Normandy where the favorites were well and truly massacred. The front row of the grid was shared by the winners of the three preceding Grands Prix. Clark had made pole position, but only just, ahead of Graham Hill (0·2 s behind) and McLaren (0·6 s behind). The Ferraris had withdrawn which was a great mistake because the three men on the front row were overwhelmed by trouble. So also were Surtees, who ran a brilliant second for a long time with his Lola, Brabham who broke the rear suspension of his Lotus, Ginther who had to push his car before he could complete the warming-up lap to have his battery recharged. . . . This time it was Gurney's turn—what a year—to win his first Grand Prix, which also gave Porsche their first victory, after a steady climb through the field. He took first place from Graham Hill nine laps from the end when the latter was having trouble with his accelerator. Second man home, Tony Maggs, finished more than a lap in arrears.

The fifth round was set against the horse-racing backcloth of Aintree. Only one Ferrari started, driven by Phil Hill, and it was forced to retire without glory when in ninth place. This race settled down into a duel between Clark, once again fastest in practice, and Surtees who clung to him like a leech until he lost second gear and fell behind, although he retained second place. Gurney's race was the complete opposite of his race at Rouen: bothered with a slipping clutch, the American fell back from third to ninth as the laps went by. Brabham scored his first two Championship points by finishing fifth with the Lotus, behind McLaren and Graham Hill whose tires were right down to the canvas at the end. Because of this placing the Londoner kept his lead in the Championship, but he now had to share it with Clark.

On the results of practice it would have been a risky business to forecast the outcome of the German Grand Prix. Gurney was certainly the fastest (with an excellent 8 min 47·2 s), 3 s ahead of Graham Hill, but the first five places were occupied by five different makes—Porsche, B.R.M., Lotus, Lola and Cooper, in that order. Only the Ferraris were out of the picture in spite of returning in force with four cars, one of which was a brand-new model entrusted to Bandini. In the end, the fate of the race, run on a soaking wet Nurburgring, was in the hands of three men: Graham Hill, Surtees and Gurney, who finished in that order with 4 s covering the three. It was a nerve-racking race and the Londoner showed that he was the toughest and most determined of this trio of hard men who, while giving nothing away, made not the slightest mistake either in the most difficult of driving conditions: a circuit full of traps, a terribly slippery surface and constant pressure from the opposition. Clark finished fourth, more than 40 s behind; he failed to join this fight because, after stalling on the line (he forgot to switch on his fuel pumps), he could not catch up with the leading trio.

However, the most notable feature of this Grand Prix was the first appearance of the Brabham-Climax. It was a very light, classic-style car distinctive for its rational suspension layout at the front where the lower wishbones were angled forward to resist braking forces. After serious engine trouble in practice, Brabham, who left the line twenty-fifth and last, was in ninth place towards the end of the first lap, but he lost this position to Clark and then followed Ginther until he was forced to retire with a jammed throttle.

Although there were three Grands Prix left, the turning-point of the 1962 Championship came at Monza. During practice, the two pretenders to the title showed that not only were they in a class of their own but they were pretty nearly equal. Clark (driving teammate Taylor's car which undoubtedly was not set up as he would have wished) was only 0·03 s ahead of Graham Hill. The suspense did not last long. Clark made the best start but failed completely to shake off Hill who was in the lead at the end of the first lap. The second time round the rivals came past together in the same order, but on the third lap the B.R.M. appeared on its own: the Lotus stood at its pit while Clark explained that he had felt his transmission seize. At that moment, he lost the Championship. Graham Hill pranced along in the lead all on his own and nobody could get near him. At a distance Ginther was trying

Overleaf: Clark at Rouen at the Nouveau Monde hairpin: the master of braking in a corner.

*Gurney's eight-cylinder
Porsche . . .*

*. . . and its
air-cooled engine.*

The Lotus 25, the first monocoque, from which all future Formula 1 cars descended.

The Lola-Climax.

The Brabham-Climax.

to make it a double for B.R.M. which was made easier for him when Surtees, with whom he was struggling hard, broke a piston. Further back still, a large bunch of Coopers, Ferraris and Porsches travelling in a tight pack swapped places and fought among themselves until the situation was resolved by a series of incidents and only McLaren and Mairesse were left to compete for third place. The game was played out in the last corner where the calm New Zealander outflanked his impetuous opponent much to the great vexation of the Milanese crowd.

Nevertheless, Clark's hopes of taking the World Championship title rose after the U.S. Grand Prix which he won in a totally convincing manner, leading from start to finish ahead of Graham Hill. So, whichever of the two won the South African Grand Prix to be run at East London on 29th December would be World Champion. Although Hill had nine points more than Clark, he had scored them in the maximum number of events allowed by the 1962 regulations—five. Should he win the South African G.P., he would

take the title; if he did not win, he could not add anything to his total. On the other hand, if Clark won, he could add the nine points to his score which was derived from only four events. In this case he and Hill would have an equal number of points but, because of his greater number of victories, he would take the title.

The fate of this title which is worth so much money both to the driver and to the constructor was decided by a tired mechanic and a spare part worth no more than 50 cents. Racing is made up of such unlikely contrasts: advanced technology and trivial errors, meticulous preparation and gross neglect, detailed research and the vaguest empiricism. Sometimes logic triumphs and the deserving cause wins but sometimes not, which is disconcerting for the spectator and discouraging for the competitor. However there is always a reason for the misfortune, sometimes technical, sometimes temperamental, depending on whether a mechanical part or a human being is behind it.

During the 1962 season Jim Clark and his Lotus 25 put on alternate exhibitions of tremendous skill and

out; on the contrary, because the season's fastest driver-car combination would have got what they deserved. However, the gaps in the organization had to be paid for. If this fact was rather heavily underlined there was in the final analysis a reason for what happened. . . . Crucial perhaps.

So, Graham Hill and B.R.M. took the title, an achievement which brought to an end fifteen years of effort, dismal failure, rebuffs and vexations. They had had more troubles than any other company could have coped with, but nevertheless they got over them. Until the year of grace 1962, the history of this team was nothing but a succession of uninterrupted disappointments during which time they proved that ridicule never killed anyone. However, the people involved—particularly Raymond Mays and the principal supplier of funds, Sir Alfred Owen—never lost heart. They deserve admiration for their persistence in pursuing the success that took so long to materialize and was so dearly bought.

Nor had it all been easy for the new World Champion. His was not the story of a brilliantly talented man rising to the peak of his profession after a meteoric career. He had come up the hard way, starting as a mechanic at Lotus who eventually gave him a drive. His most outstanding qualities as a driver were determination, professional pride and a formidable devotion to racing; off the track, his courtesy and sense of humor made him the pleasantest of men to talk to. At thirty-three, after six seasons of racing—he started at Brands Hatch on 30th April 1956 with a borrowed Lotus 1100—he was a link between the rising generation, which was led by Jim Clark, and the waning generation of people like Moss, Brooks and Salvadori. It is important to realize that he did not win a Grand Prix until 1962 and in this respect his career is similar to B.R.M.'s. However, the comparison must not be pushed too far because whereas B.R.M. were mocked and despised by the public at large during their difficult period, Graham Hill was very soon established as a popular figure, particularly in England where no other driver, and that includes Moss, had ever had, or indeed has, such a good image. In short, the new World Champion Driver was not only a great driver, he was a personality, a character of wide-ranging appeal.

To turn to the machinery, it was not the most technically advanced car that came out on top in 1962; nevertheless certain performances of the Lotus 25 had convinced observers that this was really the superior machine. At the other end of the scale, the most disappointing feature of the season was the eight-cylinder Porsche which never came up to expectations, and although it did win once, at Rouen, it owed this victory more to the failure of the opposition than to its own performance. In the final analysis it had its best race at the Nurburgring where it performed on equal terms with the B.R.M. and Lola. The latter did not win a race, but it usually went very well and gave Surtees fourth place in the Championship, ahead of Gurney. The Coopers were also fairly tame in spite of their win at Monaco which was a triumph of reliability. Bruce McLaren was their best driver and his consistent appearance in the first six took him to third place in the Championship. Ferrari were on the way down and the 1961 Champion, Phil Hill, finished a distant sixth. Finally, the Brabham looked promising.

failure and while it was undeniably a more brilliant partnership than Graham Hill and his B.R.M., it was also a less consistent one. The difference lay in the level of organization achieved by the two teams. Efficiency of this kind was a rather weak point with Team Lotus whereas B.R.M. that year ran like clockwork—was under the beady eye of their chief engineer, Tony Rudd. Given these circumstances, although Clark and his Lotus were always favorites at the start, it was usually Graham Hill and B.R.M. who came out on top, particularly in a Championship event. It was not B.R.M. but Lotus who forgot to fit the locking washer to the bolt holding the bearing of an engine auxiliary shaft; the bolt worked loose under vibration and the oil leaked out. When the bolt fell off, sixty-one of the eighty-two laps of the race had been run and Clark was well ahead of Graham Hill: with 30 s in hand and scarcely 30 min left to go it seemed all over. There was no doubt about it. Had Clark been spared this trouble and crowned World Champion 1962, no one would have been at all put

1963

the coronation of jim clark

During the close season Porsche announced that they were retiring from Formula 1. At the same time a new Italian marque appeared on the scene with engineer Chiti's latest creation—the A.T.S. Consequently a lot of drivers were up for transfer: freed by Porsche, Gurney went to Brabham (whose retirement from driving was already being rumored) and Bonnier replaced Trintignant in the Rob Walker team. Phil Hill and Baghetti went to A.T.S. from Ferrari who signed up John Surtees to join their regular driver Mairesse and Ludovico Scarfiotti, their occasional extra. Surtees had come on to the market because the Yeoman Credit team had been disbanded and their ex-team manager, Reg Parnell, bought up their equipment and ran a Lola for the very young Chris Amon. Still in England, U.D.T.-Laystall disappeared and was replaced by a new organization called B.R.P. (British Racing Partnership). They built their own chassis to which they fitted Lotus suspensions; one of their drivers was Innes Ireland and the other was American Jim Hall, at that time virtually unknown but later to become very famous as the founder of Chaparral. Another American, Tony Settember, and an Englishman Burgess, were to drive the Settember-designed Sciroccos. In Italy, the Centro-Sud team bought a 1962 B.R.M. for Lorenzo Bandini; finally, Joseph Siffert was to drive a new Lotus-B.R.M. in the colors of the Swiss Filipinetti team.

There were ten rounds in the 1963 World Championship series, a series which gave Jim Clark the opportunity of putting the Lotus 25 in what was unquestionably its rightful place. In short, he won seven of the ten events, leaving only two for Graham Hill and one for John Surtees—his first.

Most of the teams had new cars. The reigning champion, B.R.M., built a hybrid chassis consisting of a central monocoque flanked by a tubular frame at each end: it was lighter and stiffer than their previous chassis and had a higher resistance to roll. Their V8 engine had been slightly modified, particularly on the exhaust side, and had gained a bit more power. The Lotus 25s were virtually unchanged but the Climax engine had developed: the bore/stroke relationship had been altered to make it more oversquare and the Lucas fuel-injection system had been adopted. The new Cooper chassis was still a tubular structure, but it had slightly revised suspension to combat the effects of brake dive. The new Brabham was a development of the 1962 model. Ferrari had a new multitubular chassis which seemed lighter and more scientifically designed; they had given up their wire wheels and fitted the Bosch fuel-injection system to the V6 engine which now gave 205 bhp at 10,500 rev/min—this was a stopgap while they were waiting for their V8.

The A.T.S. was 100 per cent new; it had a very narrow multitubular chassis with extremely low, delicate bodywork surmounted by an enormous windscreen. The suspension was of classic pattern with inboard front springs and the rear brakes attached to the Colotti six-speed gear-box differential casing. The engine was a 90° V8 with a bore and stroke of 2·59 in (66 mm) and 2·14 in (54·6 mm) respectively. It had four overhead camshafts, dual ignition and four doublechoke Weber carburetors; it gave 190 bhp at 10,000 rev/min.

Finally, the Settember-designed Sciroccos had a hybrid chassis like the B.R.M. and also used a B.R.M. engine.

For the start of the season at Monaco only a few of these machines were ready. Hill and Ginther in particular had to use their 1962 cars. By way of compensation this race saw the first appearance in Formula 1 of a Volkswagen-based gear-box (fitted to Gurney's Brabham) built in England by Hewland and derived from the well-tried unit they supplied for Formula Junior racing; however, the first of a future great line was to be the cause of the American's retirement.

The battle for the best practice time was limited to Clark (who made it), Graham Hill, John Surtees demonstrating that the new Ferrari was competitive, and Ginther. They lined up in that order on the starting grid which had moved to a new place—instead of being on the quayside just before the Gasworks hairpin, it was now on the other side opposite the stands: a really sensible move. From the start Hill and Ginther took the lead, followed closely by Clark and Surtees, but the Scotsman did not wait long to launch his attack. On the eighteenth lap he went ahead and left the rest behind. Surtees also challenged the B.R.M.s and managed to hold second place between the fifty-eighth and sixty-second lap when, in need of a change of goggles, he had to surrender his position to Graham Hill. The latter found himself back in the lead on the seventy-eighth lap as Jim Clark, who had been 15 s in front, spun at the Gasworks with a jammed gear-box. From then on the race was over and B.R.M. won an encouraging double ahead of McLaren and Surtees who had livened up the end of the proceedings with a frantic struggle for third place, breaking and rebreaking the lap record as they went.

The A.T.S., B.R.P. and Scirocco machines were all present and correct for the Belgian Grand Prix at Spa, but they made very little difference to the outcome of a race that Jim Clark literally ran away with. The torrential rain caused an unusually high number of incidents, but Clark was quite at home and, very much the Flying Scotsman, was running a lap ahead of all his rivals; however, his toughest opponent, Graham Hill, was suffering from mechanical troubles and these eventually forced him to retire. The Ferraris also broke down and Gurney was holding a steady second place ahead of McLaren whose engine was firing on only seven cylinders; towards the end of the race this drawback lost its significance as the rain got worse and grip and visibility fell to practically zero. While John Cooper was recovering from a road accident, the Cooper pit was temporarily being managed by an English timber merchant called Ken Tyrrell. Now he noticed that Gurney had slowed down quite a lot, quite sure of himself with his 1 min 12 s lead, so he gave a discreet sign to McLaren to go as fast as he could and the gap started to close without the Brabham pit realizing what was going on. Two laps from the end McLaren let Clark through and tucked in behind him. The pair of them arrived on the heels of Gurney who, seeing only Clark in his mirrors, moved over to give him a free passage. . . . Clark went by with McLaren in his wake. Tyrrell's reputation for cool running gained further acceptance from his maneuver.

So, before the third Grand Prix of the 1963 season, the two arch-rivals of 1962, Graham Hill and Jim Clark, had once again drawn level. As it happened, this was

Monaco:
Hill ahead of Clark
and Ginther.

66

to be the only moment of uncertainty in the Championship stakes that year. After his win at Spa, Clark had a run of victories which very quickly put him out of reach of his opponent. At Zandvoort he repeated the extraordinary performance he gave at Spa and led the entire field by a lap, while Graham Hill had to retire once more, this time with a blown cylinder-head gasket. Dan Gurney kept his second place on this occasion in spite of a pit stop to have a fuel-line connection tightened up, while Surtees, who had a spin, finished third.

In the French Grand Prix at Reims, Clark once more took the lead from pole position. Graham Hill stalled on the line and was unable to restart without a push from his mechanics which earned him a minute's penalty and destroyed all his hopes of winning. Clark got away, followed at a distance by Surtees and Brabham and it all seemed to point to another Clark solo when his engine started to splutter. Out came the watches as if by magic to confirm that the Lotus's lead was gradually dwindling. Brabham was beginning to look like a possible winner when a sudden downpour soaked the circuit. Clark made magnificent use of the now slippery surface and managed to stabilize his lead, his superb braking and cornering technique winning back the time he was losing on the straight. And then the decidedly unlucky Brabham had to stop to have an ignition lead fixed. . . . So Tony Maggs and Cooper took second place. In spite of his penalty, Graham Hill finished fourth, but the C.S.I. decided to cancel his Championship points on the grounds that starting on the starter was compulsory.

Interest at the British Grand Prix, held at Silverstone, was centred on the increasingly competitive Brabhams. They shared the front row of the grid with Clark (pole position) and Graham Hill, but any doubt about the final result was soon dispelled. Brabham and Gurney, the latter trying out the new flat-crank Climax engine with independent exhausts right and left, did indeed keep in front for the first four laps. Then Clark passed them, never to be caught. When the two Brabhams broke their engines, Graham Hill took over second place only to run short of fuel on the last lap and, crawling to the finish, was forced to let Surtees beat him to the post.

However, the Ferrari driver was to do better than second in the German Grand Prix: he succeeded in breaking Clark's winning streak and temporarily obscuring his glaring superiority which was becoming a trifle monotonous. Still, it was the Scot who recorded the best practice time, though Surtees was only 0·9 s behind, very little for a lap of 14·17 miles (22·6 km) particularly as he was constantly troubled by ignition and carburation problems. The revelation of practice, however, was the young Italian Lorenzo Bandini who drove a 1962 B.R.M. for Centro-Sud into third place in front of Graham Hill.

Clark was first away from the line, but at the end of the first lap Ginther was in the lead ahead of Surtees, Clark, McLaren, Hill and Maggs. Ireland and Bandini had collided and retired. Ginther started to have gearbox troubles and slip back and Mairesse went off at Flugplatz and was seriously injured. Now there was something definitely wrong with Clark's engine. Surtees was doing all he could to take advantage of the situation and build up a clear lead; the ex-World Champion motorcyclist was over a minute in front when he crossed the line to win the first Grand Prix of his new motor-racing career.

*Jim Clark,
king of Spa.*

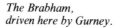

*The Brabham,
driven here by Gurney.*

The new A.T.S.
with Phil Hill at the wheel.

Jim Clark getting to grips with the Dutch police.

Mathematically, Clark's title bid was still vulnerable when the circus went to Monza at the beginning of September for the Italian Grand Prix. This was scheduled for the combined circuit, but there were so many accidents in practice that in the end the organizers decided to run the race on the road circuit only. John Surtees was trying out the brand-new monocoque Ferrari which was, however, fitted with the V6 engine. He recorded the best practice time ahead of Graham Hill who had the new B.R.M. monocoque which had not been finally sorted out. The Ferrari took the lead and kept it for seventeen laps in spite of challenges from Clark who never let go although his Lotus seemed slower. Surtees, however, fell victim to a broken valve spring and Clark found himself alone in the lead, 3 s in front of Hill and Gurney. The race was not yet over because his two rivals, towing one another along, caught him up. For twenty laps the

three men engaged in a fierce struggle: Hill was the first to go—with clutch trouble—and he was followed very shortly afterwards by Gurney, let down by his fuel-injection system. So Clark won his fifth Grand Prix of the season and with it the World Championship and Lotus were assured of the Constructors' Cup. A just reward, although a season late, for the most outstanding car, a car which would exert an influence on single-seaters for years to come.

Of the three remaining Grands Prix of 1963, Jim Clark won two—the Mexican and South African—thus finishing the season with seven victories to his credit out of ten races run; nobody had shown such superiority before. Graham Hill scored his second victory of the year in the U.S. Grand Prix and was runner-up in the Championship, with the same number of points as his team-mate Ginther. Nevertheless, it had been a disappointing season for this London

driver because his car had not come up to expectations and more often than not he had been forced to call on the services of his 1962 machine.

On the technical side, 1963 was the year when all four engines used in Formula 1 went over to fuel injection; three of these units—the Climax, B.R.M. and A.T.S.—were now V8s and although Ferrari remained faithful to the V6, it was only a temporary measure while they finished their V8. All the engines gave about 200 bhp, but B.R.M. alone was prepared to say so. The various transmission systems gave their share of trouble: only Brabham (Hewland) and Lotus (ZF) were content with five speeds, the rest had six. As for weight, the Brabham succeeded in knocking the Lotus 25 off its perch as the lightest car in Formula 1 by getting down to the minimum limit of 990 lb (450 kg), while of the relatively competitive cars the Cooper was the heaviest at 1058 lb (480 kg). Finally, everyone ran on tires supplied by Dunlop who had brought their R6s to such a high level of development that they obviously made a big contribution to the increased average speeds recorded on the various circuits.

Although there was a lot of to-ing and fro-ing of second-string drivers, the big names on the whole stayed put; the transfers that took place were as follows: Bandini went to Ferrari to take Mairesse's place; the Formula Junior champion, Peter Arundell, took over at Lotus from the unlucky Trevor Taylor who joined another Team Lotus exile, Innes Ireland, at B.R.P.; Phil Hill replaced Maggs at the wheel of the second works Cooper and Maggs, like Baghetti, found a drive at Centro-Sud. In contrast, the B.R.M. (G. Hill and Ginther) and Brabham (Gurney) teams remained unchanged.

*The start
at the Nurburgring.*

*Clark (1st)
and Gurney (2nd)
share the champagne
after the South African Grand Prix.*

1964

a cliff~hanger championship

Competition for the Championship in 1964 was to be very close, so close in fact that the name of the driver who would take the title was not known until the last round was run. There had been a similar situation two seasons earlier, but then there had been only two contenders at the finish whereas this time there were to be three: Surtees, G. Hill and Clark.

The season started, however, exactly like the previous one with a Graham Hill-Richie Ginther double at Monaco. Ferrari brought along their new monocoque fitted with the V8 engine, using a Bosch direct fuel-injection system and giving at least 200 bhp at about 11,000 rev/min. B.R.M. had abandoned the semi-monocoque structure which had proved so difficult to adjust in 1963 and instead were using a full monocoque. Their V8 engine had been improved and was now developing 210 bhp at 11,000 rev/min. The new Lotus, the 33, had been destroyed during a preparatory race in England, so Clark was using his faithful 25 which had been slightly modified, mainly so that it would take the new 13 in (330 mm) Dunlop tires now fitted to all the works cars, though the private teams were still making do with the old 15 in (381 mm) equipment. The dimensions of the Climax engine had been changed to give a larger bore and shorter stroke; its power was of the order of 200 bhp at 9750 rev/min. They were also installed in the Brabhams which kept their tubular chassis, and in the

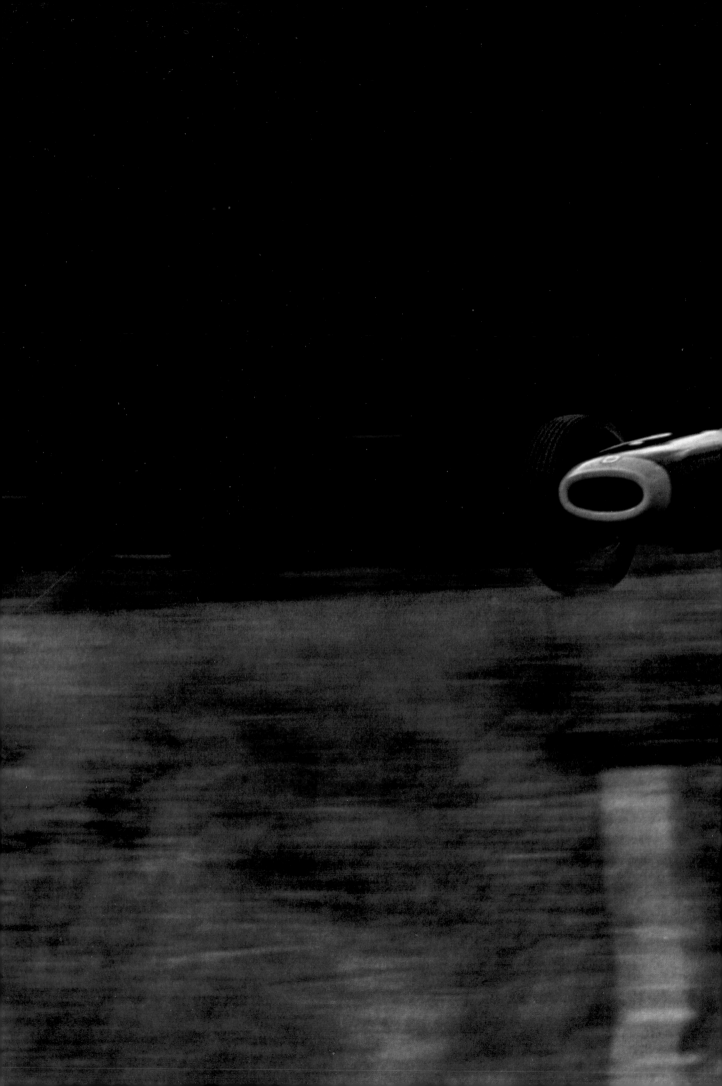

Brabham (left) and Clark:
problems at Monaco.

Start of an amazing Belgian Grand
Prix which . . .

... ended with this dialogue
between an unlucky Gurney and a
Clark, who, out of fuel after the
finish, was still unaware that he had
won.

Coopers which for the first time abandoned their simple tubular structure. This was now reinforced by riveted aluminium panels. The Coopers also had new suspension with inboard springs at the front like the Lotuses, B.R.M.s and Ferraris and an original system at the back comprising a normal wishbone and transverse arm below and a transverse arm and radius rod up above. All the other constructors had adopted the Lotus geometry, i.e. lower inverted wishbone, upper transverse arm and two radius rods.

From the technical point of view, therefore, the forces seemed fairly evenly matched and as it turned out the cars were closer in performance than they had ever been before. By the end of practice only 0·5 s separated the fastest of them—Lotus, Brabham, B.R.M. and Ferrari.

In the race, Clark took the lead at first, but coming out of the chicane he slid and hit the protective barrier with his left rear wheel. Three laps later his rear anti-roll bar came loose and he had to spend several seconds at his pit to have it removed by the mechanics. He rejoined the race in third position behind Gurney and Graham Hill, and though he chased them very hard he could not catch them because, of course, the handling was affected. In front of him, Gurney started to have trouble with his new Hewland gear-box and had to let Graham Hill into the lead before he was forced to retire on the sixty-second lap. From then on the B.R.M. had the race sewn up, particularly as Clark lost his oil pressure and had to give up eight laps from the end, thus allowing Ginther, who had driven a very steady race, to take second place behind his number one. Surtees's Ferrari had to stop with a broken gear-box on the twelfth lap when lying fifth. On the day before the Grand Prix an unknown young Scotsman had won the Formula 3 event; it was Jackie Stewart driving a Cooper-B.M.C. managed by Ken Tyrrell.

The year 1963 went on repeating itself at Zandvoort where Jim Clark took his revenge for Monaco and led from start to finish while Hill had to retire. The Scotsman and the Londoner found themselves once again sharing the top of the Championship table. The gearbox trouble which put Surtees and his Ferrari V8 out of the running at Monaco had been traced and he took second place at Zandvoort, the only competitor to finish on the same lap as the winner. Unfortunately, Dan Gurney broke his steering wheel this time.

This strange repetition of results tempted one to forecast a Jim Clark victory in the Belgian Grand Prix. Indeed he did win, but in absolutely bewildering circumstances that were not at all reminiscent of his solo 1963 performance. Never has a Grand Prix had such an unlikely end. Three laps from the finish the leader, Gurney, ran out of fuel but he managed nevertheless to get to his pit where he found that this eventuality had not been catered for. In other words they had no fuel. Absolutely furious, instead of waiting until someone found a can somewhere, Dan Gurney committed what was literally a "suicidal" act—he set off again empty and stopped, of course completely dry, a little further on. Meanwhile Graham Hill had taken the lead but his satisfaction did not last long as his fuel pump let him down at Stavelot, and so it was a surprised but delighted McLaren who found himself first with half a lap still to go. It all seemed settled, but it was at this point that the Cooper's engine started to make a frightful noise on the long climb before the La Source hairpin. The alternator belt had broken and the battery was flat. Even so, Bruce McLaren managed to drag himself to La Source, get round the bend and free-wheel down towards the finishing line. You can imagine his relief. He saw the man with the flag getting ready to greet him. . . . But as all this was happening and with only a few yards of the race left, a missile shot out of the blue and overtook the Cooper. It was Clark's Lotus which had managed to fight its way up from the back position to which it had been relegated after a minute and a half stop to take on more water for the overheated engine. After the stop, no one had given Clark another thought. It was a miraculous victory, the result of sheer luck, but all the same it gave Clark the lead in the Championship while he was still without his new car. Given these conditions, he became an even greater favorite in the race for the title. Although once again the use of the 33 was denied him at Rouen, it was thought, quite reasonably, that he was on the way to reproducing the series of consecutive victories he had achieved the year before.

However, this was to ignore the capriciousness of fate. This time it took the form of a pebble which, thrown up probably by the wheel of a back-marker, fell into one of the inlet trumpets on Clark's engine, and was digested. Result—a broken valve. The Scotsman had to retire and leave Gurney to take his revenge for the bad luck and other imponderables which, with distressing regularity, had so far prevented him from giving the Brabham marque its first Grand Prix victory. Everyone in the Australian team was overjoyed, particularly as the boss, although losing second place by a hairsbreadth to Graham Hill, had set a new lap record. After two years of constant tribulation, complete success had come at last. On the other side, the Ferrari was not yet right and Surtees had to retire at Rouen after his injection pump had jammed. As for Cooper, they were outclassed and suffered repeated suspension troubles. In the Championship, Graham Hill was now back within one point of Clark. It seemed that the fight for the title would follow the pattern of 1962 and be restricted to these two, and these two only, unless Gurney was really rid of his jinx. . . .

Brands Hatch, a short but good spectator circuit, was used for the first time for the British Grand Prix. Here it was discovered that the American was still hag-ridden. He had to retire on the third lap with ignition trouble when he was right up with Clark. The Lotus driver, however, still at the wheel of his old, considerably modified 25, had not won with the disappearance of Gurney. He still had to contend with Graham Hill whose enterprising challenges continued to the end where they crossed the line only 3 s apart. Surtees finished more than a minute behind, while Brabham in fourth place was a whole lap in arrears. Obviously the B.R.M. had made better progress than the Lotus and the four-point lead that Clark had over Hill in the Championship did not mean very much with five Grands Prix still to come.

The situation was made even more complicated by the appearance of a third contender after the German Grand Prix—John Surtees. For this race, the V8 Ferrari was perfectly in tune and now developed 210 bhp at 11,000 rev/min. Practice produced some extraordinarily close results. Variations in times for the 14·17-mile (22·6 km) lap of the Nurburgring are usually counted in seconds rather than in tenths of

John Surtees: 1964 World Champion.

78

*In full flight,
from the front (Clark)
or from behind (Hill).
(Right-hand page).*

the pedals, for example, was reserved exclusively for the smallest of the Japanese mechanics. To the rear, the monocoque stopped at the back of the seat. Then came the engine which acted as a chassis member in that it carried the suspension, a system that was to become almost universal a few years later. The suspension was of classic pattern at the front with inboard-mounted springs, but less conventional at the rear because here, too, the spring/damper units were mounted inside the "bodywork" pivoting on a small triangle operated from the top of the hub carrier by an inclined transverse rod. Wheels, brakes and tires were all supplied by Dunlop.

*Difficult start for the new Honda, driven
by the American Bucknum . . .*

seconds, but this time only 0·9 s separated Surtees (8 min 38·4 s), Clark, who was at last driving his 33 (8 min 38·8 s) and Gurney (8 min 39·3 s). However, there was as much attention focused on the back row of the grid as there was on the front because there in the rear was a brand-new machine—the eagerly awaited Honda, now making its first appearance. Besides bearing the name of the most distinguished racing motor-cycle manufacturer in the world, this car was so unusual in appearance and so original technically that it was already stealing the limelight.

Designed and built under the direction of engineer Nakamura, the Honda differed from the rest chiefly in having a 60° V12 engine placed transversely in the chassis behind the cockpit. It had a built-up crankshaft and big ends mounted on needle roller-bearings. The four overhead camshafts were driven by a train of gears situated in the middle of the engine, which was also the take-off point for the drive to the six-speed transmission. There were four valves per cylinder in the pent-roof combustion chambers, while carburation was by an incredible battery of a dozen Keihin motorcycle carburetors placed in the middle of the V. In the first version, the power output was said to be 224 bhp at 12,000 rev/min, i.e. the highest in Formula 1.

The chassis was no less original than the engine. Perhaps it was because Nakamura came from the aircraft industry—he had had a hand in the design of the famous Japanese Zero fighter planes. Whatever the influence, the chassis was not the bathtub structure used by European Formula 1 constructors, but a real monocoque closed at the top—in short a tube, with an opening only for the driver. Needless to say, access to

*. . . in spite
of an army
of Japanese mechanics.*

The transverse arrangement of the engine had been chosen to concentrate as much mass as possible round the car's centre of gravity in an effort to obtain the lowest possible polar moment of inertia and thus increase maneuverability. In addition, this layout enabled Honda to keep the wheelbase to a normal length in spite of a long engine. Although it was a technical masterpiece the car seemed outrageously complicated

and it was suspected that sorting it out would probably be a long and difficult job, particularly as the Japanese factory, finding that there was no first-rate driver available, had decided to call on the services of a young American who was completely unknown in Europe—Ronnie Bucknum. Not only had he to find out about the Nurburgring, he also had the crushing task of adjusting a brand-new and complex car to the excessive demands and peculiarities of the difficult Eifel circuit. In these conditions, nobody was at all surprised that he experienced the utmost difficulty before he got his lap time down to within a minute of that recorded by Surtees. . . .

Practice was overshadowed by the death of the colorful Dutch amateur driver Carel Godin de

The remains of
Phil Hill's car at Zeltweg.

Beaufort, who was killed when his popular orange Porsche left the road. At the start of the race, Bandini, who had achieved fourth-best time in practice, snatched the lead for a brief moment, but it was Clark who was ahead by the end of the first lap. However, Surtees, Gurney and Graham Hill were still with him. Then the Ferrari took the lead as the Lotus began to experience the first symptoms of the trouble that was to put it out of the race: Clark had to retire just before half-distance with a worn-out gear-box. Gurney battled relentlessly with Surtees until he had to give up because of the failure of a cylinder-head gasket. From then on there was nothing to stop Surtees repeating his success of the previous year, and he climbed into third position in the Championship table which Graham Hill, thanks to his second place at the Nurburgring, was now heading again, two points in front of Clark.

It is at this point that the second circuit new to Grand Prix racing that year—Zeltweg—passed beneath the competitors' wheels. But just as everyone had been satisfied with Brands Hatch, so everyone was to find himself faced with serious problems on this airfield track that was the scene of the Austrian Grand Prix. The surface of the track was in such a disastrous condition that it was to cause an unbelievable number of chassis and suspension breakages, which completely distorted the race and produced a result that had little to do with logic, although it did reward the talents of a really good driver.

Practice saw the appearance of a new face in Formula 1. This belonged to a local boy, Jochen Rindt, who was driving the Rob Walker team Brabham-B.R.M. Another unusual sight was the strange pneumatic collar wrapped round Graham Hill's neck— he had cracked a vertebra in an accident at Snetterton. In spite of it all, Graham recorded the best time in practice. His companions on the front row of the grid were Surtees, Clark and Gurney. Practice had been very rough on the cars and a lot of patching up was necessary. Where the chassis itself had not broken, a wishbone had, or a wheel or a steering arm. In such circumstances it was not possible to make any fore-

The Ferraris painted
in the colors (blue and white)
of the North American Racing Team
in Mexico.

cast about the result of the race except that it would not be the fastest driver who won, but the one whose car succumbed last to the vibrations and thumps caused by the more or less disjointed concrete slabs that formed the surface of the track. . . .

There were breakages galore. To mention only the leading performers, Graham Hill gave up on the fifth lap (distributor drive), Surtees on the eighth lap when he was in the lead (broken suspension joint), Gurney a little before half-distance when he was comfortably ahead (broken wishbone mountings), while Clark had stopped six laps earlier when in second place with a broken transmission half shaft. As far as the Championship was concerned it was a worthless round. Victory went to the young Lorenzo Bandini who, at the wheel of his V6 Ferrari, successfully warded off Richie Ginther challenging to the end. The ex-champion motorcyclist, Bob Anderson, brought his apple-green Brabham-Climax home safely in third place. Since Baghetti's equally surprising win at Reims in 1961, this was the first time an Italian driver had taken a Grand Prix.

In a strong position after two consecutive victories, Ferrari were favored to win the Italian Grand Prix held on their local track at Monza. Moreover, John Surtees lost no time in justifying the general opinion by recording the best time in practice and putting a considerable distance between his Ferrari and Gurney's Brabham (0·8 s behind) and Graham Hill's B.R.M., now powered by a new engine with the exhaust in the centre of the vee (1·3 s behind) and Clark's Lotus (1·7 s behind) and McLaren's Cooper (2 s behind). This time Bucknum and his Honda were able to take advantage of improvements to the car and a more favorable circuit than the Nurburgring to desert the back of the grid and record the tenth fastest practice lap, 3 s slower than Surtees. The twelve carburetors had given way to a fuel-injection system which looked a lot less terrifying.

Right at the start one of the stars was forced to retire: Graham Hill broke his clutch. Surtees and Gurney, closely followed by Clark and McLaren, took turns in the lead. At one-third distance, Clark's engine blew up and McLaren started to lose contact with the two in the front who were still engaged in an inconclusive struggle, but between laps 50 and 55 (of the 78 that made up the Grand Prix) the Brabham was posted as leader more often than the Ferrari. Then Gurney started to drop back as his engine began to misfire and eventually had to stop as his battery was completely flat. From then on it was Surtees's race and as McLaren was sure of second place, the interest of the Italian crowd focused on the relentless fight for third spot between their favourite Bandini and Ginther. To the huge delight of the crowd, Lorenzo Bandini finally beat Richie Ginther to it, but in order to do so had zig-zagged his way down the last straight, an action severely criticized by a lot of observers.

After this Grand Prix, Gerard Crombac wrote in *Sport Auto*: "This third consecutive Ferrari victory puts Surtees only two points behind Jim Clark. The possibility of his winning the world championship cannot be discounted."

This forecast was made when there were still two Grands Prix to be run and although it was to prove accurate, circumstances took malicious pleasure in withholding confirmation until the last possible moment. First of all, the U.S. Grand Prix gave rise to a terribly tight leader-swapping chase between the four drivers at the top of the Championship table. Originally Surtees had the edge on Clark, Hill and Gurney, but Jimmy Clark passed John Surtees and managed to get 5–6 s in hand only to be let down by his injection pump. Then Graham Hill got slightly ahead of Surtees and Gurney who once again had to retire, this time when an oil pipe burst. It is very likely that the slippery pool resulting from this incident was the cause of Surtees's monumental spin when he was still right up with the leaders. Although he did not damage anything and rejoined the race, Hill had a lead of 20 s and was now out of reach.

Apart from the very close fight involving the four star performers, this Grand Prix was notable as the racing début of a new Ferrari—the flat 12 driven by Bandini which retired when the oil pressure dropped. So, with the Honda, there were henceforth to be two twelve-cylinder cars pitted against the total domination of the V8 machines. While on the subject of Ferrari, spectators and magazine readers were a little disconcerted by the unusual appearance of these Italian cars which had swapped their traditional red livery for American colors (blue and white).... This was due to a violent row which had blown up a little earlier between the irascible Enzo Ferrari and the Italian Sporting Commission over the fact that his 250LM model had been refused homologation for which he held his national sporting organization responsible. As a sort of reprisal, he said he would not race any more . . . and had his team entered at Watkins Glen by his American satellite, the North American Racing team managed by Luigi Chinetti. In fact this was a purely symbolic, and customary, gesture of protest because, of course, works technicians and mechanics continued as ever to look after the cars "made in Maranello."

Now back to the Championship. Before the Mexican Grand Prix, the last event of the 1964 season, there were three drivers still in the running for the title. Graham Hill was the best placed of the three since, even if Clark won, he had only to finish third. If Clark won he could seize the crown, provided Surtees did not come in second, a position which would give Surtees the title unless Hill took third place.

In this matter, Clark's best friend was Dan Gurney. At least that is how it seemed on examining the results of practice which had been easily dominated by the Lotus driver. As we have just seen, though, victory was not enough to give him the title: the results of his rivals were also crucial. And who should be sitting alongside Clark on the starting grid but Gurney, who was himself out of the running. Better still, Bandini, at the wheel of the Ferrari V12, was ahead of Surtees with his V8—but Clark could not really hope that John Surtees's road to the title would be barred by his team-mate should the latter find himself in front of Surtees before the end of the race. On the other hand, Clark's new young team-mate Mike Spence (who had replaced Arundell after his serious accident at Reims in a Formula 2 race) preceded Graham Hill, who had not been able to get higher than sixth. So, if the order established by practice held good on the day of the race, Clark had the title in the bag. Indeed, things very nearly happened that way. At any rate, the final unravelling of the Championship was worthy of the best of Hitchcock.

Clark made a superb start: 2 s ahead at the end of the first lap, nobody could touch him. Behind, Gurney was installed in second place and he, too, soon put himself out of reach of his pursuers. As for Hill and Surtees, they had completely bungled their getaway and as they came round after the first lap they were lying tenth and thirteenth respectively, while third and fourth spots were filled by Bandini and Spence in that order. It was a situation that could not be better as far as Clark was concerned . . . at least until the twelfth lap when, after a magnificent climb, Hill took over third place—between this point and the thirtieth lap, a little before half-distance, he was World Champion.

However, this was to reckon without Bandini's impetuous driving. After letting Graham through, he began to attack him with rather too much dash and spirit with the result that, as they came out of the hairpin on the thirty-first lap, one of the Ferrari's front wheels touched a rear wheel of the B.R.M. which spun into the guard rails. Its exhaust pipes were completely buckled by the impact and Hill had to stop at his pit to have them removed before he could continue with the race. While this was going on, the crown removed itself from Hill's helmet and went to sit on Clark's.

At the same time Surtees, who had made his way up from the back of the field, overtook Bandini, but was still only third, a long way behind Gurney. Then, almost immediately, Bandini overhauled his team leader. They were proceeding in this order towards the closing stages of the race when, ten laps from the end, Clark's oil-pressure gauge began to tell him he was running dry; because of (another) badly secured bolt a leak had developed in the engine. He drove more slowly in an attempt to avoid doing irreparable damage to his engine and losing his lead. He almost succeeded. By the end of the penultimate lap, however, his advantage had melted away and Gurney passed him. There was worse to come: a few yards further on the engine gave up completely—this was definitely the end. At that moment, the crown went back to Graham Hill, but not for long. Bandini immediately received an order from the Ferrari pit to let Surtees through and the young Italian hastened to obey. During the course of the very last lap Surtees moved into the second place that gave him the title with a one-point lead over Graham Hill. There is nothing more to add to this exciting farewell to the 1964 season except to note the sixth position taken by Pedro Rodriguez driving a Ferrari V6. He was the brother of Ricardo who had been killed on this very circuit in 1962 in a non-Championship event. It was the first appearance of this new driver on the Grand Prix roll of honor.

It is worth stopping a moment to consider John Surtees in the light of his success. Only four years earlier this driver had set out on what was in effect a second career. Before then he had been perhaps the greatest motorcycling champion of all time, at least he had collected more titles than anybody else, i.e. seven times World Champion between 1956 and 1960. It was a record that Hailwood pursued in vain and that was not to be broken until the current two-wheel champion, Giacomo Agostini, did so in 1970.

Surtees was not the first of the great motorcyclists to take a seat in a racing car. It is a natural enough temptation after all, since the two sports have a lot in common and motor racing offers its champions far more substantial rewards than motorcycling. However, the greatest motorcyclists do not automatically make the greatest racing drivers and there are illustrious examples to prove it—Geoff Duke and Mike Hailwood. The latter was the king of motorcycling after Surtees and, like Surtees, tried to change over to cars when he reckoned that he had nothing left to prove on two wheels. What is more, this happened during the very season, 1964, we have just finished describing. It will not have escaped your notice that not once in these reports is the name Mike Hailwood mentioned—"Mike-the-Bike" as he is called by his admirers. He was racing one of the two Parnell team Lotus-B.R.M.s, his team-mate being the very young Chris Amon. While it is true that their machines could not really compete with the works cars, an examination of Mike Hailwood's results shows that his best outing of the season was at Monaco where he came sixth, a placing that earned him his single point in the Championship. A poor harvest. . . . However, in Formula 1 it is not possible to judge the qualities of a non-works driver on his results alone: it is how he does it that counts.

This was not so in Surtees's case. He started motor racing in Formula Junior, the equivalent of the present Formula 3, that is a stepping-stone formula. It happened early in 1960, the car was a Cooper-B.M.C. and the team manager who engaged him was Ken Tyrrell. The winner of the event, ahead of Surtees, was another very talented beginner—Jim Clark. During the following months Surtees was entered in Formula 1 by Lotus and he just failed to win his first Grand Prix at Portugal that year. Then he became a member of the Yeoman Credit team (with a Cooper in 1961 and a Lola in 1962) before going to Ferrari in 1963, after which he had to wait for more than a year for his first triumph—in the German Grand Prix—but at the end of the season he was World Champion.

Unlike most Formula 1 drivers, Surtees is a reserved man and not very easy to get to know. He is truly admirable for the tremendous concentration he brings to his duties as a racing driver. It seems that nothing can distract him from the job in hand, no matter what it is—preparing for the race, practice for the race, the race itself. . . . He is a relentless worker and sometimes falls prey to his own thirst for perfection. This is not, however, a fault that belongs to him alone. One could say that Dan Gurney, for example, has suffered just as much in exactly the same way. This type of character, forever unsatisfied, forever searching for some improvement, making the same demands on those around him as he makes on himself—i.e. the maximum— certainly finds it rather difficult to become part of a team. This, without doubt, is Surtees's weakness. Otherwise he is an excellent tuner and brilliant all-round driver. He was to become one of the most remarkable and highly respected figures in Formula 1 during the decade 1960-70, a decade which ended with the addition of another string to his bow— the construction of his own racing cars bearing his own name.

1965

clark
and
lotus
unbeatable

*Picture
of a perfect symbiosis
between driver and engineer:
Jim Clark
and
Colin Chapman.*

For 1965, the last season of the 1500 cc Formula 1, the new World Champion was naturally leader of the Ferrari team and he had Bandini as his number two. Graham Hill remained as number one driver for B.R.M., where Jackie Stewart replaced Ginther who had left for Honda. That year another driver from the ranks of the new generation was to become a regular competitor in Formula 1. It was Jochen Rindt who went to join McLaren at Cooper, taking the place left vacant by the semi-retirement of the ex-World Champion, Phil Hill. Obviously for the very last season of the 1500 cars, there were more changes in their cockpits than in their constituent parts, which remained very much as they had been in 1964. The most important technical event of the year in fact was the arrival on the Formula 1 scene of the American tire manufacturer Goodyear who supplied Honda and the works Brabham team. This was the first time since 1958 that Dunlop had a rival in Formula 1. However, they reacted pretty smartly and came up with a new tire, the R7, which won all the events in the 1965 G.P. calendar except the last—the Mexican. Victory in the Mexican G.P. was the occasion of a double first—for Goodyear and for Honda.

As far as engines were concerned, they all (that is B.R.M., Honda, Ferrari and Coventry-Climax) claimed more than 200 bhp for 1965. Coventry-Climax, who had been taken over by Jaguar, announced that they would not be building a 3-litre unit for the new Formula 1. However, they unveiled an ambitious experimental flat 16 which, sadly, was never installed in a car. They had also developed a fourth version of their V8, the FMWV/4 on which the stroke had been shortened yet again. The important effect of this was that it increased the area of the bores and made it possible to fit four valves per cylinder. It developed 210 bhp at 10,500 rev/min and so it was on equal power terms with the B.R.M. V8. Ferrari claimed 215 bhp at 11,000 rev/min for their V8 with Bosch direct fuel injection and 220 bhp at 12,000 rev/min for their flat 12 with Lucas manifold fuel injection. The highest power output was claimed by Honda for their V12 which was peculiar in that its crankshaft ran on roller bearings, whereas the opposition all put their faith in plain bearings: 230 bhp at 13,000 rev/min—this remains the record for the 1500 Formula 1.

The calendar for the season included a change that was to become customary: instead of being the last Grand Prix of the series, the South African was now the first. It was held on 1st January 1965, and for Jim Clark and his Lotus 33 it provided the occasion for a trouble-free solo performance. Lotus might have made it a double, but Spence spun twice thus effectively giving away second and third places to Surtees (Ferrari V8) and Graham Hill respectively. Jimmy Clark was not yet using the new Climax but the intermediate version with two large valves per cylinder which produced 200 bhp at 9750 rev/min. Honda did not enter, but Gurney had Goodyears on his Brabham, unlike Jack Brabham who stayed faithful to Dunlops. The results of practice seemed to indicate that the boss was right since he took a place on the front row of the grid (third-best time) while Gurney was back on the fourth row, more than a second behind Brabham. However, as from Monaco, the second event in the Championship, the Australian, too, was to run on the American tires.

Clark made no secret of the fact that he intended to get his revenge for the bad luck he had had in 1964 by winning the title in 1965. However, he took rather a chance on this by giving up the Monaco Grand Prix in favor of the Indianapolis 500-Mile (800 km) Race which was to be held the day after the Monegasque event and which he won brilliantly. There were no Lotus works cars at all entered for Monaco. The favorite was Graham Hill who had won the two previous editions of this race, and in fact he proved the forecasters right, as for the third consecutive time his name was inscribed on the roll of honor. It was not an unexciting race however; rarely has the course of a Grand Prix been so extraordinary.

It all began in the most reasonable manner imaginable. After recording the best time in practice, ahead of Jack Brabham giving the four-valve Climax its baptism of fire, Graham Hill took the lead, dragging in his wake his new team-mate Stewart. The pair of them steadily shook off the two Ferrariites, Bandini (V12) and Surtees (V8) in that order, and Brabham who had made a slow start.

Suddenly there was Hill, coming out of the tunnel on his twenty-fifth lap and lining himself up to negotiate the chicane, masked from the driver's sight until the last moment by a hump in the road. As he cleared the hump he saw that Bob Anderson's Brabham, slowly making its way back to its pit, was occupying a part of the track where it was impossible for the two cars to pass side by side. All Hill could do was brake violently and take to the short escape road. He managed to stop in time, but he could not engage reverse so he had to push the car himself before re-settling himself and rejoining the race. On the following lap, he was posted at 30 s behind Stewart. . . . It seemed that he was now denied all hope of winning, particularly as the two Ferraris and the Brabham were ahead of him as well on a tortuous circuit renowned for the difficulties its narrowness presents to would-be overtakers.

Nevertheless, he won and this is how. The first opening was made by Stewart, who made a big mistake at Sainte-Devote, spun and went over a curb. In doing so he bent his rear suspension and slightly tore a wheel rim. This was on the thirtieth lap. The two Ferraris took the lead, but only for five laps because Brabham let fly, overtook them and went ahead. Meanwhile, behind all this, Hill overtook Stewart who was back in the race. Brabham's joy was short-lived. On the forty-third lap the new Climax gave up the ghost. Now only 4 s separated Hill from the leaders. The B.R.M. seemed to take wings and seven laps later was right on the heels of the Ferraris. Three laps later Surtees was passed. Another twelve laps and Bandini had to give way. Hill had recovered his lead, but not his original advantage—when Surtees overtook his team-mate to head the chase, twenty-two laps from the end, there were only 2 s between the two men. It was a homeric struggle. Just as everyone began to think that they were worn out by eighty laps (the current total distance of the race to which it was reduced following Bandini's fatal accident in 1967, an accident that was attributed to driver fatigue), Hill and Surtees, lapping faster than the best practice speeds, literally let fly. However, the B.R.M. gently drew away and Hill had a 6 s lead on the penultimate lap when Surtees ran out of fuel. He had to push his car to the finishing line and Bandini and Stewart took

Bandini, Hill and Surtees approach the black yawning mouth of the tunnel at Monaco.

advantage of his predicament to claim second and third places.

So, after the first two Grands Prix of the season Jim Clark and Graham Hill found themselves together again at the top of the Championship table. But the Lotus driver soon put an end to the suspense. By winning the next five Grands Prix he was sure of the title even before the Italian event was run. Hill was beaten in this race by his team-mate Stewart, but the moustached Londoner took the U.S. Grand Prix, his second victory of the season, a season that was to end in Mexico City with success for Honda.

Clark's formidable series began with the European Grand Prix at Spa-Francorchamps in the pouring rain. In such conditions this very fast circuit, made up chiefly of sweeping curves, becomes extremely selective as is proved by the following list of best times recorded on one lap during the race—the differences speak for themselves: Clark (Lotus-Climax), 4 min 12·9 s; Stewart (B.R.M.), 4 min 16·9 s; McLaren (Cooper-Climax), 4 min 18·8 s; Hill (B.R.M.), 4 min 21·1 s; Brabham, 4 min 22·2 s; Gurney (Brabham), 4 min 25·2 s. All the same it is only fair to say that there is an explanation for the relatively mediocre performances of Hill, Gurney and Brabham. On Hill's car the suspension adjustments were completely unsuitable for the wet track—he had recorded the best time in practice in the dry—while Gurney and Brabham were handicapped by the indifferent wet-weather behaviour of their Goodyear tires. After a very disappointing return at Monaco, the Hondas acquitted themselves much better in practice at Spa. Ginther started from the second row with the fourth-best time, Bucknum from the fifth row. In the race, however, Ginther was also handicapped by his inadequate Goodyears and in addition he was bothered by the lack of progressiveness of his fuel-injection system. He finished sixth, a lap behind Clark. . . . Indeed, only Stewart succeeded in not being lapped by the winner.

For the first time, the French Grand Prix had for its setting the mountain circuit of Charade near Clermont-Ferrand. Magnificently laid out, very hilly and perfectly surfaced, it might have been made for Jim Clark who, once again, was quite untouchable. Yet Clark had demolished his car in practice and had to run with a hack car fitted with the old small-valve Climax engine which developed about 15 bhp less than the B.R.M., Ferrari and more recent Climax. However, it would have needed more than that to stop an absolutely superior Clark giving his solo recital.

Once again it was Stewart—decidedly making steady progress—who was the best of his opponents, albeit at a respectful distance. He finished nearly 30 s behind. The new hope of motor sport took second place on the second lap and did not have much trouble keeping it because Surtees, who was following him, still driving the V8, had to make a brief stop at his pit because of a failing alternator. The New Zealand driver Denis Hulme was driving Brabham's car—the organizers had refused him an entry and as he had won the Formula 2 race on this circuit the year before, Jack Brabham gave him his place—in which he finished a distant fourth. Graham Hill was an even

In the wet as in the dry,
Clark and his Lotus
became almost unbeatable.

more distant fifth: he did not like the circuit very much and could not avoid being lapped.

So far only the Monaco Grand Prix had developed into an interesting race for the spectators and this seemed to have something to do with the fact that Jim Clark had not taken part in it. He was so overwhelmingly superior that there could be no doubt about the outcome of any race in which he was entered. It has to be admitted, though, that the processional Grand Prix of the A.C.F. was a very boring race to watch. What is more, the very nature of the circuit ensured that the competitors would be separated by enormous gaps. This sort of thing is harmful to motor racing because it destroys the spectacular element and, as the specialists commented at the time, could in the long run endanger the popularity of Formula 1—but Clark and Chapman, they did not care.

Thus, two weeks later and working to a perfectly planned scenario, Jim Clark laid claim to the British Grand Prix. He naturally set the best time in practice and was leading the race at the end of the first lap. . . . Nevertheless, there was a break with tradition and it was not Clark who made the best start but Ginther. The Honda, which was gradually improving, had in fact recorded the third-best time in practice and made the front row of the grid. The American had put his power advantage to work to get the better of Clark, Hill and Stewart when the flag dropped. His moment of glory, however, was very short-lived and Clark took over the lead at the third corner. On the second lap Hill also overtook Ginther to go off in pursuit of the Scotsman, but each time round and in spite of all his efforts Graham steadily lost ground until at half-distance he was 17 s behind. However, it seemed that Clark's four-valve engine was not running properly, but the gap continued to widen inexorably and it had stretched to 30 s when, twenty laps from the end, it became obvious that Clark had started to slow down. What was going on in that spindly elegant green body with its yellow band? The oil had reached a dangerously low level, not because it was leaking out but because of the high consumption of the Climax engine through the thirty-two valve guides in its cylinder head. When he saw his oil pressure fluctuate alarmingly as he cornered, Clark reacted at once and carefully trimmed his speed to avoid melting his bearings and being caught by Hill. As it turned out, he had made his calculations to a nicety and he not only managed to finish the race, he succeeded in winning— by 3·2 s. But it had been a close thing. Hill, conscious that victory was within his reach, made a splendid finish—and the proof, a final lap in 1 min 32·8 s, a new Silverstone circuit record.

Ginther might have led for a third of a lap at Silverstone, but at Zandvoort he was to do better still. The Honda was brilliant in practice and recorded the second-best time, 0·3 s behind Hill and on equal terms with Clark. It took the lead at the start of the Dutch G.P. and kept it for five laps while the best cars that Europe could produce tagged at its heels. It is true that the Japanese team had its base in Amsterdam and that they used the Zandvoort circuit for developing and testing their cars. Be that as it may, Ginther's demonstration that day restored heart to his entire team. He then spun twice, without serious consequences, and dropped back to sixth place, but not before he had proved that the Honda was getting to the competitive stage.

Two newcomers share the front row of the grid with Clark and
Hill (furthest from camera): Stewart (B.R.M.) and Ginther (Honda).

Rindt's accide
at Charade .

. . . *where Ginther shows*
perfect courtesy and hospitality.

*Surtees at the wheel
of the V8 Ferrari
in the French Grand Prix.*

Gurney (Brabham).

Perhaps it was the effect of sand from those famous dunes that caused the epidemic of broken rev counters. The main victims were Clark and Hill during the race; but during practice Clark had broken something far more serious—his thirty-two-valve engine. Therefore, as at Clermont-Ferrand, he had to compete in the Grand Prix at the wheel of a hack car, but this time fitted with the large-valve engine. This no doubt explains why he left the line like everybody else instead of like the usual streak of lightning. Nevertheless, on the sixth lap he was in the lead ahead of Graham Hill and at the end of eighty trouble-free laps he claimed his fifth victory of the season, preceding Jackie Stewart who was runner-up for the third time that year, each time behind Clark. Then came Gurney and Graham Hill and, a lap in arrears, Denis Hulme who was again replacing Brabham. This time it is for sure, they were saying in the paddock, old Jack's hanging up his helmet. The same old story. . . . As for Surtees, he was driving the twelve-cylinder Ferrari for the first time, but the promises it made in practice (second fastest with Clark and Ginther) were not kept in the race where it could finish no higher than seventh, because of its handicap due to the wrong choice of tires. Once again the Coopers were a sorry sight. They had roadholding problems and neither McLaren nor Rindt managed to finish. . . .

From now on, Clark was virtually untouchable in the Championship, but Lord Jim still lacked a victory at the Nurburgring. At the mere mention of this name legend, mystery and magic take over. It is undoubtedly magnificent, but it is hostile as well. A driver triumphs *at* Brands Hatch, *at* Monza, *at* Zandvoort but he triumphs *over* the Nurburgring. There the most dreaded, the most relentless opponent is not another driver but the circuit itself. Both car and driver are given very rough treatment. For over 14 miles (22 km) they are first flung into the air and then crushed into the ground by gravity and centrifugal force. They have to contend with bumps and hollows, sudden steep climbs and dizzy drops. The Nurburgring is something which cannot be learned. It has to be broken in, tamed, brought to heel like a wild animal which is just waiting for the slightest sign of weakness on the part of its trainer to jump at his throat. So, on 1st August 1965,

Clark of the velvet gloves changed into Clark of the iron fist. In appearance, Jimmy Clark was not very impressive. Wearing his racing overalls he looked like a rather reserved young man of average build without distinguishing marks. He appeared almost the antithesis of the archetypal racing driver burning the candle at both ends, breakfasting off champagne and caviar, gambling his prize-money at the tables in Monte Carlo. In fact he was a man of steel with the looks of a child. Well hidden beneath the natural and simple courtesy was a wild and vigorous strength.

As a good Britisher, Jim Clark was fascinated by the idea of 100 mile/h (160 km/h) and he had promised himself a lap of the Ring at that speed. The record, established by John Surtees the previous year, stood at 8 min 39 s, an average of 99·3 mile/h (158·2 km/h). By the time practice for the 1965 Grand Prix was over, Jim Clark had not only reached his objective, he had gone well beyond it. He had recorded a staggering 8 min 22·7 s, an average of 102·1 rev/min (163·4 km/h). He left Stewart trailing by 3·4 s, Hill by 4·1 s, Surtees and his V12 Ferrari by 5·1 s. . . .

The Hondas, which had made their début on this circuit the year before, were not entered. The cars and their technicians had returned to Japan to make the modifications that experience in the previous Grands Prix had suggested were necessary. It was a pity they withdrew because it would have been interesting to see how much progress this impressive Japanese single-seater had made in just one year.

Although the race was dominated from beginning to end by the excellence of Clark, Dan Gurney gave a particularly splendid performance. The big American was using an old small-valve Climax engine which was giving away more than 15 bhp to the engines used by Clark and Hill. Gurney resisted the strain imposed by Hill in a magnificent fashion and finished third, only 5·5 s behind the B.R.M. driver, which, in the circumstances, undeniably ranks as a feat. As far as the public were concerned, however, this fine drive went largely unnoticed because of the brilliance of Clark's solo performance in the lead. By crossing the line 16 s

*Jackie Stewart
wins
his first Grand Prix
at Monaco.*

*The flat 12 Ferrari: destined to
have a famous descendant in
1970.*

ahead of Hill, he had averaged over 100 mile/h (161 km/h) for the whole Grand Prix had received the ovation that such prowess deserved. The unlucky men of the day were Surtees who had gear-box selector troubles on the first lap, and Stewart who hit a curb on the following lap and bent his front suspension.

The World Championship 1965 was over; with six victories, five of them consecutive, Jim Clark was completely out of reach even though there were three Grands Prix still to be run. So he took the title for the second time and embellished it with his Indianapolis victory. This total success was naturally shared by Lotus. The season had shown both driver and constructor to be possessed of a superiority that was almost insolent. They could not go any higher.

However, their Formula 1 rivals recovered some of their pride at the end of the season. Beginning with the Italian Grand Prix, success deserted Lotus for the B.R.M. camp. It was expected that at Monza Ferrari would react in their usual way. In any case, the 1964 World Champion, John Surtees, had not won a single race in 1965, and everyone thought that the Italian team would make a special effort to break their string of failures in front of the enthusiastic home crowd.

Surtees appeared at Monza at the wheel of a twelve-cylinder car which had had detail modifications made to its cylinder heads. There was some doubt, however, as to whether that would be enough to cope with the four-valve engines of Clark's Lotus and the B.R.M.s which had been specially tweaked for Monza, as had the Hondas, making their eagerly awaited reappearance.

The results of practice suggested that if the Ferrari had not shown an overwhelming superiority, it did at least have the ability to win. Surtees, in fact, recorded the second-best time, 0·2 s behind Clark and 0·5 s and 1·0 s ahead of Stewart and Hill respectively. Then came Bandini, ahead of Bucknum and his Honda. Because he had had engine troubles early in each practice session, Ginther was a long way back.

When the flag dropped, the crowd let out a howl of disappointment as they saw Surtees remain stationary. His clutch had started to slip and at the end of the first lap, as the still tightly bunched pack, led by Clark, came past, he was marked down in fourteenth position.

However, the clutch was in proper working order again and, taking easy advantage of the tow, Big John set himself the task of cutting his way through to the front. By the seventh time round the Ferrari was up with the leading bunch which comprised Clark, Hill, Stewart, Gurney, Bandini, Spence and Siffert. The Hondas already seemed beaten.

On the eleventh lap the spectators in the stands rose to their feet with a shriek of delight. Surtees, continually advancing, had made it to the front. The tables had been nicely turned, but it was not all over yet by

*The extremely original Honda 1500
which in the end won the last
Grand Prix of the Formula at Mexico.*

*Engineer Nakamura,
standing in front of Ginther.*

a long chalk. It was not long before Surtees felt his clutch begin to slip again, but he managed to hang on by sheltering in the wake of his rivals. Then, just before half-distance, the Ferrari had to stop at its pit and stay there. Everything suggested that the race would be fought out between Clark, Hill and Stewart who were taking fairly equal turns in the lead. Twelve laps from the end, however, the injection pump on the Lotus gave up the ghost and the way seemed open for a B.R.M. double. The decision as to which of the two men, veteran Hill or newcomer Stewart, would be the winner was taken on the penultimate lap in the Parabolica curve which is situated just before the finishing line. Travelling on the outside of the corner, Hill put himself completely sideways on the loose gravel, and though he got his car back under control, Stewart had disappeared in the meantime and the race was over. Thus the young Scotsman won his first Grand Prix before he had even completed his opening season in Formula 1. Readers of *Sport Auto* found the following comment at the end of Gérard Crombac's report on the 1965 Italian Grand Prix ". . . Stewart winged his way to his first Grand Prix victory . . . I'll guarantee there will be many more to inscribe on his roll of honor."

In the U.S. Grand Prix, held at Watkins Glen near New York, B.R.M. continued the offensive launched at Monza. This time, however, it was Graham Hill who won. He thus took his third consecutive U.S. Grand Prix victory and, curiously enough, equalled his Monaco hat-trick. Of course, the favorite at the start was Clark, but for once he did not take pole position on the grid—Hill beat him to it by 0·1 s. The two of them quickly pulled away from the rest of the field, but on the twelfth lap Clark's engine swallowed one of its thirty-two valves and Hill found himself alone at the front. Once his lead over Gurney and Brabham had reached 20 s, it seemed that the race was all over. Until it started to rain. Suddenly the gap ceased to widen. Apparently the Brabhams' Goodyears were more effective in the wet than the B.R.M.'s Dunlops. Then, with one-third of the race over, Hill made a monumental mistake—he went into Fast Bend too fast and left the road. Luckily for him, he did not hit anything and was soon back on the track, but the Brabhams were now only 3 s behind and they quickly caught up with him. Black Jack made an all-out assault and, taking advantage of Hill's difficulties in lapping the squabbling Rindt and Bandini, cunningly overtook him and went into the lead. Not for long though, because he in his turn went into a corner too fast and spun. So Hill took the lead again, followed very closely by Gurney in his less powerful car. Brabham was some way behind. Hill took advantage of the gradually drying track to draw away from Gurney who could not retaliate, and finish without further ado an exciting race well ahead of the Brabhams, the only other cars on the same lap. Next came Bandini and Pedro Rodriguez with twelve-cylinder Ferraris. The third Italian car, with American driver Bob Bondurant at the wheel, took ninth position. The important absentee at Watkins Glen was in fact John Surtees who had had a serious accident a few days earlier in a prototype Lola. It was an unhappy end to a barren season for poor Surtees and the seeds of his forthcoming break with Ferrari were already germinating.

Since taking the cure in Japan, the Hondas had not really shone and the half promises they made at Silverstone and Zandvoort were never fulfilled. The

Mexican Grand Prix was to be the last of the 1500 Formula which meant that the Japanese factory might never again have the chance of winning a Formula 1 race since the decision to build a 3-litre car for the 1966 formula was yet to be made. Honda's V12 was the most powerful of the 1500 cc engines and their chassis and suspension seemed to have improved, particularly after Ginther's arrival on the scene. The central part of the chassis was a light alloy monocoque fitted at each end with a tubular structure to carry the suspension which had been modified, notably by being stripped of its complicated, cranked elements. Thus it now had a neater and more classic appearance. At the front it comprised upper swinging arms acting through tie-rods on the inboard-mounted combined spring-damper units, and large lower wishbones, while at the rear it had inverted lower wishbones, upper arms and double radius rods. The engine was still transverse, but mounted rather differently with a forward slope which lowered the centre of gravity by facilitating the use of forward-facing exhausts. As for the engine itself, it was a 60° V12 with a 58·1 mm (2·26 in) bore and 47 mm (1·83 in) stroke. Each pent-roof combustion chamber had four valves and the four overhead camshafts were driven by a train of gears situated in the middle of the block where the power take-off for the transmission was also placed. The main new feature of the transmission was the multiplate clutch, completely exposed to the air stream as on the Ferraris. Needle roller bearings were used for the big ends and for the main bearings of the built-up crankshaft. Here the influence of motorcycle technique, of which Honda were the masters, was obvious.

Unlike their rivals, however, Honda had also designed and manufactured their own direct fuel-injection system, which was peculiar in that it allowed independent adjustment for each cylinder by means of different-length inlet pipes. The aim of this arrangement was the ability to give preference to the high- or low-speed power ranges by tuning the system as required. In theory it was a very attractive system, but undeniably too complicated. It was the weak point of a magnificent piece of machinery and often made driving very difficult because of its uncertain response to the throttle. It so happened that the Mexico City circuit, situated at an altitude of some 6500 ft (2000 m), was notorious for the problems it posed in the delicate matter of carburation adjustment. Honda were certainly aware of this and since their unresolved tuning difficulties concerned carburation, they took themselves off to Mexico for a week on the day after their disappointing exhibition at Watkins Glen. This extra period of training was turned to good account by the Japanese technicians who managed to come up

with a satisfactory answer to the carburation question, and by Richie Ginther who had plenty of time to sort his chassis out properly. Thus it was that Honda, at their ninth attempt and much more meticulously prepared to meet the unusual conditions of the race than their rivals, finally managed to win the very last Grand Prix of the 1500 Formula 1; it was also Richie Ginther's first Formula 1 victory.

However, by the end of practice the Californian had achieved only the third-best time 0·4 s behind Jim Clark and Dan Gurney. When the flag dropped Ginther rocketed away from the second row and at the end of the first lap he was something like 300 yd (270 m) ahead of Stewart and Spence. For once Clark had made a bad start and came round in tenth place. After his triumphant finish, Richie Ginther was talking to journalist Bill Gavin about the race and made this marvellous comment: "I looked in my mirror at the end of the first lap and there was no one there. Then it occurred to me—I must have spilt a gallon of oil on the track and they had all spun behind me."

Ginther's toughest opponent was his friend and fellow American Dan Gurney, who was decidedly consistent in achieving good results, but whom victory was just as consistent in avoiding. After passing Spence, Gurney got to within 3 s of Richie Ginther, but that was the best he could do. Ginther explained afterwards that he had adjusted his pace to that of his pursuer, thus saving 1000 of the 12,000 rev/min permitted by his engine. Clark, at the wheel of an obviously tired machine, never got a look in before his retirement and the same applied to Hill and Stewart.

Such was the unexpected end of the 1500 Formula which, though widely cursed at birth, blossomed out superbly between 1961 and 1965 both as a technical and as a sporting exercise. One of the most outstanding points of a quick but objective summary of the period is that it was within the framework of the 1500 Formula 1 that such interesting and advanced techniques as the monocoque chassis and fuel injection were developed, techniques that are now almost universal. It was also during these years that racing tires began their fantastic evolution, first in shape—diameter reduced from 15 in to 13 in (381 mm to 230 mm), increase in width—and then in the composition of their rubber. Colin Chapman declared that they were the most important contributor to the recent improvements in roadholding. Finally Clark, Stewart, Surtees, Hulme, Rindt, Rodriguez, Siffert, Amon, a whole new and extremely brilliant generation of drivers, proved beyond doubt that this formula had given valuable encouragement to the emergence of an élite corps at the very top of motor racing.

the 3~litre formula: the return to power

A storm of protest had greeted the 1500 cc Formula 1, but when the C.S.I. announced the 3-litre formula they were hailed with a chorus of praise. There was only one discordant note: by the end of 1965 it was quite clear that the preparations made by the various constructors for the new formula were of a very precarious nature and a cry went up asking that a year's suspension be granted. However, the C.S.I. remained deaf to this appeal and the 1500 Formula 1 was truly dead and buried at the end of the 1965 Mexican Grand Prix.

The usually cautious legislators decided to give Formula 1 a shaking by choosing a capacity limit twice as big as that allowed since 1961. Perhaps they wanted to atone for their previous mistake and restore to Grand Prix racing a character that was both more distinguished and more spectacular. Perhaps they desired to close the performance gap between the single-seaters, the pinnacle of motor sport, and the then considerably more powerful sports prototypes. Perhaps; but the strongest motive behind the C.S.I. decision was their wish to obtain world-wide unity for the sport in fact rather than just in principle by encouraging American constructors to get involved in Formula 1. It was obvious, as much for commercial reasons as for technical ones, that no American constructor had the slightest interest in cars powered by 1500 cc engines, since nothing could be more dissimilar to the products of the U.S. motor industry. In fact, the American delegation to the C.S.I. had asked that the capacity for the new Formula 1 be increased to 4·5 litres. This would bring it close to the limit specified for single-seaters running in the United States Automobile Championship (the best-known event in this series is the Indianapolis 500-Mile Race), but in the end it was decided to fix the limit at 3 litres only. Though General Motors, Chrysler and American Motors did not rise to the bait, Ford, in the framework of the offensive they launched in great style on all levels of motor sport, gave a push at the half-open door.

However, by the beginning of 1966 the American giant had made no more preparations than most of their future European opponents. One of the leading Europeans, the most successful manufacturer of engines for the previous formula, announced their retirement from competition: Coventry-Climax, taken over by Jaguar, would not be building any 3-litre units. This was not the case with B.R.M. who were working on an H16, but the design was so complicated that it

was easy to foresee that it would not be ready on time. Encouraged by their Mexican success, the Honda team had gone back to Japan with the firm intention of constructing a 3-litre for the new formula. Here again there seemed to be little hope that it would be finished before the season was well under way. Dan Gurney had decided to build his own cars under the name American Eagle and he had secured the services of Lotus technician number one, Len Terry. He lost no time in designing and constructing a chassis in the brand-new workshop at Santa Ana in California, but the engine that was to power it, a V12 designed by the famous English engineer, Harry Weslake, was still just a heap of plans in the winter of 1965–66.

In short, by the beginning of the first season of the 3-litre formula, only three projects had materialised and of those three only that of Ferrari seemed to hold any promise of success. It seemed that, as in 1961, the first year of the 1500 formula, there was to be total domination by the Italian team; domination due not only to the performance of their cars but also to the lack of preparation of their rivals, the British in particular, especially since the other two cars that were ready to confront the Maranello single-seaters, theoretically as equals, seemed much less well equipped.

The first was Cooper, an undeniably illustrious name, but undoubtedly on the decline since 1960. However, the enthusiasm at Surbiton was undiminished and they signed an agreement with an engine supplier, no less famous but whose successful sporting activities lay even further in the past. It was Maserati who had last appeared in a Grand Prix in 1957. Cooper, for their part, had decided to start from scratch and had taken on Tony Robinson to produce their first monocoque; engineer Alfieri, on the other hand, had to be content with doing up an old V12 that had been in a state of suspended development since Maserati's retirement from competition all those years ago. On the whole, even if the project roused kindly feelings, there were not many specialists ready to put their money on it.

This was even truer of the Brabham project. Brabham's company had been brilliantly successful in Formula Junior, then in Formula 3 and in Formula 2, but unfortunately not in Formula 1, and when the contracts had been signed, Brabham did not exactly find himself rolling in money. Jack Brabham, however, had no intention of giving up Formula 1. At forty he felt at the top of his form and was ready to prove it, wheel in hand, to Messrs Clark, Surtees, Hill and the rest, but in the circumstances, i.e. financially depressing, he found he had to limit his ambitions drastically.

Then he thought of Repco. This was a small Australian firm, quite unknown in Europe, whose chief engineer, Phil Irving, had earlier made quite a reputation for himself in motorcycling circles as the designer of the famous 1000 cc Vincent HRD. Brabham had turned to him for a cheap answer to the Tasman Formula* (2500 cc single-seaters). In fact, most of the competitors in this series used an engine that was no longer made: the good old four-cylinder Coventry-Climax. Owing to the lack of spare parts, keeping this unit in running order became a real Chinese puzzle.

Because the cost of the engine had to be kept as low as possible, Irving realized that he must start with a mass-production block and his choice fell on that of the V8 Oldsmobile which had the advantage of being made of light alloy. In its normal version this engine had a capacity of 3·5 litres but this could be reduced. Ever mindful of the need for economy, Irving then looked around for mass-production connecting-rods and found what he wanted in the Daimler Majestic engine at a price of £7 each. However, if the engine was to be at all competitive, something had to be done about the timing gear and cylinder heads. Brabham explained to Irving that he had better not go too far because the engine had to fit into an existing chassis, one that had been built in 1965 to take the 1500 cc flat 16 Coventry-Climax but for which it was never used. This restriction prevented Irving from designing double overhead camshaft cylinder heads, long considered an absolute necessity for a competition engine, because such equipment would make the engine too wide for the BT19 chassis. Too bad, the Repco would have to be a s.o.h.c. unit with two in-line valves per cylinder. This really was something to make every enthusiast, however lacking in sporting technical knowledge, smile pityingly, just as they had done twenty years earlier. The gallant Repco had Lucas fuel injection and hardly more than 250 bhp for its 2·5 litres. In other words, it had the modest output of 100 bhp per litre which was already exceeded by certain tuned touring cars. The imperturbable Brabham then asked Irving to make him a 3-litre version so that he could have a go at the Formula 1 World Championship. No sooner said than done, but not without

a loss of specific power. The early examples just reached 275 bhp at the absolutely maximum limit of 8200 rev/min—any more revs and the engine exploded irreparably.

So much for the engine. Now about the chassis. For the 1966 season Brabham and Tauranac remained the sole supporters of the multitubular chassis which was now considered as unsuitable by every single one of their opponents. It was quite all right for Brabham, however, because his engine was low powered and therefore not a great user of fuel. This meant that he did not have to provide huge fuel tanks, which would have been a difficult job with a tubular trellis. Since there was no problem, Brabham and Tauranac did not feel at all obliged to build a monocoque merely to keep up with fashion. Wisely, as was their way, they were quite happy simply to make detail improvements here and there to a structure which on the whole had remained practically unchanged since 1962.

On paper there seemed to be nothing at all to recommend the 1966 Formula 1 Brabham-Repco except its weight (1170 lb (530 kg)) which was very close to the minimum permitted by the regulations (1100 lb (500 kg)). It did not take great powers of prophecy to foresee that the more complicated machines would have difficulty in getting down to this limit, or even near it, at least at first. Sure enough, as they made their appearance, one by one all the other 3-litres weighed in at more than 1320 lb (600 kg), the Lotus and B.R.M.s fitted with the H16 engine being closer to 1540 lb (700 kg). The lightness of the Brabham was not only a partial compensation for the lack of power, it was also an advantage where tires were concerned because it permitted the use of much softer rubber. The heavy opposition was condemned to more wear-resistant and less adhesive mixtures.

This brings us to a fundamental issue which, though now well established and taken for granted, dates back only to 1966: the decisive influence of tires on the performance and design of Formula 1 cars since the three big manufacturers brought their fierce rivalry to the race-tracks. Goodyear had already made their appearance as suppliers to Brabham and Honda, and in 1966 Firestone, the third party, arrived in their turn to dispute the traditional superiority, or more precisely ex-monopoly, of Dunlop. The really frantic struggle that these three giants were to indulge in determined, directly or indirectly, the most decisive developments in Formula 1 during the years that followed. The wide tire with its completely flat rolling

---

* Championship held every winter in Australia and New Zealand.

surface, so familiar to us today, in fact started its career in 1966. It goes without saying that the rivalry of Firestone and Goodyear alongside Dunlop also had a fundamental and beneficial influence on the ever unstable finances of Formula 1. The money they put into racing replaced the funds about to be withdrawn by B.P. and Esso. If the gap left by these two important sponsors had not been filled, the result might well have been an impasse and—who knows—the signing of the death-warrant of Formula 1.

Let us return to the constructors. We have noted the reservations prompted by the Cooper-Maseratis and the Brabhams. B.R.M. and Lotus, the two most successful marques under the previous formula, had to use V8 1500 Climax or B.R.M. engines bored out to 2 litres in a ballasted 1965 chassis. Gurney had to fit a completely out-of-date, four-cylinder 2·7-litre Climax unit in his Eagle. McLaren, who had left Cooper, also had his chassis ready. Bruce McLaren had no fear of originality and had built his monocoque of mallite, a sandwich material composed of two sheets of aluminium enclosing a core of balsa wood. According to some estimates McLaren's monocoque was ten times as rigid as the Brabham BT19 or 20 for a still acceptable weight. On the other hand it is a difficult material to shape and McLaren did not persevere with it. However, his most serious problem was not the chassis, but finding a competitive, and existing, engine. His choice fell on the Indianapolis Ford V8 which he had to modify considerably to get the capacity down from 4·2 to 3 litres. It was not a success.

The same applied to Ferrari. Ferrari who, as usual, were ready in time for the change in formula and for whom the 3-litre capacity was an old acquaintance. Ferrari who, according to general opinion, would dispose of their disorderly, late, ill-equipped, makeshift rivals in one mouthful. They punctually introduced their new V12 3-litre Formula 1 car at a non-Championship event in Syracuse which opened the European season. They won, without brilliance perhaps, but without trouble either. The name of the 1966 World Champion was already on everyone's lips. John Surtees would reclaim the title he had won in 1964 and lost to Jim Clark in 1965. What in fact happened was quite a different story.

brabham's return to success

1966

For the first Grand Prix, held at Monaco, the Italian team was not convinced that their new twelve-cylinder car, undeniably powerful (350 bhp) but relatively heavy and clumsy (1329 lb (604 kg)), was a sufficiently effective weapon to use against the bored-out 1500s of B.R.M. and Lotus which would obviously find the tortuous streets of the Principality more favorable to their cause.

These cars had 1965 chassis slightly modified to enable them to carry a drop more fuel. They weighed no more than the specified limit (1100 lb (500 kg)) and developed 240 bhp at 10,000 rev/min (1·9-litre V8 B.R.M.) and 250 bhp at 8000 rev/min (Clark's 2-litre V8 Lotus-Climax).

Only Brabham's car had the V8 Repco engine. The chassis for team-mate Hulme's car was not yet ready and he had to make do with a 2·7-litre four-cylinder Climax in a Formula Tasman chassis. Its weight was down to the minimum limit, but it could not count on more than 225 bhp while Jack Brabham's BT19, which had just won a non-Championship event at Silverstone, had 300 bhp for only 66 lb (30 kg) more.

Like the Ferrari V12, the Cooper-Maseratis seemed too heavy and cumbersome to be at home on the Monaco circuit. They weighed the same as the Ferrari but developed only 320 bhp. As for McLaren's V8 Ford, though undeniably the noisiest car on the track, with its 305 bhp at 9600 rev/min it was not the most powerful.

So, theoretically, Brabham, Clark and the B.R.M. drivers, Jackie Stewart and Graham Hill were the best placed. Bandini, however, driving the second works Ferrari, a very different car from Surtees's V12, found that he had a machine perfectly suited to the demands

The V8 Repco:
an unexpected success.

The V8 Ford Indy:
a complete failure.

of the circuit. This fact was so obvious that Surtees, the team's number one driver, asked that he be given this car, a 1965 1500 chassis fitted with a 65° V6 increased to 2·4 litres and giving 260 bhp at 7800 rev/min; it weighed 1200 lb (550 kg). However, Eugenio Dragoni, the Ferrari team manager, refused his request and there followed a row which was to reach its climax several weeks later at the Le Mans 24-Hour race and involve Surtees's departure from the Scuderia.

Happy or not, Big John was not the man to sulk. Beaten only by Clark in the struggle to record the best practice time, he went into the lead at the start of the race and it was not long before there was a big gap between him and all his rivals except Stewart who was hanging on to him like a shadow. The big disappointment was Brabham who had broken his good Repco engine in practice and was forced to fit his less powerful spare for the race; he was not in the picture. As for Clark, he had been unable to engage second gear just after the beginning of the race and was passed by the whole bunch. He was thus condemned to climb through the field, an undertaking which the narrowness and overtaking difficulties of the circuit made very tricky. The Cooper drivers—Rindt, Ginther, Bonnier and French privateer Guy Ligier, a newcomer to Formula 1—not only had to get the better of their too-heavy cars, they also had to cope with the dreadful handicap imposed on them by the totally unsuitable gearing of their ZF boxes.

Only ten laps from the start, the differential on Surtees's car failed which left Stewart alone in the lead, while Bandini, who had made a poor getaway, was now in second place but some 30 s behind the leader. From then on, the gap between the two men gradually diminished until it fell to 12 s twenty laps from the end. During this hard struggle, the young Italian driver broke and rebroke the lap record, leaving it at 1 min 29·8 s which represents a very substantial improvement compared with the previous year's best lap (1 min 32·5 s) recorded by Graham Hill at the wheel of the 1500 B.R.M. Stewart, however, who was driving brilliantly and very steadily, was ceding ground only yard by yard, and it became clear six laps from the end that the Ferrari could not make it. Dragoni told Bandini to be satisfied with what he had got and so B.R.M. won the Monaco Grand Prix for the fourth consecutive time. Only four competitors were classified (Graham Hill, who was third one lap behind, and Bob Bondurant, also driving a B.R.M., five laps behind), while not one of the "real" new Formula 1 machines was present at the end, the four Cooper-Maseratis, the Ferrari V12, the Brabham-Repco and the McLaren-Ford all having broken.

Stewart (B.R.M.) first winner of a 3-litre Formula Grand Prix, using a V8 increased to 1·9 litres.

*The V12 Maserati
—half success or half failure?*

Those who thought that in view of the constructors' lack of preparation the new 3-litre formula should have been put off for a year did not miss the chance of using this rather miserable result as evidence for their case.

If the gods who look after racing had not shown clemency during the Belgian Grand Prix (which followed Monaco) by allowing the two participants in a superb duel to reach the finishing line in one piece, these Cassandras would have been overjoyed and the C.S.I. ridiculed unmercifully. The circuit at Monaco is very short and if necessary can cope with the pyrrhic situation of a field reduced to four or five competitors at the end of the race. This is intolerable at Spa where a driver comes round only once every three and a half minutes after a lap of 8·76 miles (14·01 km), and there is nothing for the poor spectator to do except

consider himself swindled out of his entrance money. Only seventeen cars turned up for practice for the Belgian Grand Prix and two of them had to withdraw at the end of it. McLaren found that his Ford was not running properly and launched himself into an even more hazardous undertaking: he fitted an Italian-built Serenissima V8 into his chassis but it did not take it long to run its bearings.

The new H16 B.R.M. had been glimpsed at Monaco, but at the Belgian Grand Prix it was used for the first time on the track, strangely enough mounted in a Lotus chassis. At B.R.M. they were in a position to know that it was not yet in proper working order so once again the 2-litre V8 was called into service for Graham Hill and Stewart. An H16 had, however, been delivered from Bourne to Chapman who put it into the specially built Type 43 chassis. The car was then assigned to Peter Arundell, Clark preferring to entrust himself still to the 2-litre Climax. On the third practice lap the H16 broke a valve and all they could do with the 43 was trundle it back into the Team Lotus transporter and postpone the début of the engine to a better day.

Of the fifteen survivors, only seven were equipped with real 3-litre engines. There was only one Ferrari V12 (Surtees) and one Brabham-Repco (Brabham) to take on the five Cooper-Maseratis that had been entered—the two works cars of Rindt and Ginther and the three private machines of Bonnier, Siffert and Ligier. It seemed obvious that on a circuit as fast as Spa the 3-litres would be unbeatable. Bandini (Ferrari V6 2·4-litre), Spence (Lotus-B.R.M. V8 2-litre), Bondurant (B.R.M. V8 2-litre), Hulme (Brabham-Climax four-cylinder 2·7-litre) and Gurney (Eagle-Climax four-cylinder 2·7-litre) seemed irretrievably cast in the role of extras while Clark, Hill and Stewart had to be content as makeweights.

Rindt (Cooper-Maserati), poorly rewarded for a heroic drive in the rain at Spa.

It was expected that Ferrari would take their revenge on this mixed bag of bones, and in fact Surtees largely dominated practice, finishing with 3 min 38 s, more than 3 s ahead of Rindt; Stewart and Brabham were within a second of the Austrian but after that it was a rout.

The race started under a threatening sky and Surtees went straight into the lead as predicted. The pack disappeared behind the steep road at Eau Rouge, and as the noise of the engines died away everyone in the pits and stands waited. Some four minutes later Surtees's red Ferrari surged out of the Welcome curve, braked hard for the La Source hairpin and flew away downhill towards Eau Rouge once again. Surtees's lead was considerable, Jack Brabham and his green Brabham being posted some 10 s behind. He was followed by Bandini, and there was another gap of 8s before Ginther appeared. After that, strung out, came Rindt, Ligier, Gurney. Then nothing, just silence again, heavy, threatening. Where were the other eight? Anxiety followed bewilderment when a very pale Phil Hill, driving a McLaren hack car fitted with a camera to take pictures for *Grand Prix* then being filmed, stopped and announced that he had just witnessed a massacre.

This is what happened. The pack arrived at the Malmédy S-bend to find that rain had already fallen and that the track was soaked. Bonnier, taken unawares, spun off as his dry-weather tires suddenly lost their grip. Spence, Siffert and Hulme who were close behind had to brake to avoid him and they, too, lost control of their cars. They all disappeared into the

scenery. The four cars were put out of action, but fortunately the four drivers were unharmed.

Meanwhile, a few hundred yards further down in the even faster Masta S-bend, Rindt was also spinning—according to witnesses he went round no fewer than nine times before he stopped, miraculously still on the track but a long way from where he started. He managed to get going again at once but Stewart, who lost control in the same place, was not nearly so lucky. The B.R.M. went into a ditch and turned over, trapping the driver underneath. Like Rindt and Stewart, Graham Hill and Bob Bondurant could not control their machines and they, too, went off. Safe and sound they rushed towards the upside-down B.R.M. and tried unsuccessfully to extricate poor Jackie Stewart who was wedged in by the steering wheel. Fortunately Graham Hill managed to borrow a spanner from a farmer whose house was on the edge of the track and he got the wheel off. Stewart had only broken a shoulder and a rib, but he had been through a period of terror. He was literally soaked in fuel which had flowed over him in torrents from the full tanks. This accident had a profound effect on him and since then he has always made sure that a spanner is fixed in a conspicuous position in the cockpit and labelled in the relevant language, "Spanner for removing steering wheel in the event of an accident." It's an odd thing, but hardly anyone else has followed his example.

Thus, of the eight men involved in incidents on this incredible first lap, only one managed to rejoin the race—Rindt, posted some 25 s behind Surtees the first time round. The other seven were eliminated as was

Clark who had over-revved at the start and damaged the timing. There were seven drivers left in the race and twenty-seven laps to be run. Happily for the spectator interest of this Grand Prix, Rindt went on to prove that it takes more than nine spins at 125 mile/h to put a man like him off his stroke and he set off with amazing panache in pursuit of the leaders. It took him only a little more than two laps to dispose of his handicap and take the lead ahead of Surtees who hung on, unwilling to declare himself beaten. Right until five laps from the end, in spite of his persistent nagging, he was kept at a distance by the driver of the Cooper which seemed better adapted to the slippery conditions than the Ferrari. Then, just when everyone thought that the young Austrian was about to win his first Grand Prix—over another three years were to pass before that happened—the differential on the Cooper gave up the ghost. The car became almost undrivable and Rindt had to slow down and let Surtees through to a victory that had first been predicted then despaired of. Bandini was a lap behind, but he nevertheless finished in third place and took the lead in the World Championship in front of his team leader and Stewart with the same score. Everything suggested that Ferrari's position was firmly established.

Then the wind changed—in fact a hurricane blew up in the shape of Jack Brabham who, by winning the next four Grands Prix one after the other, claimed possession of the crown even before the season was over.

It all happened in just over a month. The calendar was crazy: first came the French Grand Prix at Reims on 3rd July, then the British G.P. on 16th July, then the Dutch on 24th July and finally the German on 7th August. Brabham's four consecutive victories were quite astonishing and showed how well he had managed to sort his car out. He did not have the slightest trouble during this hectic period while all his rivals, one after the other, suffered more or less from the disastrous effects of this lunatic scramble.

At Reims, which vies with Spa for the title of the fastest circuit in Europe, the thing that counts above all is speed, particularly as driver ability is less important at Spa. Obviously therefore the Ferrari V12s were the favorites despite the fact that Surtees had left for Cooper where he took over from Richie Ginther. The latter in any case had only been in Europe on a temporary basis. By this time he was already in Japan and about to start testing the new Honda which, it was understood, he would of course be racing. Lorenzo Bandini became Ferrari driver number one and a second V12 was entrusted to the English engineer-driver Mike Parkes who was making his début in Formula 1 racing. With Stewart injured, B.R.M. entered only one car, but this time Graham Hill got to the heart of the matter and drove the H16 into fourth place on the grid. However, Graham Hill still lacked confidence in the strength of the engine and ran in the race with the 2-litre V8. Clark was a non-starter: during practice he was travelling at full speed when a bird crashed into his face. He just had time to stop before he lost consciousness. Suffering from shock, he had to withdraw and Pedro Rodriguez took his place in the V8 Lotus-Climax. As at Spa Peter Arundell was at the wheel of the B.R.M. H16-engined 43, and this time he succeeded in getting this engine to make its official racing début. Several times in practice the distributor drive shaft broke and he consequently found himself on the back row of the grid. During the race he was the first to retire—with a broken gear-box.

In spite of all the determined efforts of new Cooper driver, Surtees, who was bursting to get his own back on his ex-team manager Dragoni, Bandini achieved the best practice time, 0·6 s ahead of John Surtees. At the other end of the front row was beginner Parkes, and behind him came Brabham and Rindt. The race, it seemed, would be fought out between these five and more particularly between Bandini and Surtees.

However, Surtees's fate was decided at once. At the start his engine spluttered, the injection-system control had broken. Bandini's main rival had gone but he found another in Jack Brabham, and the two of them raced ahead of Parkes and Graham Hill. All the Coopers were handicapped and had to stop more or less often with overheating injection systems.

Undeniably the Brabham weighed less and was lower than the Ferrari, but the V8 Repco engine had 75 bhp less than the Ferrari V12, so it was reasonable that Bandini should inch ahead of Brabham. He seemed all set for the most straightforward of victories when on the thirty-second of the forty-eight laps of the race his throttle control broke. At that point Parkes was more than 40 s behind Brabham. He made an attempt to close the gap and did in fact reduce it, but the time sheets for the two men show that the Australian, on instructions from his pit, slowed down rather than that Parkes speeded up. It was all over and Jack Brabham was still 10 s ahead of Mike Parkes when Toto Roche lowered the checkered flag. Bandini was still at the top of the Championship table, but Brabham went into second place on equal terms with Stewart, Surtees and Rindt who scored the three points for fourth place at Reims. Hulme, trying out his Repco-engined BT20, finished just in front of him.

The great success of the Brabham team at Reims became a triumph at Brands Hatch, venue for the British Grand Prix. This time it was a different deal. The circuit is difficult and not very quick and it was suspected that it would not suit the Brabhams. Jack Brabham explained later that at the start of the season this was the only Grand Prix he thought he had a chance of winning. He was too modest, although of course he could not have foreseen that his rivals' troubles and lack of preparation would leave the way to the Championship open for him.

Beset by strikes—at least that was the official reason put about—Ferrari withdrew and so Bandini was prevented from defending his place at the top of the Championship. At the end of practice, which was marked by the return of Stewart and the open rivalry between Cooper drivers Surtees and Rindt, the two Brabham-Repcos were side by side on the front row. Gurney gave an amazing demonstration of his ability as a driver and the excellence of the Eagle chassis by recording third-best time although he was still only using the venerable four-cylinder Climax engine. Thus equipped, he treated himself to the luxury of beating Hill and Clark driving 2-litre V8s.

It was an uncomplicated race. At the start Brabham took the lead on a rain-soaked track and, gaining an average of half a second a lap, went on his way unopposed. His team-mate, Denis Hulme, was passed by Gurney—whose engine soon failed him—Rindt and Surtees. These two were engaged in a pitiless, spectacular battle, as were Clark and Hill just behind them. As the track dried out the roadholding of the heavy Coopers deteriorated and they were submerged by the

Clark-Hill-Hulme trio. Hulme then decided that he had watched the other two for long enough and overtook the pair of World Champions who retaliated magnificently, much to the delight of the crowd, enchanted by such an exhibition of driving skill; but Hulme was secure in second place. This happened in the middle of the race. On the eightieth and last lap the situation was unchanged. Brabham and Hulme achieved their first Grand Prix double, following the tradition they had established in Formula 2, where they were the only competitors using the Honda engine which outclassed the opposition. Jack Brabham was now at the top of the Championship table ahead of Rindt (who finished fifth) and Hulme and Bandini who had the same score. However, it was a catastrophe for Jimmy Clark and Graham Hill, the king and prince of the 1500 formula. There was nothing they could do about being left behind. They did not even have the prospect of a speedy cure because their engine still was not ready and had not even appeared in the paddock at Brands Hatch. As for Ferrari who had seemed so strong, it was beginning to dawn on people that they were in fact in a dangerous position. First of all, there was the loss of Surtees. Then there was the fact that the V12 virtually had not improved since the season began and that its performance was really quite disappointing; and the two Grands Prix where it should have had the edge (Spa and Reims) had already come and gone.

Eight days later among the dunes at Zandvoort, Clark rebelled superbly against the situation. It was the reaction of a great champion who will not settle for second best. He could not stop Brabham winning his third Grand Prix in a row, neither could he do any better than third place, two laps in arrears. At least that is the story the scoreboard tells. For those who watched this splendid race, nothing is more misleading than a perusal of these dry results. In spite of being one-third down in capacity, the peerless Jimmy Clark well and truly outpaced Jack Brabham and he did so by taking advantage of the difficult track conditions provoked by a mixture of sand, rubber and oil—the conditions were so bad that the average speed was lower than it had been the previous year under the 1500 formula. He was only a few seconds ahead but it seemed enough. Then, two-thirds of the way through the race, the crankshaft damper on the 2-litre Climax broke. This made the water pump break and Clark had to stop twice to refill his radiator. So Brabham won again, a whole lap in front of Graham Hill who had abandoned his usual Dunlops for Goodyears. Hulme had to retire with ignition failure when he was right up with his team leader and acting as a splendid shield against attacks from Clark in the opening stages of the race. The Ferraris were outclassed, particularly as Bandini had difficulty in changing gear because he had injured his right hand when he went off the road in practice.

At the end of the German Grand Prix on 7th August, Jack Brabham was practically sure of the crown, the third of his career, even though three Grands Prix remained to be run. Thus he became the first man to experience the supreme satisfaction of winning the Drivers' World Championship at the wheel of a car which bore his own name. However, he spent a very painful weekend. He broke down in practice and the race was held in pouring rain which aggravates the snags and difficulties of that most difficult of circuits, the Nurburgring. Last but not least, for nearly the whole race he was under strong pressure from that master of the Ring, John Surtees. But Jack Brabham gritted his teeth and withstood the challenge magnificently. Finally, it was Big John the indomitable who had to give way when the Cooper's differential ceased to function properly.

It is worth noting that this was the "old man's" first victory at the Nurburgring and, in spite of all his other honors, this must have given him particular pleasure. It is true that there are Nurburgring specialists. The reason for this is the length of the circuit coupled with a large number of hidden corners and changes of surface. These features make detailed knowledge of the circuit more difficult to acquire than elsewhere and this has its effect on lap times. This explains why drivers who compete often at the Ring, for example in the 625-mile (1000 km) race for sports prototypes, perform better than those who race there only once a year in the German Grand Prix.

Jim Clark recorded the best practice time (8 min 16·5 s), beating his record lap of the previous year by 6 s. Because it rained on race day the 1965 World Champion's Firestones constituted an unbeatable handicap in such conditions, even for him. Chapman considered for a moment replacing them with Dunlops, but concluded that he dare not risk offending his usual supplier. This was to give up all hope of victory and Clark, skating along in sixth position, ended up by going off the road.

In fact, the Grand Prix boiled down to a long struggle between Brabham, in the lead, and Surtees some lengths behind. All the others were outpaced, Rindt, Gurney, Hill, Stewart and Clark battling for the remaining scoring places. Once again, the Ferraris were out of the picture in spite of Bandini and Parkes being reinforced by Scarfiotti. Ludovico Scarfiotti and his 2·4-litre V6 had managed to get a place on the front row of the starting grid, but he could not repeat this in the race and broke down.

This was the occasion of the entry into Grands Prix of the young French marque Matra. Not with a Formula 1 machine (they were not building them yet) but with four 1000 cc Formula 2 cars. The Formula 1 entry was as thin in August as it was at the beginning of the season and the organizers of the German G.P. had been authorised by the C.S.I. to bring the numbers up to strength with Formula 2s. The exceptional length of the Nurburgring ensured the safety of this procedure. Nine Formula 2s lined up with the eighteen invited Formula 1s, and comparatively their performance was more than honorable if you take account of the fact that they were two or three times smaller in capacity and that the theoretically best, or at least the most experienced, drivers were in the Formula 1 machines. The quickest in practice was the young Belgian Jacky Ickx who returned an astonishing 8 min 52 s. Unfortunately, he was eliminated on the first lap of the race following a collision with the English driver John Taylor who suffered serious burns. It was Jean-Pierre Beltoise who won the Formula 2 section with his Matra-Cosworth. He was eighth in the general classification, one lap behind Brabham. He was the ex-motorcycling champion of France and it had been thought that he was lost to motor racing as a result of his serious accident in the Reims 12-Hour Race of 1963, but he recovered completely from his injuries.

Everyone took advantage of the welcome rest in August to prepare in relative calm for the Italian

At the Nurburgring Surtees takes the lead at the wheel of the Cooper-Maserati.

Grand Prix, held as usual on the first Sunday in September. At Monza, again it was power that mattered above all, and it was expected that important new developments on the technical side would be disclosed.

First of all, Honda were back. The Japanese team appeared at the rendezvous with two brand-new 3-litre machines for Ginther and Bucknum and they stole the scene. In structure these cars were more classical than the old 1500s; the engine was no longer transverse but longitudinal in the monocoque chassis. It was a 90° V12 beautifully designed to be as compact as possible. The crankshaft was divided in the middle by the power take-off, a layout which resolved the vibration problems of the crankshaft itself and of the camshafts, and split the V12 into two V6 units. This allowed smaller diameter crank pins and thus reduced friction losses. The choice of a 90° angle for the vee is explained partly by the fact that it allows closer bores than the classic 60° angle and therefore the engine can be shorter. They also wished to have the great tangle of twelve exhaust pipes coming from the centre of the

vee for the sake of the frontal area of the whole car. Four overhead camshafts controlled four valves per cylinder and carburation was of course by injection. The power of the new engine was not officially disclosed but they spoke of 400 bhp quite openly. On the other hand, it was a very heavy machine clocking up 1650 lb (750 kg) on the organizers' scales.

Brought with the intention of being run, the B.R.M. H16s were not much better off in this respect (1529 lb (695 kg)). The engine had been designed to weigh a maximum of 418 lb (190 kg), but because of all the modifications it was now well over this. They should be given credit for their adventurous spirit as they launched into a project that was not only original but ambitious, and though it may not have seemed very logical, it was. Their basic idea was that the best way to increase specific power is to increase the number of cylinders. This is attractive as a theory, but as a practical proposition it involves a number of snags that B.R.M. did not escape entirely. What is in fact the main advantage of a multicylinder engine? Firstly, the forces of inertia are diminished principally because

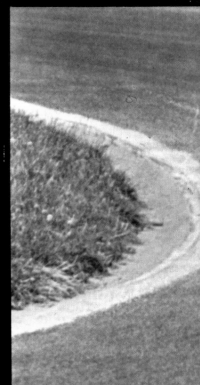

Top: Scarfiotti (Ferrari) gets the better of Clark (Lotus-B.R.M. H16) at the start of the Italian Grand Prix which he goes on to win.

Right: Brabham, surprising winner at Reims in spite of his lack of power compared with the Ferraris.

piston speed is reduced, and secondly the breathing is better. In addition, the question of combustion is simplified by the smaller length of flame travel in a smaller chamber. On the other hand, the big drawback of the multicylinder engine is that it tends to be rather cumbersome and therefore ill-suited to being used in a racing car which must be kept as light and compact as possible.

B.R.M.'s solution to this problem—sixteen cylinders in an H formation—was perfectly reasonable. First, the block had been designed to act as a chassis member so that its front face matched up exactly with the car; the chassis stopped at the front engine bulkhead. Since it was a short engine there was room in front of it for the petrol tanks, which otherwise would have to have been carried along the sides. Finally, the arrangement of the sixteen cylinders into an H kept the centre of gravity low. The layout was equivalent to two flat eight-cylinder engines placed one on top of the other with common crankcases and cylinder heads, the two crankshafts being connected by gears at the rear. Bore and stroke were 2·6 in (68·5 mm) and 2 in (50·8 mm) respectively.

The H16 thus had a high power potential and in spite of the number of cylinders it was compact. In practice, however, the designers fell foul of their own good intentions which provoked all sorts of tuning complications and led to the increase in weight mentioned above. There is no doubt that once developed, this engine would have been capable of producing appreciably more than 400 bhp but, unfortunately, its racing career was cut short because the disasters it heaped on the B.R.M. team were just too discouraging. During the winter of 1966–67 they decided to abandon the H16 in favour of a much more classical V12.

The third newcomer at this Italian Grand Prix, which really marked the beginning of the 3-litre Formula 1, was the V12 Gurney-Weslake engine installed in the Eagle chassis that had been designed for it. The unit was particularly remarkable for its small dimensions and moderate weight. The Eagle was the lightest 3-litre car on the track at Monza apart from the Brabham. At 1315 lb (598 kg) it was lighter by 44 lb (20 kg) than the Ferraris and the Cooper-Maseratis, and by some 220 lb (100 kg) than the B.R.M.s, the Lotus-B.R.M. and the Honda. The engine was designed by Harry Weslake and Aubrey Woods, the former being principally responsible for the cylinder heads and the latter for the bottom end. The V12 formed the classical angle of 60° with the intake (Lucas injection) in the centre and the exhausts at the side. The four valves per cylinder had a very small inclined angle in order to obtain a high compression ratio (12·5:1) and a good combustion chamber shape. Bore and stroke were 2·8 in (72·8 mm) and 2·3 in (60 mm) respectively, and the weight (though the engine had not been designed to have a block rigid enough to form a chassis member) was 363 lb (165 kg). In its first version at Monza, where it had numerous carburation bothers, the Gurney-Weslake was producing about 350 bhp at 10,000 rev/min.

Finally, Ferrari had not been idle and arrived at "their" Grand Prix with V12s sporting cylinder heads with three valves per cylinder. The new engine developed nearly 400 bhp and gave the Italian team a very popular victory.

This time Clark had abandoned his faithful 2-litre 33 for the H16 B.R.M.-engined 43. Although it was as heavy as the B.R.M.s, this car was quicker, as apparently it had better roadholding. Clark finished practice in third place, beaten by 0·5 s and 0·2 s by the Ferraris of Parkes and Scarfiotti respectively; but he was on the front row of the grid and ahead of the third Ferrari driven by Bandini. It is interesting to note that for the first time that season differences in performance were slight, six drivers being covered by 0·9 s and ten by less than 2 s. It promised to be a very open race. Ginther was on the seventh row with the Honda while Brabham, who had only 300 bhp at most, was on the sixth, a pretty amazing feat on this very fast circuit. Such are the virtues of slipstreaming. Gurney on the other hand started from the back row.

The question of tires was more prominent than ever. Firestone had just produced a new profile designed by Colin Chapman himself, and Dunlop unveiled their reply to the American challenge, the low-profile CF70. The latter, however, was not fully developed. In the end, Ferrari and Cooper chose Firestones while B.R.M. plumped for Goodyears. Only Siffert's Cooper wore British tires and they were the conventional ones.

Bandini was the first to take the lead but he soon had to stop. He was succeeded by Parkes, Surtees, Brabham and finally Scarfiotti who drew away, well shielded by Parkes from Hulme's attacks. So Ferrari pulled off a convincing double which was received with indescribable enthusiasm by the delighted crowd. However, it had not escaped the notice of keen observers, nor of the Ferrari drivers, that the fastest car on the track was in fact the Honda. In spite of its undeveloped chassis and the weight of his car, Ginther seemed a very likely leader when a tire burst and he went off the road in the Curva Grande at more than 125 mile/h (200 km/h). He broke a collar bone. Sixteen laps had given him enough time to show that the Japanese engine was the most powerful of them all. Although he fell prey to a host of troubles (carburation, battery, tires, gearbox), Clark had shown that his Lotus-B.D.M. H16, too, had possibilities. He even overtook Scarfiotti between two pit stops; and that did not go unnoticed either.

However, Jimmy Clark was not entirely convinced about the Lotus-B.R.M., and at Watkins Glen for the U.S. Grand Prix he sulked his way through practice even though he managed to record second-best time, only 0·11 s behind Brabham. He was sure he could have gone faster with the 2-litre 33, but Chapman insisted he use the 43 and Jimmy reluctantly did as he was told. The two H16 B.R.M.s also seemed to have improved: Graham Hill and Jackie Stewart were only 0·45 s and 0·75 s respectively behind the Brabham. However, they had Bandini (Ferrari) and Surtees (Cooper) in front of them as well, while just behind were Ginther, scarcely recovered from his accident and victimized by gremlins, and Hulme. Further back was Bruce McLaren making his reappearance; he had replaced the Serenissima with the V8 Indy Ford which was delivering 325 bhp and now running properly. Bruce McLaren was in front of Gurney whose V12 Weslake had gained some 25 bhp since Monza, bringing the power up to 375 bhp, but was now suffering from ignition trouble.

The first third of this Grand Prix boiled down to a dispute between Bandini and Brabham and they took equal turns in the lead until the Italian broke a piston. At that point, Brabham, who had a 16 s advantage over Clark, looked a certain winner and continued to do so until half-distance when he, too, had to retire—with a broken timing chain. Thus Clark found himself quite comfortably in front and he took his first Grand Prix victory of the season a lap ahead of Rindt. For once it seemed that the great Scottish driver had been helped by a fortunate set of circumstances. Besides Brabham and Bandini, there was another man faster than Clark that day. Indeed he was the fastest of the lot, recording the best lap of the race: it was John Surtees who finished only third when really he should have won. The turning-point came on the seventeenth lap when, following Brabham and Bandini, Surtees was all lined up at the entrance to a corner, ready to lap Clark's team-mate Arundell. The latter saw the leaders but not the Cooper which he chopped brutally. Surtees was taken completely by surprise and could not avoid a collision. The damage was superficial but it meant a stop for the Cooper, and while it was being restored to order two laps went by, only one of which Big John managed to make up.

This called for revenge, and it was taken in masterly fashion in the next event, held a fortnight later in Mexico. This Grand Prix was also the last of the season, a season of which Cooper had hoped so much but which so far had brought only disillusion. Nevertheless, after the arrival of Surtees, there was a sense of a renewed fighting spirit in the team from Surbiton.

At the end of practice, Surtees, who had recorded the best time, found himself with three rivals: Clark whose 43 now seemed fairly well sorted out, Ginther, who was still having handling problems, and of course, Brabham. These four men were covered by under 0·8 s. It was the Japanese car which, taking advantage of the snap start given by Clerk of the Course Velasquez, jumped into the lead from the second row of the grid. However, on the second lap Brabham took over, only to be relieved on the sixth by Surtees making a surprise come-back. From then on these two drew steadily away from the rest of the field, duelling all the way. It was the German Grand Prix all over again, but this time the other way round as it was Brabham's turn to keep an eye on Surtees and make sure that he got no more than a 3 s lead. Eventually he had to declare himself beaten and take the last few laps at a slower speed. At the end of this Grand Prix they were the only drivers on the same lap, having lapped their immediate followers, Hulme, Ginther and Gurney. The last was using the four-cylinder Climax engine because the V12 had refused to adapt itself to the Mexican altitude. The Ferraris had not been entered and Clark was out of the running because his engine was not working properly and finally he broke his gear-box.

So Jack Brabham reclaimed the crown that he had renounced in 1961. Already it was suspected that B.R.M. had taken the wrong turning with the H16, that Cooper could not hope for much from Maserati for 1967 and that Honda and Eagle would pay serious attention to their cars in an attempt to make them winners. Yet by far the most important news that concerned the forthcoming season was that Ford had decided to enter the ring. The English firm Cosworth, well known for their remarkable Ford Anglia-based Formula 2 and Formula 3 units, had been chosen by Ford and given the necessary funds to design and build a Formula 1 engine which was to be mounted in a Lotus chassis. The man principally responsible for this move was the extremely dynamic Director of Public Relations for Ford-Europe, Walter Hayes. He performed a brilliant operation on his company's image for the remarkably small capital outlay of £100,000. This was the budget allotted to Keith Duckworth and Mike Costin, a very modest sum compared with the vast amount of money spent in achieving victory at Le Mans which was no less astronomical for not being disclosed.

Today Cosworth are famous throughout the world and are established in an ultra-modern factory in Northampton. Keith Duckworth has his own personal helicopter for calling on his suppliers, which gives some idea of the success and the originality of this man who is a curious mixture of the unconventional, common sense and, of course, genius. Although still very young—a little over forty—and relaxed in appearance, Duckworth's hair is more salt than pepper. Like a good British citizen, he maintains a sense of humor and quite genuinely does not care to take himself seriously. Before the move to Northampton the firm camped in various wooden sheds in Florence Road, on the outskirts of London. That is where the marvellous Ford Anglia-based 1100 cc Formula Junior units came from in the early 1960s. There was a tiny room about 12 ft (3·6 m) square which was filled by a desk piled high with precarious heaps of papers, files, old books and magazines. Behind the desk was a chair and just above it, in a conspicuous position on the wall, a piece of cardboard inscribed with the motto of the house, "Perfect organisation is a sign of decadence." Then came the Formula 2 SCA s.o.h.c. 1600 cc unit which, in spite of its 140 bhp, was beaten by the Honda; after that the FA d.o.h.c. 1600 which was to dominate the new Formula 2 from 1967; finally the DFV 3-litre which will be discussed later. This, too, appeared in 1967 and was immediately confirmed as the best engine in Formula 1 and remained so for several years to come.

The Honda V12, a magnificent piece of machinery.

1967
ford arrive
but brabham's
success continues

They were hard at work at Cosworth when at the end of December the circus embarked for South Africa where the first round of the 1967 World Championship was to be run on 2nd January. On this occasion, the East London circuit had been abandoned in favour of Kyalami, situated in the suburbs of Johannesburg at an altitude of 6000 ft (1800 m). In other words, the carburation problems which the technicians had to deal with in Mexico for the last Grand Prix of 1966 were to recur on the occasion of the first event of the new season.

Everyone was feverishly preparing something new, particularly on the engine side, but nobody was finished by the beginning of January so that from the technical point of view there was absolutely nothing in the way of novelty at this South African Grand Prix. On the other hand, there had already been some notable transfers among the drivers. John Surtees had left Cooper for Honda and had been replaced by Pedro Rodriguez. Richie Ginther joined his friend and fellow American Dan Gurney at Eagle. Graham Hill went back to Lotus to become Jim Clark's team-mate because Ford wanted to make sure of having the services of two first-rate drivers. Thus Stewart became driver number one for B.R.M. who entrusted their second car to Michael Spence.

This Grand Prix, held in oppressive heat, very nearly had a phenomenally surprising end: to wit, the victory of Rhodesian driver John Love (ex-Formula Junior star for the Cooper-Ken Tyrrell team) who was competing with his own 1964 Cooper fitted with a four-cylinder 2·7-litre Climax engine. Love had already somewhat embarrassed the leading performers in practice by achieving the fifth best time and beating the likes of Surtees, Rindt, Stewart, Hill . . . however, the two Brabhams caused no surprise when they made it to the front row of the grid ahead of Clark and Rodriguez. In the race, when Hulme, who had led all the way, had to stop seven laps from the end with brake trouble, Love found himself in the lead, 20 s ahead of Rodriguez who for some while had been without the use of second gear. The Rhodesian was about to win the first Grand Prix of the year without any trouble when he in turn was forced to stop due to shortage of fuel. The mechanics filled him up as quickly as they could, but Rodriguez had been gone for 30 s by the time Love was able to get going again. So it was the Mexican who had the good fortune to win the first Grand Prix of his career which also coincided with his entry into the Cooper team. Surtees took the Honda into third position a lap in arrears and, with split-second timing, one of his tires burst at the very moment he was crossing the finishing line. Hulme, who had dominated the race before his troubles started, came in fourth without brakes. It had been a massacre of a race for the machinery and particularly for the B.R.M.s and Lotuses (with B.R.M. engines) which all had to retire. The Ferraris had not put in an appearance. On the whole, hardly anything worth remembering came out of Kyalami, except that after a year's racing many of the 3-litre Formula 1 machines were still a long way from being right.

There was to be further proof of this at Monaco four months later. Meanwhile there was a non-Championship event at Brands Hatch which Gurney, demonstrating the progress of the V12 Weslake, won ahead of Bandini driving the new Ferrari with the exhaust coming from the centre of the vee. The 1967 season really opened at Monaco. For the first time

Lorenzo
Bandini
(Ferrari):
he was
to die
in the Monaco
Grand Prix.

Brabham was using his new Repco engine—it was still a single overhead camshaft V8 but it had a shorter stroke and no longer used the Oldsmobile block. Its rev limit had risen to over 9000 rev/min and although the power was not disclosed it must have been more than 350 bhp. Hulme, however, still had to make do with the 1966 engine, now developing some 330 bhp at 8200 rev/min.

The young New Zealander, Chris Amon, was making his start with Ferrari; and like his team leader, Bandini, was driving a new V12: 390 bhp at 10,000 rev/min. This was less than the power claimed for the Weslake V12: 410 bhp at 10,500 rev/min, making the Eagles the most powerful of the Formula 1 machines entered for the Monaco G.P. Honda were running a version of the V12 which had been specially tuned to give good low-speed torque and which developed only 380 bhp at 9200 rev/min. The Maserati engine fitted to the Coopers had to be content with 370 bhp also at 9200 rev/min—a new three-valve-per-cylinder Maserati had been brought along but it was not used. Only Spence ran an H16 B.R.M.: 400 bhp at 11,000 rev/min. Stewart (like Clark and Hill at Lotus and McLaren who was driving a Type M4B Formula 2 chassis) preferred to go back to the 2-litre Tasman engine; depending on the one in question, these developed between 230 bhp (Hill's 1916 cc B.R.M.) and 275 bhp (Stewart's 2070 cc unit).

There was rather a commotion when the organizers announced that they had officially qualified eleven competitors and the Eagles were not among them. This unfair decision had dramatic consequences. Gurney managed fairly easily to achieve a time that gave him a place on the fourth row of the grid, but poor Ginther, wrestling with an unmanageable chassis and various other problems, suffered the humiliation of being thrown out, while newcomer Servoz-Gavin driving a 1600 Formula 2 Matra-Cosworth ballasted up to 1100 lb (500 kg), succeeded in qualifying. This made Ginther very bitter and he decided there and then to give up racing.

The new Repco seemed to come up to Brabham's expectations and he easily recorded the best practice time of 1 min 27·6 s, a very noticeable improvement on Clark's 1966 time of 1 min 29·9 s. Bandini was alongside him (1 min 28·3 s) on the front row. Surtees and Hulme shared the second row, Clark and Stewart the third. Bandini took the lead at the start, followed by Brabham who put a rod through the side of his engine at Mirabeau. He spun off and provoked tremendous jostling in the pack close behind. It was Jo Siffert who suffered, puncturing his oil cooler against the rear of McLaren's car, and the worst result was that Brabham and Siffert motored back on to the track, not realizing that they were spilling oil all over the road and turning it into a real skating rink. On the following lap there was total panic at the chicane; everybody went sideways but everybody got through nevertheless, except Clark who was convinced that a wholesale collision was inevitable and chose to take the escape road. Hulme then took the lead, and Bandini was passed by Stewart who raced after Hulme. He took him braking for Sainte-Dévote and vanished. However, he did not have long to consider the possibility of a second consecutive victory on this circuit which was usually so

Bottle-neck at the entry to the chicane at Monaco: Hulme (9), Bandini (18), Stewart (4) leading Surtees (Honda), Gurney (Eagle), McLaren (McLaren) and Clark.

The new Ford Cosworth V8.

The Eagle's V12 Weslake.

Ferrari V12.

B.R.M. H16.

Repco V8.

Maserati V12.

kind to the B.R.M.s, for on the fifteenth lap Stewart had to give up with a worn-out gear-box.

This left Hulme alone in front and he went on to pull out a lead that had reached 19 s by the thirtieth lap, nearly one-third distance; behind him, Bandini seemed to be having more trouble with the very slippery surface. Then, as the track recovered its grip, the Italian driver launched his attack, just as he had done in 1966 against Stewart, and after an exciting drive was within 7 s of the Brabham by a little after half-distance. However, Hulme had anticipated this and speeded up enlarging the gap again. It had grown to nearly 20 s when, on the eighty-second lap, catastrophe struck. For some unknown reason, but which specialists were later to attribute to fatigue, Lorenzo Bandini made a mistake in braking for the chicane and hit the straw bales. The Ferrari turned over and caught fire, and in spite of the fact that there were firemen on the spot, the driver was not pulled from the blaze until too late. For a long time Lorenzo Bandini hovered between life and death in the hospital at Monte Carlo before finally succumbing to his frightful burns. He was just thirty. His Italian admirers were really devoted to him and saw this excellent driver and eternally smiling and splendid young man as Ascari's successor.

The horrifying accident unleashed a violent controversy on the subject of safety. The fact that the firemen had been powerless to save Bandini, even though they were in a position to take immediate action, said much about the effectiveness of their equipment. The race was being transmitted live to the television screens of Europe and as there was a camera covering the chicane, millions of viewers saw the tragedy as it happened. Obviously this provoked a reaction from the news media and involved the feelings of the whole world. The Grand Prix Drivers' Association had some very harsh words for the organizers, and they were also strongly attacked by witnesses of the event who did not hesitate to categorize the members of the safety service as incompetent and cowardly. After this accident the drivers felt very strongly that something must be done to improve the safety of the circuits where they were called upon to race. Some of them, who had competed in the United States, and at Indianapolis in particular, were fully aware of the efforts that had been made in this direction on the other side of the Atlantic, while in Europe, in the sacred (and in this case very convenient) name of tradition, conservatism prevailed. As lap speeds steadily increased so did the risks taken by the drivers, and it was obvious that the provision and careful investigation of more effective safety measures was becoming a matter of urgency. The only systematic progress that had occurred over the past few years concerned the drivers' equipment and they were now starting to wear clothes made of fireproof materials and helmets of better design. There had been no broad-based, concerted attempts to do anything about the circuits, however. Any improvements that were made still stemmed from a few individuals acting in isolation on a purely goodwill basis without any real understanding of the seriousness of the problem. Because it was so spectacular, because of the publicity (by no means always in the best of taste) it received and because it aroused such passionate and violent emotions, the accident which cost Lorenzo Bandini his life served as a trigger. The public, however little interested in motor racing, felt that the situation was an intolerable disgrace. Unfortunately, the C.S.I. took

no action even though they were the governing body of motor sport and therefore responsible for ensuring that this fundamentally dangerous activity was practiced in the best possible conditions. The drivers noted this dereliction of duty and decided that, as there was no other solution, they must take matters into their own hands.

Hulme was the winner of this Monaco Grand Prix and went to the top of the Championship table, one point ahead of Rodriguez who finished fifth, four laps behind. Hulme had lapped all his rivals: Graham Hill once—he had clutch trouble; Chris Amon twice—he had to have a wheel changed after a tire had been damaged in a bump when he was secure in second place; McLaren three times—he had to have a flat battery changed. As usual, the Monegasque circuit had shown no pity for weakness, whether mechanical or human. It has already been stated that the 1967 season really began at Monaco and a comparison of Brabham's lap practice time with Clark's of the previous year gives support to this view: a 2·3 s improvement in less than a minute and a half. However, the improvement at Zandvoort was amazing. In 1966, practice ended on a lap in 1 min 28·1 s by Brabham, but this time he got down to 1 min 25·6 s yet it only secured him third place on the grid. Gurney, driving an Eagle lighter by 99 lb (45 kg) following the use of magnesium for the monocoque and titanium for the suspension and even the exhaust pipes, beat him by 0·5 s, while Graham Hill, at the wheel of the brand-new Lotus-Ford 49 powered by the Cosworth DFV V8, was a good second ahead: 3·5 s gained in just one year, it was absolutely stupendous.

Ford had indeed made a grand entrance. The others had not been caught napping either—witness the Eagle (which must have cost a fortune). Brabham also had something new to show—the BT24 chassis. It was another tubular affair, but so astonishingly compact that its dimensions were practically the same as those of a Formula 2 chassis. However, he was not able to use it. B.R.M. also introduced a narrower, shorter and lighter (by 77 lb (35 kg)) monocoque, but more than this was needed and everyone was already waiting for the new V12s from Bourne.

The new Lotus-Ford was certainly not as revolutionary as the 25 had been in its day and generally there was nothing very extravagant about it at all. At first sight its most striking feature was the purity and elegance of the design as applied both to the car as a whole and to the smallest detail. It consisted, of course, of a light alloy monocoque which stopped at the seat back bulkhead; behind this, bolted to the monocoque by plates, was the engine which acted as a chassis member and carried the rear suspension. An interesting point was that the whole transmission/suspension unit could be dismounted from the engine without any of the suspension parts having to be removed. This meant that the settings remained untouched so that in the event of an engine-change a lot of time was saved. Otherwise the suspension was still classical in its geometry with inboard-mounted front springs. The brakes, particularly at the rear, were moved from the inside of the wheels and mounted directly in the air stream.

The Ford engine designed by Cosworth was a 90° V8 and apart from the cast-iron liners was made entirely of light alloy. It was very compact, measuring 22 in (558·8 mm) long and 26·5 in (673·1 mm) wide and it was also light (369 lb (168 kg)) because of the

The Eagle Weslake.

Right:
The Cooper-Maserati.

Below:
The Brabham-Repco,
the B.R.M. H16
and the Honda.

The Lotus 49.

The Ferrari.

simplicity of the design and despite the fact that it acted as a chassis member. The centre of the vee was filled by the Lucas injection system; the exhausts were at the side and of a simplified design because of the adoption of a flat crankshaft. Each cylinder head had two overhead camshafts which were fairly close together; they were driven by gears and acted on sixteen valves (four per cylinder at an angle of 32°). Bore and stroke were 3·3 in (85·7 mm) and 2·5 in (64·8 mm) respectively and the exact capacity was 2993 cc. It had Lucas electronic ignition and a single 0·4 in (10 mm) plug per cylinder and it was probably about 400 bhp at 9000 rev/min.

Once it has been said that the gear-box was a five-speed synchronized ZF unit, all the main features of the 49 have been mentioned, except the tires which were of course Firestones—15 in (381 mm) diameter front and rear. Nothing very special in fact, but it was all of a piece and was down to the minimum weight limit 1100 lb (500 kg). In other words, right from the

start it was the best of the 1967 Formula 1 machines in respect of power-to-weight ratio, and this is the factor that enabled it to establish itself immediately as the fastest.

After his fierce struggle with Gurney, Graham Hill was assured of the best place on the starting grid for the Dutch Grand Prix. At the drop of the flag he took advantage of his pole position and at the end of a flat-out first lap he was already 2 s ahead of Brabham who was followed by Rindt and Gurney. Jim Clark had broken a wheel bearing in practice and had not been able to get his chassis set up properly. The braking distribution was unbalanced and for the first part of the race he had to be content with conserving his strength.

However, Graham Hill's brilliant solo did not last long because on the tenth lap his timing gears broke and Brabham took the lead. Clark caught up with Rindt and the two of them gradually closed on the leader; then the Lotus overtook the Cooper, beset by

Gurney's dream comes true at Spa where he drove his Eagle to victory.

handling problems, and moved in on the Brabham which had to give way in its turn. Jack Brabham hung on grimly but there was nothing he could do to stop Clark pulling away and finishing 23 s ahead. Hulme was only 2 s behind Brabham and his third place strengthened his position at the head of the Championship table, but the performance of the Lotus suggested that the fate of the title was far from decided.

In the Belgian Grand Prix Clark gave yet another superb demonstration of his supremacy on the very fast but difficult circuit at Spa. By the end of practice Gurney had been put down by 3·1 s, Hill by 4·7 s, Rindt and Amon by 6·2 s and the Brabham, still short of power, by an even larger margin. At the beginning of the race Hill was unable to start, and when he finally motored away he was over two and a half minutes behind. Meanwhile Jim Clark had shot ahead in a manner reminiscent of his best 1500 Formula 1 years. He was already some 20 s in front of Stewart (who for once had the satisfaction of using a B.R.M. H16 that was in proper working order) and Gurney (who had paid a 2 s visit to his pit without the mechanics doing anything) when he had to stop to have one of his plugs changed. This operation took nearly two minutes and cost Clark the race. Victory therefore lay between Stewart, now in trouble with a recalcitrant gear-selector, which meant that he had to steer with one hand while he held on to the gear-lever with the other, and Gurney, who made capital out of Jackie Stewart's

predicament. The Eagle took the lead on the twentieth of the twenty-eight laps of the race and went on to win its first Grand Prix. Dan Gurney was overjoyed. By driving to victory in a car that he had constructed himself, he had accomplished the same feat as his ex-boss Jack Brabham. Everyone, or nearly everyone, shared his delight—he is an infinitely popular man and his persistent lack of success in the face of all the effort he put into racing was really upsetting. This win, so widely and sincerely celebrated, came just one year after the Eagle had competed in a Grand Prix for the very first time on the very same circuit. Gurney now became a possible pretender to the title since Clark had scored only one point for his sixth place and Hulme, like Brabham, had been forced to stop, both for the same reason. The Repco lubrication system depended on acceleration and deceleration for scavenging the sump, but as Spa is a circuit which causes a car's speed to alter very little, the Brabhams' sumps gradually filled with oil. Hulme was brought to a standstill at half-distance and Brabham only one lap later. Rodriguez was classified ninth, three laps behind, and thus did not score at all.

The French Grand Prix, held on the new Bugatti circuit at Le Mans, was the occasion of the Brabham team's complete revenge for their failure at Spa. This circuit is made up of fairly slow corners joined by straights and calls above all for good acceleration; consequently the lightest cars come off best there.

Next page: Once again Clark and Lotus (with the Ford-engined 49) were at the top in terms of sheer performance, but reliability was still lacking.

Therefore no one was at all surprised to see the two Lotuses immediately get the better of Brabham and Gurney, but this exhibition from Chapman's cars was not to last long. The same weakness showed up on both Lotuses which had to retire, one after the other: the sides of the gear-casing were not sufficiently rigid and the crown wheel and pinion gave way. Brabham, driving the compact BT24, found himself in the lead ahead of Gurney, who fell prey to injection troubles, Amon, whose throttle cable broke, and Hulme, who finished second, a lap in front of Stewart and his 2-litre V8 machine. This was another double for the Brabhams, and while it consolidated Hulme's position in the Championship it also improved Brabham's chance of the title.

Team Lotus had been very confident after their thunderous début at Zandvoort, but at Le Mans they seemed to be in trouble throughout the weekend. The cars arrived late and missed the first practice session, then all day Saturday Clark's engine refused to run properly in spite of Keith Duckworth's personal attention. It had to be changed that evening although no one really knew what was wrong with it. Since there was no practice scheduled for the Sunday, there was only one way of finding out whether the new engine was functioning correctly and that was to try it on the road. That is why the inhabitants of the peaceful little town of Mayet heard (they could not see it because it was almost dark) a Formula 1 car charging blindly down the local main road. Meanwhile, Chapman, Duckworth and the rest (among them the author, stationed at a level crossing) kept watch.

The gear-casings had to be strengthened as a matter of urgency. Chapman rapidly designed some strengthened sides, the gear-boxes were sent off at once to ZF at Friedrichshafen for modification and it was all sorted out in time for practice for the British G.P. at Silverstone. The result of this extremely speedy operation was that Clark recorded the best time and Hill the second best ahead of Brabham and Hulme; thus four men and two marques filled the front row of the grid. For the first time Denny Hulme was at the wheel of the second BT24 which had just been finished. In spite of it all, the Lotus team still looked worried. The suspension was the problem now; in practice a radius-rod mounting on Hill's car had broken and he had written off the machine. A third 49 was under construction in the workshop at Wymondham and this was hastily completed during the night with the aid of undamaged bits taken from the wrecked car. The outlook for Lotus was not as bright as it seemed.

At the start of the race, however, Clark and Hill went into the lead with no trouble while Hulme, fairly typically, let most of the field stream past him. At the end of the first lap he was in eighth position. Brabham immediately attacked Hill successfully, but Hill responded and got his place back. Then violent vibrations began to shake Brabham's car to such an extent that the rear-view mirrors fell off. It was poor Amon who suffered by being blocked by Black Jack for nearly the whole race. Hulme had climbed through the field and passed these two, but the Lotuses were too far ahead for him to have any hope of challenging them.

However, a little after two-thirds distance, a bolt holding a strut on Hill's car sheared just when he had overtaken Clark and seemed all set for his first victory of the year. He went off the road again, but this time the only consequence was that he had to crawl back to his pit for repairs. In any case he would not have won,

because nine laps after rejoining the race he was let down by his engine and was unable to finish. Meanwhile, Clark continued to keep Hulme in his place and the two men ended the race nearly 12 s apart and Amon, who had eventually managed to pass Brabham and quickly lose him, came home a good third, less than 20 s behind the winner. Clark, Hulme and Brabham, who had scored 9, 6 and 3 points respectively, remained in the running for the Championship. It was obvious that one of these three men would take the title even though, mathematically, Rodriguez (who finished fifth) and Gurney (who broke his engine) still had a chance.

It seemed that the American driver was going to take his chance at the German Grand Prix. Clark undeniably outclassed everyone in practice, getting down to within 4·1 s of the magic eight-minute barrier at the Nurburgring. Hulme, the second fastest, was 9·4 s behind, Stewart 11·1 s, Gurney 13·6 s as was Bruce McLaren who, since the French Grand Prix, had been driving the Eagle abandoned at Monaco by Ginther. Jim Clark's performance undoubtedly aroused admiration, but the achievement of the young Jacky Ickx, driving a 1600 Matra-Cosworth, was simply staggering: at 8 min 14 s his lap time was the third best of practice, 0·5 s behind Hulme and 21 s ahead of Oliver the next fastest of the eight Formula 2 drivers with a place on the starting grid. In addition, he beat Brabham by 4·9 s, Amon by 6·4 s, Rindt by 6·9 s and Rodriguez by 8·2 s. It was sensational. There is no doubt that the maneuverability of a light Formula 2 machine was a decisive factor but it does not explain everything. The brilliance of this virtual beginner was self-evident and it was supported by his knowledge of the circuit and its innumerable corners and hidden hazards, a circuit where not even the most experienced professionals always feel at home. In fact the Belgian driver had competed in two eighty-four-hour endurance events for touring cars at the Ring and had thus acquired an intimate knowledge of its snags and subtleties. This was his reward for the tedium of the tasks he undertook.

At the start of the race Clark took the lead in front of Hulme and Gurney, the three of them well ahead of the McLaren/Brabham duo who were followed by the Stewart/Amon/Surtees trio. In spite of his practice time, Jacky Ickx was placed on the sixth row of the grid because all the Formula 2 machines, whatever their performance, had to line up behind all the Formula 1 cars. However, in two laps the driver of the little Matra had climbed up to ninth place, overtaking all the Coopers and Irwin's B.R.M. H16 in the process. Contrary to expectations, Hulme and Gurney managed to keep right on Clark's tail. When they came round for the fourth time, it was not the Lotus that appeared first but the Eagle. Meanwhile Clark was making his way back slowly with a broken front suspension; first of all a slow puncture had affected the handling, then the suspension collapsed in the Karusel.

Thus Gurney was in front and he quickly pulled out a substantial lead over Hulme. While the American was stepping up the pace, recording the fastest lap of the race (8 min 15·1 s), Hulme decided to ease off. He could undoubtedly have taken a tow from the powerful Eagle as he had done in the early stages of the race but his engine, forced to run at 800 rev/min above its maximum limit, would probably not have lasted the distance. Hulme wisely lifted his foot. Behind these two, Ickx was the focus of attention as he continued his climb through the field; on the fourth lap he took over fifth place, on the sixth lap he moved up again at the expense of Amon and by half-distance he was challenging Brabham for the third spot. Unfortunately, the Matra's front suspension broke and the sensational performance of Ken Tyrrell's young protégé came to a premature end.

Everyone was waiting for the Eagle to come round for the thirteenth time when it was discovered that it had stopped on the circuit with a broken drive shaft. Once again success had eluded the American who had looked like a certain winner after Clark's retirement. Hulme found himself in the lead with a 45 s advantage over Brabham who, with his customary ease, had warded off the spirited but vain attacks from Chris Amon. The independent French driver, Guy Ligier, brought his 1966 Brabham-Repco into sixth place and thus scored a point in the Championship. With four Grands Prix to go, Hulme was securely established at the top of the table, twelve points ahead of Brabham and eighteen ahead of Clark and Amon.

The next event, held on the Mosport circuit in Canada, was the occasion of another triumphant double for the Brabham team. This time Brabham won but Hulme took yet another step towards the title. However, it would be wrong to imagine that they had a walk-over as in fact it seemed that they would be beaten by Jim Clark until two-thirds through the race when the Lotus ignition failed.

The two essential factors at Mosport were the rain and the tires rather than the engines, chassis or even drivers. The rain was intermittent and the situation changed dramatically according to the dampness of the track. This was largely due to tires: when the flood-gates of the heavens opened, Goodyear's rubber proved more effective than Firestone's.

The best practice times stood to the two Lotus-Fords, and at the start of the race Clark, as usual, shot away from the line like an arrow. It was already drizzling; gradually the road got more slippery and Jim Clark's solo performance was brought to an end. Hulme steadily reduced the initial gap until by the end of the third lap he was up with the Lotus which he successfully challenged at the start of the fourth. Meanwhile Brabham was climbing up in similar fashion from fourth place and once he had passed Hill and Stewart, he too, closed in on Clark.

As Hulme pulled away in the lead, the spectators were treated to an even more exciting demonstration by Bruce McLaren. His car was fitted with the eagerly awaited V12 B.R.M. engine making its first appearance in a race (the B.R.M.s themselves were still powered by the H16). The McLaren was very classical in conception and, by virtue of its monocoque and suspension with outboard-mounted springs, reminiscent of early 1967 Formula 2 machines. The engine itself was a derivation of the old Formula 1 1500 cc V8 with cylinder heads at an angle of 60°; the four overhead camshafts, however, were chain driven. Bore and stroke were 2·9 in (75·2 mm) and 2·2 in (57·2 mm) respectively and there were two valves per cylinder; its power, announced by B.R.M., was relatively modest at 356 bhp at 9000 rev/min. However, Bruce McLaren had done a good job and got the weight of the car down to 1122 lb (510 kg) so that from the start it looked like a competitive machine. On the second lap the New Zealand driver/constructor was lying twelfth after a spin but this did not discourage him and he set off to do something about it, lapping faster in the rain than the leader himself. Twenty laps later he overhauled Clark and took second place. Everyone was waiting to see him tackle Hulme when the rain stopped, and hope moved into a different camp. It took Clark six laps to get ahead of McLaren again. So it was he who challenged Hulme whose 30 s lead shrank visibly. It was down to 6 s when, on the fifty-second lap, it started to rain once more. Still pressing on, Clark managed to pass Hulme five laps later but he was put back into second place almost immediately; another lap went by, Hulme made a mistake and Clark retook the lead. The trouble was that Hulme could not see because his goggles were steamed up and eventually he had to stop at his pit to have them changed. Just as Clark was beginning to look the certain winner his engine gave up with a drowned ignition. This put Brabham in the lead, well ahead of his team-mate and rid of the menacing McLaren who had also been forced into a pit stop with a flat battery. Owing to the fact that he wanted to keep his car as light as possible and since it used a mechanical rather than an electrical fuel pump, Bruce McLaren had not fitted an alternator. This was a mistake for which he paid heavily. With an alternator the McLaren-B.R.M. would probably have won the first Grand Prix it contested and equalled the Zandvoort achievement of the Lotus-Ford.

Back in Europe, the Formula 1 circus found itself at Monza for an Italian Grand Prix that was to become legendary. Clark's performance in this race was fantastic: it undeniably ranks with Fangio's fabulous drive at the Nurburgring in 1957 when he fought his way through the field to beat Collins and Hawthorn, and with the feats performed by Moss in 1961 at Monaco and Monza, this very same track. Unfortunately for the Scotsman, and unlike his two illustrious predecessors, he was not to be rewarded for his prodigious efforts by victory.

Practice revealed quite a number of developments and in particular the new Honda which was immediately christened the "Hondalola". John Surtees had managed to convince those responsible for the Japanese team that they had no hope of winning while they continued to run with such a heavy car and that what they really needed was a much lighter chassis. To gain time, Surtees had suggested that this chassis should be built in the workshops of his associate Eric Broadley, or in other words at the Lola Works in England. Meanwhile in Japan they should concentrate on reducing the weight of the engine/transmission unit. His plan was adopted.

From the chassis point of view, the Honda was practically identical to the Lola which had won the Indianapolis 500-Mile Race the year before and the reason for this was that they wanted quick results that did not entail any risks. Hence the nickname. The treatment was effective and the new car scaled 165 lb (75 kg) less than the old so that the weight was now down to 1320 lb (600 kg). This was undoubtedly still excessive compared with the weight of the Lotuses and Brabhams, but even so it was a big improvement. In addition the fuel consumption of the V12 had been reduced by changes to the injection system and this further reduced the weight of the car in starting-line trim. On the other hand, the power output had fallen below 400 bhp but what power there was could now be put to better use.

Another important, if less spectacular development was a new V12 engine fitted in a Ferrari chassis which was also considerably lighter at 1122 lb (510 kg). The

The outcome of the Italian Grand Prix was decided at this very moment in this very place: Brabham has overtaken Surtees in braking, but he is on a line that takes him over a patch of oil and his rival is first out of the Parabolica curve after a perfectly executed trick.

engine had four valves per cylinder and was distinctive from the outside in that, due to the closeness of the camshafts, it had only one cylinder-head cover for each bank of cylinders.

Maserati had at last got their three-valve-per-cylinder V12 sorted out and this was installed in the Coopers of Rindt and Jacky Ickx, the latter replacing Rodriguez who was recovering from an accident he had had in a Formula 2 race at Enna. So the young Belgian was making the start in Formula 1 that had been predicted after his outstanding performance in the German Grand Prix at the wheel of the Formula 2 Matra.

In practice the McLaren-B.R.M. V12 showed up well once again and, due largely to McLaren's slipstreaming know-how, managed to secure a place on the front row of the grid alongside Clark (1 min 28·5 s) and Brabham (1 min 28·8 s). Compared with the big improvements recorded at Spa and Zandvoort for example, these times were relatively disappointing since 1 min 31·3 s had been achieved the previous year by Parkes and his Ferrari.

The start of the race was chaotic and Gurney went ahead while Amon and Rindt were taken completely by surprise. On the third lap Clark took the lead. Then Gurney, in second place, broke a connecting-rod. It was not long before the leading drivers grouped themselves into two quartets: the first composed of the

Lotuses of Clark and Hill and the Brabhams of Hulme and Brabham (this took care of the four V8-engined cars), then, 10 s behind, the second comprising the four V12s of Amon, Surtees, McLaren and Rindt. By careful application of slipstreaming techniques the men in these two groups changed their position on every lap, but it was all of little significance. However, from now on it was clear that victory must fall to one of these eight.

On the thirteenth lap they were reduced to seven. Clark stopped in a panic at his pit with a punctured right rear tire. By the time he was back in the race, Hill, Hulme and Brabham were a lap and several seconds ahead. He soon made up the odd seconds, passed the other three and started to unlap himself, but although the race was only one-third over, it was reckoned he had no hope. However, first Hulme stopped, with cylinder-head gasket trouble, on the thirty-first lap. Then Brabham's throttle jammed wide open: the engine over-revved, the valves were damaged and the Repco lost power. Hill was now alone in the lead, travelling like the wind with only Clark moving faster. Brabham was being caught by Surtees, Amon and McLaren, but one by one the last two were eliminated: the Ferrari had suspension trouble and the McLaren-B.R.M. broke a connecting-rod. Meanwhile, Clark was on a fantastic progress through the field; he caught up with Rindt who was having trouble with his brakes and took over fourth place. By the fifty-fifth of the sixty-eight laps which made up the race, Hill seemed to have it all sewn up, but the fate of second place still had to be decided by Brabham, Surtees and Clark.

The excitement was only just beginning. On the fifty-ninth lap Hill had to go into his pit with broken timing gear. Brabham was now in the lead but losing ground steadily to Surtees at a rate that meant the Honda would overtake him before the end. Then something even more extraordinary happened. Clark arrived at full speed, caught up with Surtees, overtook him and pulled away with ridiculous ease. He now had Brabham within sight and on the sixty-first lap (seven left to go), Jim Clark, after making up a lap on all his rivals, went into the lead and vanished towards an incredible victory.

The fate of second place was still in the balance. Three laps from the end Surtees took it over. Then Clark suddenly started to slow down and this heralded yet another change in the situation. There was not enough fuel left in the Lotus tank—it was filled with a synthetic foam which prevented the pumps from sucking up the last few pints of petrol. During an unbelievable last lap, Surtees, closely followed by Brabham, overtook the slowly moving Clark, and as they approached the Parabolica the two men began to brake for the last time in the race. Then Jack Brabham played his last card: he challenged Surtees and got past him at the entrance to the corner. John Surtees, however, was no less cunning than the Australian and forced him on to a line that took him over a patch of oil. The Brabham went sideways and the Honda was first away on the straight that leads to the finishing line which it crossed 0·2 s ahead. Twenty-three seconds later Clark free-wheeled his way over the line to a tremendous ovation from the crowd who broke through the barriers, closed in on Clark and nearly suffocated him.

It was an unpleasant moment but the reaction was understandable: to overcome such a handicap was and is a unique achievement in the history of modern Formula 1, one of whose main characteristics is that performances vary so little that even the shortest stop automatically entails the sacrifice of all hope of victory. At Monza on 10th September 1967 Jim Clark proved that for him, and for him alone, nothing was impossible.

In the United States Clark secured the victory that had been denied him in Italy, but it was another emotional event for him and, in the final analysis, it was a miracle he won. This Grand Prix was remarkable for the superiority of the Lotus-Fords which only the Eagle, and to a certain extent the forty-eight-valve Ferrari, were capable of resisting on a circuit like Watkins Glen where acceleration is of particular importance. Although they weighed the same, the Brabhams had 40 bhp less power and were outclassed. It was reasonable, therefore, that as a result of practice Clark and Hill should be on the first row of the grid ahead of Gurney and Amon. It was no less reasonable that, after the quick disappearance of the Eagle with a broken rear upright, the two Lotuses should pull away and seem all set for an unopposed double. However,

Colin Chapman's 49s had not yet reached the stage of total development, and although Graham Hill was in the lead he had been without a clutch since the second lap. The Londoner, who was having a decidedly unsuccessful season, was unable to avoid being overtaken by his team-mate or even being caught by Amon. However, the latter was no more lucky than Hill because towards the end of the race his engine broke. So the two Lotuses again seemed sure of the double when, two laps from the finish, the upper mounting point of the right rear suspension on Clark's car gave way. Fortunately, this happened as he was getting ready to negotiate a right-hand corner so he managed to keep control of his machine. He continued at a slower speed with one rear wheel semi-horizontal, held on only by the lower wishbone and drive shaft. Everyone began to wonder whether he would make it to the finishing line or if he was to be beaten at the line yet again, this time by Graham Hill. There were seven seconds left but the Monza mishap was not repeated. Hulme (third, one lap in arrears) also just made it by the skin of his teeth as he ran out of fuel on the last lap and free-wheeled across the line. Rarely have the first men home in a Grand Prix had such an intense desire to take the flag.

With only one event left before the end of the 1967 Formula 1 Championship season, the title was still unclaimed. There were two drivers in the running for it, Denny Hulme at the top of the table and Jack Brabham right on his heels. The rivalry between these two team-mates made for a lively situation, particularly as it was complicated by the fact that the one was the employer of the other. However, there was no doubt that both men were determined to play to win without making any concessions to one another.

In order to take the crown for the fourth time, Jack Brabham simply had to win in Mexico. However, things did not start very well for him as in the first practice session he broke his timing chain. Meanwhile, Clark, with sovereign ease, was playing with the old lap record and the following day easily made sure of pole position. Jim Clark also had a strong reason for wanting to win this event because if he did, he would equal Fangio's illustrious record of twenty-four Grand Prix victories, something much more significant than a World Champion's crown.

This time the only problem Clark experienced was caused by the snap start. He was taken by surprise and left behind by Hill and Amon while Gurney's chances disappeared completely as he punctured his radiator against one of the exhausts on Clark's car which was immediately ahead of him and slow to move off.

On the third lap Clark took the lead and pulled so far ahead that he was never again to have the slightest worry. Brabham's engine was overheating and he had to be content with following Hill and Amon at a distance, while behind a particularly attentive Hulme watched his every move.

Clark's victory meant that Hulme took the title. It was soon clear that he would easily win. However, it had only needed one small thing to reverse the situation and give Brabham the crown at the end of an apparently unemotional race.

In fact the affair was settled on Saturday evening in the Team Lotus garage. During the previous day's

Dennis Hulme,
1967 World Champion.

practice the Mexican driver, Moises Solana, who had been entrusted with the third Lotus, had broken his engine and it had been replaced by a new one. The following day Clark took pole position driving his own car, but it seemed to him that the engine was starting to show signs of fatigue so he said that for the race he would like to use the unit that had been installed in the Mexican's machine. The only snag was that such a swap would mean a whole night's work for the mechanics who were already worn out. After a lot of hesitation Clark decided to run with Solana's car while Solana took over his. This turned out to be a wise decision, because on the eleventh lap a suspension joint broke, bringing the Mexican's race to an untimely end.

If this is added to the fact that Graham Hill had to retire when in second place with a broken universal, and that Amon, who took over second place, ran short of fuel three laps from the end, it comes to the fact that Brabham who finished second would have won if Clark had driven his own car as expected. It is true that even in this case Hulme would have taken the title because he finished just behind Brabham, which was enough to secure him the crown whether Brabham

won or not. Nevertheless, this shows what victory or even a World Championship depends on in motor racing.

Thus, at thirty-one, Denny Hulme took the title and surprised a lot of people. First because never until now had a team's second driver managed to do such a thing, and second because of the character of Denny himself: the anti-hero.

In fact no one could be more different from the popular image of the racing driver than this placid young man with his slow measured speech and movements; never a self-promoter, always quiet and reserved. He is so self-effacing that he represents the only mistake (he was underestimated) in Ken Tyrrell's celebrated talent-spotting career. After winning the Driver for Europe prize in New England in 1960, Hulme settled in England and bought a Formula Junior Cooper with which he set out to get to know the principal British and Continental circuits. He was very short of cash and travelled around in an old Ford Zodiac, with his racing car in tow behind, acting as his own mechanic. The following year he had several drives for the Cooper-B.M.C. works team, managed by Ken Tyrrell, but these did not lead anywhere.

Denny Hulme was undeniably sure and steady but he seemed to lack dash and aggressiveness. However, in order to improve his standard of living, he found a job as a mechanic in Jack Brabham's garage and it was Jack who gave him his chance at the end of 1962 when he was given the works Formula Junior to drive. At the wheel of this car, Hulme really showed himself for what he was, winning seven times during the course of the 1963 season and making his mark as one of the toughest (if not the toughest) opponents of Formula Junior king Peter Arundell and his works Lotus.

The following year Hulme started in Formula 2, where he had all the star performers to contend with, and gave such a good account of himself that in 1965 he found himself driving his employer's Formula 1 machine, his first Grand Prix appearance being at Clermont-Ferrand in the French G.P. in which he finished fourth. In 1966 Gurney left the Brabham team and quite naturally Hulme replaced him. He collected a lot of good results and from then on everyone got used to some extent to thinking of him as a good Formula 1 driver, but he still was not considered World Championship material.

Nevertheless, 1967 was to be his year. He not only won the title but also the two Grands Prix that do most for a driver's reputation—the Monaco and the German. These are run on the most searching of circuits where only the truly great champions can triumph. It was the consecration of the talent of a quiet man who undoubtedly does not have the ability of Jim Clark but who is regarded as a redoubtable opponent by the best, particularly if the race conditions are hard and demand strength and a cool head from the driver rather than dash. He is the championship man *par excellence*, certainly very capable of winning races, but never asking too much of his car, and always intelligently tailoring his aims to suit the means at his disposal. Denny Hulme's tactic is to finish the races he starts (where he always gives of his best), in the best place possible, rather than to try and win at all costs or throw in the sponge because he has no chance. In short the new World Champion was a thoroughgoing professional, and his success, coming after a relatively long period of obscurity, did not change him in any way: he was still the placid, accessible, amiable young man he had always been despite the fact that fame and fortune had smiled on him.

1968

the death of clark

but, with graham hill, ford and lotus triumph

"Negotiation" was the name of the game during the winter of 1967–68 and when the Formula 1 teams turned up at Kyalami for the first Grand Prix of the new season, there was a different face to be seen in all but three of them. The exceptions were Honda and Eagle, still running one car each for John Surtees and Dan Gurney respectively, and Lotus whose two Ford-engined 49s were again entrusted to Jim Clark and Graham Hill.

The most important driver transfer involved the new World Champion, Hulme, who had signed with Bruce McLaren. His place at Brabham was taken by Rindt, finally free of his contract with Cooper who had also lost Rodriguez, now replacing Stewart at B.R.M. To fill this total gap they engaged the Italian Ludovico Scarfiotti, now bent on making a full-time career in Formula 1, and Brian Redman, a British hope disclosed by Formula 2. Ferrari had changed their policy entirely and instead of the single car they had run in 1967, had three machines in the lists for 1968 with two very promising drivers as support for Chris Amon: Jacky Ickx and Andrea de Adamich. The latter had come to notice through some brilliant performances for Alfa Romeo in touring-car events and some good drives in Formula 3. Michael Spence remained with B.R.M.

Jackie Stewart, the rising star of racing, already considered by some as Jim Clark's future rival, had left B.R.M. for a French marque making their start in Formula 1—Matra Sports. This company, established in 1965 with the acquisition of Automobiles René Bonnet, was the motorcar division of a company specializing in the construction of missiles. The first Matras, which appeared on the circuits in 1965, were Ford-engined Formula 3 machines and they gave Jean-Pierre Beltoise, the multi-titled ex-Champion motorcyclist of France, an opportunity to prove himself the leading driver in France by carrying him to his first national title on four wheels. Matra followed this up by building some excellent Formula 2 machines that impressed Jackie Stewart and his mentor Ken Tyrrell so much that they entered into an agreement with the French firm. The Tyrrell team had some convincing successes with the Matra-Cosworths and their second driver, Jacky Ickx, won the Formula 2 European Trophy, reserved for non-graded drivers, in 1967.

However, Matra were ambitious and determined to break into the magic circle of Formula 1 constructors. After obtaining a loan of 6,000,000 francs from the State and securing the support of the new and go-ahead French oil company Elf, Jean-Luc Lagardère, Matra's extremely dynamic director, announced in 1967 that they were going to build Formula 1 chassis and engines with a view to taking the drivers' World Championship and the Constructors' Cup before 1970. It was a bold statement and while the comments that greeted the challenge were favorable (the enterprise was after all not lacking in style), they were also somewhat tinged with skepticism.

By then Matra already had substantial experience to draw on from the point of view of chassis since their Formula 2s and Formula 3s were proving at least as good as the best. However, as far as engines were concerned, they were going into the totally unknown and despite his optimism, M. Lagardère was fully aware that he really must not expect miracles from the projected V12—this layout had been chosen even though at the time the V8s ruled the roost. It was then that Stewart and Tyrrell approached him with the proposition that a chassis should be committed to their care which they would equip with a V8 Ford-Cosworth. Since this offered the possibility of quickly notching up a few wins while Matra waited for their 100 per cent French car to become competitive and at the same time secured the collaboration of one of the best team managers and one of the fastest drivers in the world, M. Lagardère approved the idea. Thus was created the Matra-International stable, which was run from Ken Tyrrell's timber business in England.

Apart from Stewart's new Matra-Ford, the first Grand Prix of the 1968 season had little to offer in the way of technical originality. There were no important changes to be seen on the Brabham-Repcos, the Lotus-Fords, the Ferraris, Hulme's McLaren-B.R.M. (Bruce McLaren was not running), the Cooper-Maseratis, the Eagle-Weslake, the Honda or Spence's H16 B.R.M. Rodriguez, however, had been given a B.R.M. Formula Tasman chassis fitted with a 3-litre V12 similar to the one in the McLaren. Interest, however, centred on the Matra, an interim model based on the Formula 2 monocoque which was reinforced with a tubular structure round the Ford V8. It had been finished in a great hurry and was not even painted when it arrived at Kyalami, the only covering on the bodywork being a coat of strange matt green primer. The suspension components were largely borrowed from Matra's sports prototype and the car was fitted with Dunlop tires.

Although in no way a final product, the Matra-Ford was confirmed right away as a competitive machine and at the end of practice, during which all the runners experienced serious cooling and carburation problems, it found itself with a place on the front row. Stewart was only 0·1 s behind Graham Hill, but he had conceded 1·1 s to a supreme Jim Clark. At all events, it was a magnificent demonstration of strength by the Ford-Cosworths installed in the three cars which had returned the three best times. This comment can be extended to cover the V8s in general since the two cars occupying the second row were the Brabham-Repcos, ahead of the seven V12s of which the Honda was the fastest but with a time that was already 2 s slower than Clark's.

After a brief duel with Stewart, who made the best start and led for a little under two laps, Clark went ahead and steadily pulled away to finish some 25 s in front of his team-mate Graham Hill. In twenty-nine laps the latter had climbed up from seventh position. On his first outing at the wheel of a Brabham—in this case the one used by Hulme the previous season—Rindt achieved a good third place, 5 s behind Hill. Brabham had been obliged to retire with valve-spring trouble on the forty-fourth lap as had Stewart, who had been holding third place after being forced to give way to Hill. Classified fourth, ahead of Hulme, Amon was the best placed of the V12 drivers but the pair of them were two laps behind the leaders. Beltoise, driving a ballasted Formula 2 Matra-Cosworth, scored the first championship point of his career by taking sixth place.

The next grande épreuve was scheduled for April on the brand-new Jarama circuit in Madrid. Henceforth the Spanish Grand Prix took over from Monaco as official opener of the European season. Meanwhile, however, the Race of Champions, a non-championship event held at Brands Hatch, saw the appearance of some important new features. First two McLaren-Ford M7As designed by the young engineer Robin Herd: they were very small bathtub monocoques which, because of the horizontally inclined position of the radiator and the air outlets situated just behind and above the hood, were flat at the front. These very elegant cars were fitted with a new version of the Ford engine which Cosworth had pushed up to 410 bhp and which of course served as a rear chassis member. They weighed 1133 lb (515 kg).

There were also two new B.R.M.s: Tasman-type chassis, designed by engineer Len Terry; improved two-valve-per-cylinder V12 (non-stressed) engine developing 380 bhp. Weight 1144 lb (520 kg).

Finally there was a new V12 B.R.M.-engined Cooper (again the engine was not used as a chassis member). The designer was still Tony Robinson and his new monocoque was very similar to previous ones; the suspension (inboard front springs) had not been modified. The weight was 1188 lb (540 kg).

The honor of driving the new McLaren-Ford to victory on its first outing fell to McLaren himself. The B.R.M.s had a good race, demonstrating in particular their convincing roadholding characteristics. The Matra-Ford MS10 on the other hand, now in a definitive state, was unable to come to terms with the bumpy Brands Hatch track.

What promised to be an exciting season of Formula 1 was deeply scarred by an event that happened in a Formula 2 race at Hockenheim on Sunday 7th April. It was on that day that the greatest of the contemporary champions, Jim Clark, the man who had just beaten Fangio's record by winning twenty-five Grands Prix in six years of competition, met his death while driving a Lotus, the marque to which he had remained faithful throughout his career. With two World Championships to his credit, Jim Clark was the great favorite for the title at the beginning of the 1967 season: he was already at the top of the table following his victory in South Africa, and the Lotus 49, which was now sorted out, certainly seemed capable of carrying him to further success. From the sporting point of view, his death deprived motor racing of an irreplaceable standard: it had become customary to judge the performance of all the other drivers against him. He had thus taken over the role once played by Fangio and Moss.

Jim Clark was only thirty-two when he died. Although he had had a number of accidents he had never been hurt and he came to be regarded as invulnerable. Behind the wheel he was the personification of thoroughbred talent, overcoming every difficulty with astonishing ease and matchless elegance, and even when he had the opposition on the run, the perfection of his technique never wavered. The close working relationship between him and his constructor, Colin Chapman, is an example of what friendship between two exceptional men can achieve.

Jim Clark came from a comfortably off Scottish family and was one of the last great champions to race simply for his own pleasure; the money was incidental. Shy, but very courteous and wonderfully straightforward, he was a true gentleman and quite the opposite of the bumptious character he might have become, given his superiority and the columns of praise it received in the world's Press.

Why the fatal accident happened was never explained. Clark was out on his own when the Lotus 49 went off the road in a long corner and smashed into a tree. His neck was broken by the violent impact. Although the track was damp and the tires on the Lotus were not the most suitable for the conditions, the drivers reckoned that the corner where Jim Clark lost his life was not sharp enough to constitute a real danger. There were various theories about what went wrong: engine seizure, puncture, breakage of a suspension or steering component; all these causes were suggested but none of them was ever verified. There was even talk of evidence pointing to the fact that he must have swerved abruptly to avoid a trespassing child who ran across the track in front of him. However, the mystery was never cleared up. There remains to those who had the good fortune to know him and see him drive the undying memory of the greatest driver of his time; and in a hollow in the Hockenheim forest there is a simple commemorative stone.

Unfortunately that was not the only fatal accident as Mike Spence was killed very soon after Jim Clark. Indeed he had been assigned to the seat left vacant by Clark in the Lotus Indianapolis turbine car. It was in training for the 500-Mile Race, just after he, a rookie, had recorded the second-best time ever achieved at Indy, that he drifted out in a turn and hit the wall. The front right wheel of his car was torn off by the impact and struck his head with such violence that his helmet was not strong enough to protect him from the blow. When Mike Spence drove for Team Lotus, Jim Clark considered him an excellent stable-mate. He resembled his team leader, if not physically, at least in personality as he was shy, courteous and quiet. He was also an outstanding driver and he, too, had come up from Formula Junior.

So, Lotus and B.R.M. entered only one car each for the Spanish Grand Prix, held on the new circuit at Jarama, while the cockpits of the other two machines unfortunately remained empty. Gurney had refused to enter on the grounds of the inadequacy of the Madrid organizers' offer. The field was thus reduced to fourteen runners. It fell to thirteen when Brabham broke his one and only brand-new thirty-two-valve Repco engine in practice. Finally, Jackie Stewart, who had injured his wrist in an accident during a Formula 2 event on the same circuit, had not recovered and Ken Tyrrell appointed Beltoise to take his place at the wheel of the Matra-Ford.

Although it had a poor entry, this Grand Prix nevertheless had plenty to offer in the way of technical attractions. First of all there was a very much modified Lotus 49 whose rear suspension in particular had received attention and the wheelbase had been lengthened. However, it did not run. Then there was a new Ferrari which was lighter (1115 lb (507 kg)) and a little more powerful (410 bhp) than the 1967 models and fitted with 13 in (330 mm) wheels at the front. That, too, stayed in its pit. Next, there was a new Brabham, the BT26, which arrived very late and, as has already been said, did not take part in the race either. Finally there was a new Honda, the RA301, with a reworked V12 (420 bhp at 9600 rev/min) but still very heavy (1276 lb (580 kg)). This one did line up for the start—in the seventh place on the grid.

Chris Amon had recorded the best practice time and Rodriguez and Hulme (confirming the Brands Hatch performance of the McLarens and B.R.M.s) shared the front row with him. Bruce McLaren and Beltoise, who had both had practice accidents, though not serious ones, were on the next row with the same time (1 min 28·3 s) as Hulme and only 0·4 s away from

First appearance of the Matra-Ford: driven by Stewart at Kyalami.

Amon. A hard fight was expected from these five men, not to mention Graham Hill who had recorded 1 min 28·4 s.

It was Pedro Rodriguez who managed to make the best start while Rindt, who was having tea when the drivers set off on their warming-up lap, had not quite caught up with the pack when the flag dropped. Immediately a furious struggle for the lead began with Beltoise and Amon harassing Rodriguez. However, when it came round for the tenth time the Matra was trailing a wisp of blue smoke which proclaimed its approaching end. Nevertheless, it did not seem to hinder the driver at all and he continued to attack as though nothing were the matter. Two laps later he even took over the lead. The French fans were torn between delight at seeing their driver at the head of a Grand Prix (the first time this had happened since Behra had led the Monaco G.P. in 1959, nine years earlier) and consternation at knowing that it could not last. Four laps later in fact Beltoise went into his pit where the mechanics changed a leaky oil-filter seal.

Amon then took the lead. He, too, had managed to overtake Rodriguez who was running in front of Hill, Hulme, Surtees, McLaren and Siffert at the wheel of the ex-Clark Lotus 49 now painted in Rob Walker's colours. Amon and Rodriguez steadily drew away until Pedro went off the road; his B.R.M. went through the first protective barrier and half broke the second, just missing the spectators' feet. At half-

distance, therefore, the Ferrari was alone and secure in first place, 17 s in front of Hill, 23 s in front of Hulme and 45 s in front of Surtees who was having brake trouble; he was a minute in front of McLaren.

In the circumstances, everyone thought that the New Zealander was about to win his first Grand Prix when, on the fifty-seventh lap, he went missing. The cause of his breakdown was at least as ridiculous as that which had stopped Beltoise. In the case of the Ferrari it was a fuse on an electrical pump. Graham Hill became the new leader, but his position was more precarious than Amon's had been since he had scarcely a 5 s edge on Hulme. The latter was aware that he was fighting for victory from now on and made a magnificent effort which on the seventy-fifth lap took him right up behind the Lotus. However, just as it was expected that he would make a decisive challenge at any moment, the reigning World Champion noticeably slowed down as his second gear had broken. It was all over. It had undoubtedly been a lucky race for Hill, but in the final analysis it was not unjust that fate should give a helping hand to a very demoralised Team Lotus. At all events, Graham Hill secured a precious lead in the Championship which he was to increase in a decisive manner by winning (once again) his favorite race, the Monaco Grand Prix.

For this event, Clark's place at Lotus had been filled by Jackie Oliver, a British hope who had never before competed in Formula 1, and Richard Attwood, an excellent British driver already well known in Formula 2, was at the wheel of Spence's B.R.M. Gurney was back but the Ferraris did not turn up. It was the middle

At Madrid it was taken over by a skilful Jean-Pierre Beltoise. The Frenchman was to hold the lead until he was forced to stop.

of a period of trouble in France. The general strike and the political crisis made the situation uncertain and for quite a while it was thought that it would not be possible to hold the Grand Prix. There was not a drop of fuel in the service stations and there was some speculation whether enough fuel would be found to fill the tanks of the competing cars. Not to mention their transporters which, for the most part, made the return trip across France without being able to fill up. Everyone, except Ferrari, managed to sort things out, including Matra who had entered their MS11 V8-engined car for the first time, and it was to have its first race in the hands of Jean-Pierre Beltoise.

In general layout this machine differed essentially from its half-sister the MS10 in that the monocoque did not stop at the back of the driver's seat but continued to the rear suspension mountings, forming a cradle for the engine which was not designed as a stressed member. Otherwise, suspension, brakes, steering, track and wheelbase were completely identical. However, the MS11 was appreciably heavier (1320 lb (600 kg) against 1210 lb (550 kg)) than the MS10 and in starting-line trim this handicap was increased because the extreme thirstiness of the engine meant that an extra 11 gal (50 litres) of fuel had to be taken on. The workmanship that had gone into the construction of this car was superb, but the back end seemed to be a mechanical jumble which was rather lacking in elegance.

The Matra engine was a 60° V12. It had a bigger bore and consequently shorter stroke than all the other engines of this type. The following table gives the bore, stroke and weight for all the 1968 Formula 1 units:

Make	Type	Bore (mm)	Stroke (mm)	Weight (lb)
Matra	V12	79·7	50·0	380
Weslake	V12	72·6	60·0	411
Ferrari	V12	77·0	53·5	396
Honda	V12	78·0	52·2	462
B.R.M.	V12	74·6	57·0	429
Ford	V8	85·7	64·8	354
Repco	V8	85·9	64·8	358

The valves were operated of course by four overhead camshafts driven by a train of gears at the front. It had four valves per cylinder forming an angle of 55°, fairly large compared with the 32° of the Ford, 30° of the Weslake and 26° of the Ferrari. The intakes (Lucas injection) were situated in the middle of the vee, the exhausts were at the side. The claimed power was 420 bhp at 11,500 rev/min.

Stewart was still not fit enough to drive and as Beltoise had been assigned the Matra V12, Ken Tyrrell had chosen to give Johnny Servoz-Gavin, a young French hope and national Formula 3 champion, his start in Formula 1. At Cooper, Scarfiotti's team-mate was now the Belgian Lucien Bianchi, who replaced the Englishman, Redman. This time there was to be a better chance of seeing the new Brabham

A study in concentration: Rindt.

Beltoïse.

Rodriguez.

Surtees.

A study in style. At the Station corner in Monaco: from top to bottom and from left to right—Hulme, Courage, Hill, Rodriguez and Attwood, Amon, McLaren and Siffert, Stewart and Elford.

177

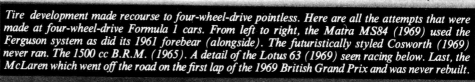

Tire development made recourse to four-wheel-drive pointless. Here are all the attempts that were made at four-wheel-drive Formula 1 cars. From left to right, the Matra MS84 (1969) used the Ferguson system as did its 1961 forebear (alongside). The futuristically styled Cosworth (1969) never ran. The 1500 cc B.R.M. (1965). A detail of the Lotus 63 (1969) seen racing below. Last, the McLaren which went off the road on the first lap of the 1969 British Grand Prix and was never rebuilt.

however, was the consideration that it did away with the problem of wheel spin under acceleration, something that it was impossible to avoid with an ordinary transmission despite the large contact area of modern tires. This became a very important factor once the C.S.I. had issued the constructors with precise instructions on the subject of wings; they were now permitted to use only very much smaller aerofoils (stumps) and forbidden to connect them to the suspension. It was therefore reasonable to assume that the transmission of power to all four wheels would compensate for expected and unavoidable loss of output. The point that tipped the scales in favor of four-wheel drive was better weight distribution between the front and the rear of the car. Also it should have made driving easier in that theoretically it demanded less delicate throttle control since the effects of acceleration were split four ways instead of two.

After practical experience of the cars, however, the drivers were not exactly ecstatic. The three who tried them, Stewart, Rindt and Hill, all had their usual mounts available as well and it was in these cars that they recorded the three best practice times in the order Rindt, Stewart, Hill. It is true that the Matra MS84, like the Lotus 63, was hardly a finished product, but the comments the pair of them provoked were not flattering: heavy steering, difficulty in feeling the breakaway point. Obviously Lotus and Matra still had a long way to go. And no driver wanted to spoil his chances in the race for the sake of progress, even though Hill drove the Lotus very fast during the final practice session in the rain.

So on race day these cars remained in their respective garages and, after a superstart by Hill, there were two Lotus 49Bs and a Matra MS80 out in front. Soon Rindt claimed the lead and, taking advantage of the fact that Hill and his badly vibrating car were slightly blocking Stewart, in two laps put 4 s between himself and the Scotsman. The latter had the greatest trouble in overtaking but managed it in the end, and the crowd expected to see him take off in pursuit of Rindt. But although Jackie Stewart had easily left Hill behind, he continued to lose ground to the leader. Rindt was undoubtedly by far the fastest and he was over 7 s ahead when on the sixteenth lap a universal joint on the Lotus gave way. Barring incidents, Stewart now had the race tied up and in fact he went on to win the Dutch Grand Prix for the second year running. Because of a stop to have his rear suspension checked, Hill could get no higher than seventh place and so he scored no points at all, while Jackie Stewart took a magnificent stride forward in the Championship where he was now twelve points ahead of his nearest rival.

Stewart got interest on this capital from the next Grand Prix, held on the beautiful Charade mountain circuit at Clermont-Ferrand. The layout of this circuit is very varied but very smoothly flowing, and its perfect surface allows both driver and car to exercise their talents to the full. The MS84 and the Lotus 63 again turned out for practice and this time the British car, in the hands of the young John Miles, even started the race, but it lasted for one short lap before it stopped with carburation troubles.

Because Stewart, now well on his way to the title, was so overwhelmingly better than everyone else, this race might have foundered in boredom had it not been for a magnificent duel that lasted right until the end between Jean-Pierre Beltoise—appearing in front of his home crowd—and Jacky Ickx, whose Brabham

was at last functioning to his satisfaction. Malicious tongues put this down to the fact that Jack Brabham had been forced to withdraw because of injuries to his foot sustained in an accident he had had while testing in England; thus Ron Tauranac's small team had been able to prepare the Belgian driver's only car very carefully. Beltoise had made a poor start and was posted seventh at the end of the first lap, while Ickx came round in third place behind Stewart, who was already well ahead, and Denis Hulme. Jean-Pierre Beltoise then began a splendid climb, successively peeling off Hill (who does not like this circuit very much), Amon and finally Rindt (who was unwell). At that point he was 10 s behind Ickx now in second place as a result of Hulme's disappearance with a broken front suspension. It took the Matra ten laps to catch up with the Brabham. Then, for the sixteen laps that remained of the race, Beltoise tried everything he knew to get by: he challenged Jacky Ickx on the inside, on the outside and in braking, at times almost going too far. This tremendous pressure, which brought the crowd to its feet as one man every time the two cars came round, paid off on the very last lap. Ickx was being forced into making a mistake and in the end he succumbed and Beltoise took him coming out of a corner on the dizzy downhill swoop to Gravenoire. From then on their roles were reversed and it was the Brabham's turn to lie in the wake of the Matra. In this order the two cars approached the last bend before the finishing line. Beltoise, wishing to avoid making a mistake and at the same time prevent his rival from making some desperate braking maneuver, moved into the middle of the track, braked early and then slowly turned. But this is exactly what Ickx had expected him to do and he deliberately eased back so that the Matra should not be in his way; he went through the corner in a straight line like a bullet from a gun. It was a good try but not good enough because the finishing line was too close and Beltoise crossed it first by about a length. The crowd went mad with delight. Nearly a minute earlier Jackie Stewart had won his fourth Grand Prix of the season—to the accompaniment of polite applause.

And Jackie Stewart had not yet finished. Definitely riding the crest of a wave called success, at times unapproachable, at times helped along by events, he notched up his fifth victory by winning the British Grand Prix, the next round after the French. This time, however, success came at the end of a very hotly disputed race and after serious alarm in practice when Stewart went off the road and destroyed his Matra against a bank.

While Stewart had spent the year so far collecting first places, Rindt had been piling up failure. When it was announced at the end of 1968 that he was going to Lotus, it was expected that he would be Stewart's toughest opponent and a serious candidate for the world title. Yet the season was half over and Jochen Rindt had still to finish a race. In public he said it was just bad luck, but in private he blamed the bad organization of Team Lotus who were suffering from strain brought on by their desire to run too many horses at once: Indianapolis, the development of the 63, the maintenance of the 49Bs—it was clearly too much for a single team. In addition, the question of the 63 had provoked deep dissension between Chapman, who believed in the car, and his drivers, who did not want to know about it; the atmosphere was heavy with bad feeling. The tension in the Lotus pit and the sullen, haggard faces contrasted sharply with the singularly relaxed air surrounding the Tyrrell crew. According to the specialists and to Jackie Stewart himself (and he never failed to say so), Rindt was a driver of the highest class, of his own class. Yet, while Jackie Stewart flitted from victory to victory, Rindt achieved nothing. The MS80 was certainly a car of more recent design than the Lotus 49B, but the difference in performance, if any, was extremely slight which Rindt demonstrated time and again until something broke. In fact it was lack of confidence and lack of concentration on one single objective that put Rindt at a disadvantage to the benefit of Stewart; this is why the one was a systematic failure while the other was a complete success. There was to be a repetition of the situation in the British Grand Prix at Silverstone.

Yet this event seemed far from having Stewart's best interests at heart. After smashing his own car in practice he had to borrow Jean-Pierre Beltoise's machine and establish his grid position with hardly half an hour of practice left (Beltoise was thus forced to give the MS84 its first outing in a race). He adapted himself incredibly quickly to the strange vehicle (every driver has his own little idiosyncrasies and particular style of driving and since practically everything on a Formula 1 is adjustable, two cars which start by being identical soon become totally different) and recorded the second-best time, only 0·4 s behind Rindt.

Two new cars were making their début at Silverstone: first, the four-wheel-drive McLaren M9A, a fairly large machine, reminiscent in lots of ways of the 1968 Indianapolis Lotus. It is worth noting that the whole transmission system was the work of the McLaren team and that, as the engineer responsible for the construction of the M9A, the Swiss Jo Marquart, pointed out, the car was lighter than the classical M7. It was entered in the race for Derek Bell but the handling was far from right; he had a puncture on the first lap, went off and damaged the suspension. The car was never seen again.

John Surtees was trying out a new classical-style B.R.M., the P139, a lighter machine than the P138 he had driven without success. This car was sixth fastest and in fact seemed more competitive than the previous model, but the suspension broke on the first lap. If such a thing were possible, then Surtees's face was even longer than Rindt's.

Finally, a novelty of another kind: Pedro Rodriguez was part of the Ferrari team—yet another set-up that was not very happy and whose leader, Chris Amon, was visibly downhearted.

There was in fact another new four-wheel-drive machine making its first appearance at the British Grand Prix: the one built at Cosworth under the direction of Robin Herd. Yet it was seen only briefly turning a few laps in private practice when it was found to be far from competitive. To look at it was quite revolutionary, particularly at the front with its long, tapered, elaborate sections.

At the start of the race Rindt jumped into the lead. Stewart followed him one wheel away and the two of them soon forgot their pursuers in their concentration on a duel that was close, fierce and exciting. At half-distance, the nose of the Matra was still glued to the Lotus exhausts when the two men found themselves faced with the prospect of lapping a bunch of five cars. Rindt showed himself to be more skilful—or luckier—at this delicate operation than Stewart and he pulled out a 3 s lead and took an option on victory.

Then Jackie Stewart retaliated in superb style, breaking and rebreaking the lap record in spite of his lack of clutch, and little by little the gap closed up. Rindt did all he could to fight back but he noticed that the left longitudinal section of the wing, which was bent and half detached, was rubbing against the tire on right-hand corners and threatening to cause a puncture. Utterly dispirited, once again victim of an ill and decidedly implacable fate, Jochen Rindt had to resign himself to stopping to have the section ripped off. When he rejoined the race Stewart was already 34 s ahead and had victory in his pocket.

This was not the end of Rindt's troubles. During the last ten laps, the onlookers watched in amazement as one after the other the three Lotuses of Rindt, Hill and Siffert came in for more fuel. It was panic stations because apparently Lotus were taken unawares as they had miscalculated their fuel consumption and had not fitted the supplementary fuel tanks. Tauranac had made the same mistake and Jacky Ickx, second one lap behind Stewart, coasted to the finish, lucky to get across the line on a dead engine.

In spite of this last-minute alarm, the Ickx-Brabham BT26 was clearly making progress. In the last two Grands Prix Ickx had taken first a third and then a second place, and in the German Grand Prix at the Nurburgring he did better still, achieving what was believed to be impossible: winning the race by well and truly beating Jackie Stewart.

Jacky Ickx had made his ambition quite plain in practice when he recorded the best time: a fantastic new official record—7 min 42·1 s. Moreover, he seemed to have obtained this time with the greatest of ease, putting in only very few laps so that he would not tire the car. Stewart tried to reply but had to concede 1·3 s, while Rindt, who had various bothers to cope with (roadholding, carburation), had to be satisfied with 7 min 48 s. It was interesting to see that Elford had recorded a good time (7 min 54·8 s) at the wheel of an ex-works McLaren now owned by the British historic car specialist Colin Crabbe, and that Andretti had returned and been assigned a 63 by Chapman. Unlike his European team-mates, Mario Andretti showed no distaste for this car and, despite his total ignorance of the circuit, achieved a very encouraging 8 min 15·4 s after only three practice laps.

Practice, for which Ferrari did not appear, was unfortunately overshadowed by grief for the death of the excellent German driver, Gerhard Mitter, the ex-European hill-climb champion. He went off the road in a Formula 2 B.R.M. and was killed instantly.

Surtees withdrew as his suspension had proved too fragile for the harsh layout and uneven surface of the Nurburgring. In contrast to the year before, the weather on race day was brilliant. This did not make much difference to Ickx though who once again started this event badly. Stewart, however, managed a perfect getaway and at the end of the first lap he was already well ahead with a 5 s lead over Rindt and Ickx who had meanwhile recovered and shot up to the front. Next came Hulme, Hill and McLaren, Beltoise and Courage. Andretti and Elford were no longer circulating: they had had a bump and although the only human injury was Vic Elford's broken arm, the cars were very badly damaged. On the second lap Courage bottomed on a bump and lost control of his Brabham. This impressive accident, which was televised, happily damaged only the car.

While Stewart was increasing his lead over Siffert,

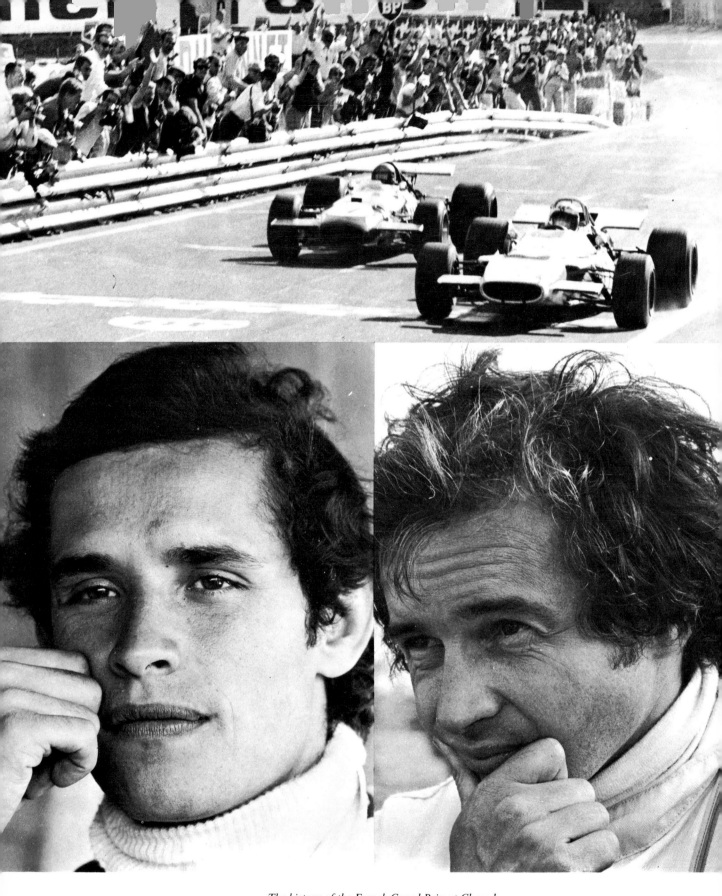

The history of the French Grand Prix at Charade summed up in five pictures. Watched by an enthusiastic crowd, Beltoise (right) kept his lead of a length over Ickx to win a fascinating duel which lasted the whole race. But they were only playing for second place; the winner was Stewart who to a certain extent was not considered by the crowd to be part of the race.

Magnificently determined, Jacky Ickx first caught and then drew away from the Champion who was in trouble, thus asserting himself as Stewart's number one rival.

As usual, Stewart took
the lead at the start of
the German Grand
Prix.

Ickx was closing on the Swiss. He overtook him on the third lap, and now in his stride he went off in pursuit of the Matra which was running 10 s ahead. It took Jacky Ickx two laps to catch up with Jackie Stewart, and just after they had been round for the sixth time he launched a decisive attack in braking for the South curve, taking the lead in an uncommonly spirited way. Continuing at his extravagant pace, Ickx established a new record on this lap (7 min 43·8 s) and pulled out a 2 s advantage over Stewart. What the spectators were watching was really a battle of the titans, for Siffert, in third place, was more than a minute behind at half-distance. Stewart, however, hung on with the energy born of despair and until the tenth round was conceding no more than 1 s a lap to a truly unsurpassable Ickx. From then on, the gap got appreciably wider. The Matra driver had not surrendered, he had lost the use of three gears and had to be satisfied with a second place that no one else was in a position to contest. Rindt had retired, Hulme also, and Siffert, who had given a splendid performance, went off the road on the penultimate lap when his front suspension broke. Jacky Ickx therefore won easily what had been the best race of the year, and of his career. In fact this prestigious victory raised him to the level of the greatest and the future would confirm time and again that he was worthy of the honor.

Although Stewart was well and truly beaten for the first time that season, he had again increased his lead in the Championship so all he needed now to be mathematically sure of the title was victory in the Italian Grand Prix. For a long time nobody had really imagined that the Championship would fall to anyone else.

Monza, however, is a slipstreaming circuit where anything can happen since the driver of a modern Formula 1 car, no matter how excellent he is, can no longer hope to shake off the opposition. More than skill or courage, it is tactical sense that this circuit puts to the test because a final sprint for the line is practically inevitable. Stewart proved to be just as good at this game as he was at all the others.

It has become a tradition that the Italian Grand Prix provides the occasion for Ferrari to unveil a new model and the very latest creation from Maranello was awaited with much interest since it promised to be technically very exciting: the V12 had been abandoned in favor of a flat 12 layout, the ideal solution, in theory, according to Keith Duckworth. Unfortunately, a lubrication fault had come to light in private tests at Modena and rather than cut a shadowy figure with the uncompetitive V12, Amon withdrew to the enormous disappointment of the Italian enthusiasts. Ferrari gave the old 68 car with central exhausts to Pedro Rodriguez who had to be content to finish two laps behind the leaders.

There is nothing more exciting for the uninitiated and nothing more boring for the specialist than the unfolding of a Grand Prix at Monza. The continual changes of position in the pack have no significance whatsoever, the situation is only clarified as competitors retire and, in the final analysis, the race is won and lost on one single lap—the last. Perhaps even on one braking, also the last—before the Parabolica which leads to the finishing line. For more than an hour and a half, as they motor along at more than 140 mile/h (224 km), the drivers are thinking of only two things: not letting themselves fall off the band wagon and being well placed for the final sprint.

At this crucial moment there were three drivers with a chance: Stewart, Rindt and Beltoise. There was no question of team racing between Ken Tyrrell's two drivers. Beltoise was set on making his bid and he had never been nearer winning a Grand Prix. Rindt was also trying for his first victory, but he suspected that yet again he had little chance of making it since he did not have the right gearing. Stewart, however, was quite calm.

So the three men appeared in a group on the straight before the Parabolica. Utterly determined, Beltoise was the last to brake. He outflanked his two rivals on the inside and led into the corner, followed by Stewart and Rindt. At that point he could have been considered the winner: he was in the lead and he was the only one of the three whose car was fitted with a wing which meant that he could take the corner and accelerate away a little more quickly and stop Stewart and Rindt from coming back in his slipstream for just long enough. However, perhaps the Frenchman was rather tense, in any case he made a mess of changing down into third and so cancelled out his advantage. At the exit of the corner, Stewart moved to the left and overtook him while Rindt did the same on the right. And Jackie Stewart with a lead of a short length won the Italian Grand Prix and with it the 1969 World Championship. As far as the title was concerned, the results of the last three events that still had to be run could not change anything.

As it turned out this was lucky for Stewart as from then on success was to avoid him as persistently as it had courted him hitherto. The new World Champion did not win another Grand Prix that season. He had to retire in Canada and the United States while in Mexico he could not finish in a higher place than fourth.

In fact a close look at this change of fortune shows that it must be put down to two things: an incident during the race on the Mosport circuit when once again he was engaged in a very close duel for the lead with Jacky Ickx. The latter, attacking a little too enthusiastically, touched his left rear wheel at the entrance to a corner and sent him spinning off the track. The only damage was to a wheel rim but the engine stalled and refused to restart. Without more ado Ickx won his second victory of the season, helped this time by a bit of luck, while Brabham confirmed that his machines were now extremely competitive by taking second place. However, it must be pointed out that they were assisted in this by some new Goodyear tires (G20s) which were obviously much more effective than Stewart's Dunlops (and this must be regarded as the second reason for Stewart's sudden relegation to the ranks) and Rindt's Firestones. After being first away from the line Jochen Rindt had to give way to Stewart, Ickx and Brabham one after the other.

Strangely enough, the superiority of the new Goodyears, so noticeable at Mosport and so overwhelming at Mexico, where G20-shod machines monopolized the first three places, was not at all in evidence at Watkins Glen. This race proved beyond doubt that racing-tire technology had reached such a level of sophistication that the classical distinctions between rain, damp and dry qualities were no longer sufficiently precise. It had become necessary to add to the equation the notion of matching the tire to the circuit, each circuit naturally presenting a special case for the manufacturer to deal with. Taken to extremes, this meant that they would have to produce a different tire for each circuit, designed to suit not only the atmospheric conditions but also the surface and layout of the track.

So the situation at the end of the season was that while the G20s were unbeatable at Mosport and Mexico, they impeded the progress of those who used them at Watkins Glen. This point was proved by the fact that Courage, whose Brabham was fitted with Dunlops, maintained station ahead of Ickx and Brabham. Piers Courage, now a noticeably mature driver, was rewarded for his very good race by another second place (the first was at Monaco) and thus confirmed his status as one of the surest hopes of the new generation.

Yet neither he nor anybody else, except Stewart who led—marginally—for nine laps in the early stages of the event, was in Rindt's class. Finally justice was done and he won a Grand Prix for the first time. Finally is the right word. There was something offensive, something that ran counter to the idea of a sporting ethic in the way that this driver, whom Stewart considered as his equal, was continually submitted to defeat. Jochen Rindt had been kept waiting too long for his hour of glory, though for several seasons he had ruled as king of Formula 2. It was almost ironic that he should collect so many victories in this formula—as though a strange malicious fate had chosen to put him down eternally in Formula 1 merely for the sake of offering him meagre compensation in Formula 2.

In view of his continual lack of success and because of the way he drove—always with spirit and sometimes with too much—there was a lot of support for a theory which claimed Jochen Rindt to be a brutal driver, quite without mechanical sympathy, unpolished and lacking nervous and physical stamina because he threw himself around too much when he was racing. The theory went on to say that although his undeniably exceptional skill was enough to enable him

to win shorter Formula 2 races, his extravagant style put him at a disadvantage in Formula 1.

Of course this was nonsense and was soon to be demonstrated as such. In fact what Jochen Rindt had never had in Formula 1 was a good car and more specifically a perfectly prepared car. The 1966–67 Coopers he started on were outclassed. Then at Brabham in 1968 he was up against a combination of mechanical failure and an insoluble problem concerning the way the team was organized. Finally, when he went to Lotus it was just at the time Colin Chapman was losing interest in the 49 and devoting his attention to what in the end was nothing more than an illusion—the 63. These were the real reasons behind Rindt's persistent failure but he never lost heart. His Watkins Glen victory led to a reconciliation between him and Chapman and once they were pulling together they found they had signed a contract with success for 1970.

Sadly it was only a short-term contract but the success was dazzling.

For Lotus, however, the delight in winning the United States Grand Prix (the richest in the history of Grands Prix with a first prize of $50,000) was clouded by a serious accident involving the unfortunate Graham Hill. His car turned over after the right rear tire punctured. The circumstances of the accident were quite remarkable: first of all Hill spun as a result of the progressive deflation of the tire, gradual loss of pressure being customary with a tubeless cover provided the object that pierces it is not over large. The engine stalled and Hill had to get out of the car to push it back on the road. He was therefore fully aware of the slow puncture and indeed he made an explicit signal to his pit to have a spare wheel ready. He was motoring along at a relatively reduced speed, getting prepared to stop on the next lap, when the tire unexpectedly flew off the rim. The car went sideways and the impact of the bare rim against the track heeled it over. Graham was half thrown out because after the spin he had not been able to refasten his safety belts and both of his legs were so badly damaged that for a long time it was feared he would never be able to drive again.

An analysis of the accident makes it very plain just how dangerous losing a tire can be and it was as a result of this that retaining screws were fitted through the outer flange of the rim to prevent a punctured tire coming off the wheel. Rather a makeshift remedy perhaps, but one that has been generally effective.

The final Grand Prix of the year, the Mexican, was not the crowning achievement that Stewart hoped it would be: it was a real procession of the Goodyear men.

The race was fought out by Jacky Ickx and Hulme, watched from a distance by Brabham who kept ahead of Stewart apparently without any difficulty. The scales tipped decisively in favor of Denny Hulme's machine when at three-quarter distance Jacky Ickx

From the beginning of the season, Stewart regarded and named Rindt as his most dangerous rival. The World Champion's opinion was vindicated at Watkins Glen when Jochen Rindt finally won a Grand Prix for the first time. It was too late for the 1969 Championship, but in 1970. . . .

suddenly flagged completely and literally bemused conceded 12 s to Hulme in four laps and although he recovered and even went on to finish at a sprint, the handicap he had imposed on himself was too great to be entirely overcome.

Stewart and Matra (and Elf, their fuel supplier) thus won their first title at the end of a season that had confirmed the total supremacy of the unbeaten Ford engine.

However, for political reasons and because they were now convinced that their V12 was fully developed, the French marque had already decided not to use the Anglo-American V8 for 1970.

Though they would have wished it otherwise, this decision brought the Stewart-Tyrrell/Matra partnership to an end.

This was to put a very different complexion on things.

the tragic success of jochen rindt

Just after he had won the German Grand Prix, thereby assuring himself of a very solid lead in the Championship, Jochen Rindt declared: ". . . My only ambition in life at the moment is to be World Champion. What I'm most looking forward to is the day when I've got enough points to stop anyone else catching up with me." Jochen Rindt had no idea that he had already reached his objective. He suspected even less that, in the event of his keeping his lead, he was destined to be denied the satisfaction of tasting the fruits of victory— the World Champion's title, his supreme ambition and the dream he had chased for ten years. On Saturday, 5th September, in practice for the Italian Grand Prix Rindt lost control of his Lotus while braking for the Parabolica; at the same moment he lost his life. Although there were still four events left, none of Jochen's rivals was able to equal the score he had made before his death. He won his crown. Posthumously.

The career of this very high-class driver, whom many had long regarded as a potential World Champion, came to an end in the most dramatic manner imaginable: glory and tragedy arrived hand in hand.

This was the man Chapman had chosen to groom as Clark's successor at a time when the distressing regularity of his failure in Formula 1 made it seem doubtful that he would ever win a Grand Prix. But his moment came at Watkins Glen, just less than a year before his fatal accident. It portended a complete change in Rindt's sporting career, a change brought about with the construction of the Lotus 72 for the following season. Success, which had so persistently avoided him in Formula 1 now began to favor him, almost to the point of insolence. Once the car was sorted out it quickly established itself as the best in the field. Equipped with such a machine, Jochen Rindt suddenly matured, his talent developed and he became quite a different driver, bringing to the job the same sort of concentration, intelligence and moderation as Jackie Stewart himself. Perhaps the influence of the Scotsman also had something to do with the transformation; the two men were very close friends and neighbors on the banks of Lake Leman where they had both settled.

However it happened, at the wheel of the 72, Rindt drove in a style that had been pared of its excesses. He had decided to conserve his nervous energy for Grands Prix and this was reflected by his declining performance in Formula 2: he wanted to exchange the title "king of Formula 2" for the World Champion's crown and he had realized that if he were to succeed he would have to devote himself exclusively to the task. As a result he rose in Formula 1 to the level of a Clark, a Stewart or a Brabham. Only Jim Clark, Jackie Stewart and Jack Brabham had managed to achieve a series of wins in a Championship so far; in 1970 Jochen Rindt did the same. Phil Hill, Graham Hill, John Surtees, Denis Hulme, all the other drivers who had won the Championship since 1959 certainly had not swindled their way to success but none of them had shown that almost crushing superiority exerted by Clark in 1963 (7 victories out of 10 Grands Prix contested, 4 of them consecutive) and 1965 (6 out of 10, 5 consecutive), by Brabham in 1966 (4 out of 8, all of them consecutive) and by Stewart in 1969 (6 out of 11, 3 consecutive). By winning five Grands Prix, four of them in a row, out of the nine he contested in 1970, Rindt earned his place in the gallery of super-champions. It matters little that only six Grand Prix victories stand to his credit, it is the manner in which he achieved them that qualifies him for a place among the stars.

Sadly there were other victims in 1970. Bruce McLaren was killed while testing a prototype Can-Am machine at Goodwood on 2nd June, just a few days before the Dutch Grand Prix during the course of which the young British hope, Piers Courage, also met his death.

Like Jack Brabham, whose team-mate he once was, Bruce McLaren grew up with modern Formula 1. In fact the start of his Grand Prix career in 1959 coincided exactly with the technical revolution that opened this period. He had come from New Zealand the previous year with a "scholarship" from his national Federation and had been signed up by Cooper. At the end of the

193

1959 season he took his first Grand Prix victory (in the U.S.) at the age of twenty-two.

Eleven years later Bruce was naturally regarded as a veteran even though he was only thirty-three. He became a constructor in 1966, but he did not relinquish his seat at the wheel of either his Formula 1 cars or his Can-Am machine which brought him so much success before one of them proved fatal. He was a wonderfully well-balanced man, a fast and very steady driver and a first-class constructor. His wife Pat and his associates decided to carry on his work and it was a good decision: today the cars bearing McLaren's name continue to win races on all the circuits of the world.

Another driver disappeared from the scene in 1970 but fortunately in less unhappy circumstances. The colorful French driver, Servoz-Gavin, who had been engaged by Ken Tyrrell in the winter of 1969–70 as Jackie Stewart's number two, suddenly decided he had had enough when he failed to qualify for the Monaco Grand Prix.

All these losses and the fact that a much larger number of cars had been built as a result of the availability of Ford-Cosworth engines, explains why so many young drivers got a start in Formula 1 in 1970: there were no fewer than nine newcomers, not counting Pescarolo, Eaton, de Adamich and Miles who had appeared before but only very briefly. They were Clay Regazzoni and Ignazio Giunti (Ferrari, where Ickx was employed once again), Rolf Stommelen (Brabham), Peter Gethin (McLaren), Emerson Fittipaldi and Reine Wisell (Lotus), François Cevert (Tyrrell), Tim Schenken (Frank Williams) and Ronnie Peterson (Antique Automobiles). All of them (with the exception of Stommelen and Giunti) were fresh from Formula 3. They formed the nucleus of a new generation of great drivers and the big stars of the future.

Many things were changing, and not only in the drivers' seats. The 1970 season was a turning-point in every respect, a fact that will emerge more clearly no doubt in a few years' time. A wave of disputes—about values, customs, etc.—swept over the world of Formula 1 and no one escaped becoming involved; the ruling bodies of the sport, the organizers, the constructors, the drivers—they were all affected.

At the end of the 1969 season divorce between Stewart and Matra was known to be inevitable. Although the World Champion had a very high regard for the quality of the French chassis, he was not at all convinced that the V12 was a competitive engine, particularly after a couple of test sessions with it. He had every intention of continuing his association with Ford in spite of the signs which foretold the end of the V8's supremacy, but first he had to find a constructor willing to sell a chassis to the Tyrrell team. As one man, the established marques refused to co-operate with the World Champion. This may seem rather strange but there were two good reasons for it: first, the question of contracts. Stewart was tied to Dunlop while McLaren and Brabham, probably his two most likely sources of supply, were contracted to Goodyear. Lotus on the other hand were with Firestone. Secondly, none of them was particularly thrilled by the idea of providing a stick for Stewart to beat them with.

There was another important man on the market: Chris Amon. He had had enough of the never-ending problems that Ferrari ran into and decided to change teams. Matra approached him at once, but in vain.

Like Stewart, Amon was convinced that the Ford engine was the best and wanted to be absolutely sure that the motor in his next car had four cylinders fewer than his old one. However, in the Ford camp, all the number one driving seats were occupied.

Then along came March, and with it, crazily ambitious project that it was, a fantastic upheaval. In early summer 1969, it had become known that efforts were being made to set up a new firm in England to build chassis. The impetus came from four men: Robin Herd, an engineer, who already had the McLaren M7 to his credit; Alan Rees, a well-known Formula 2 driver; Max Mosely, a young lawyer; and Graham Coaker, an experienced workshop manager. Their reputation assured them of backing and they duly drew up their plans of what was a very conventional car. Nearly everyone agreed that this was a shrewd move since the chassis was by far the least important factor in the Formula 1 equation as laid down by Ken Tyrrell. According to his formula, the essentials for winning a Grand Prix were, in order of importance, a good engine (Ford), a great driver, the best tires, a shrewd team manager and last, but definitely least, a well-set-up chassis. Indeed, chassis and suspension construction had hardly progressed since 1967 and the Lotus 49.

So, thought likely customers for the March chassis, no risk there. What particularly interested Stewart and Tyrrell was that it involved the minimum of sorting out and guaranteed that there would be no nasty surprises. It was a sensible way of looking at things. After all, as far as the engine went, Ford certainly would not put them at a disadvantage and naturally they had no worries about the rest.

Tyrrell therefore ordered three March 701 chassis. At the same time Andy Granatelli, boss of the American S.T.P. additive company, did likewise for his young protégé, U.S. champion Mario Andretti, who wanted to compete in Formula 1 Grands Prix on a more regular basis. In addition, Granatelli gave March a contract to advertise his product. This put them in a position to run a team of their own and they engaged no less than Chris Amon and Jo Siffert to drive the works cars. They also took on the young hope Ronnie Peterson; they built a chassis for him and gave Colin Crabbe the responsibility of looking after it and organizing the Swede's racing program. During the winter of 1969–70 a total of eight chassis were put under construction in a small workshop in Bicester, all destined to be driven by a rare line-up of star performers. It was the result of an extraordinary exercise in public relations which March had applied vigorously to a far from commonplace situation.

The first consequence of March's success was a considerable increase in the number of cars in running order compared with the 1969 total. As a result the organizers, who had complained with some justification about the poor entries the year before, now found themselves faced with the problem in reverse: in 1970 there was a glut of machines looking for a place on the Grand Prix grids. Besides the March hordes, it was common knowledge that de Tomaso were building a chassis for the Frank Williams team; that Surtees, who had left B.R.M. (where he was replaced by Rodriguez) and bought a McLaren M7C for the start of the season, had decided to build his own car; and finally, that McLaren and Alfa Romeo had agreed that a Milanese V8 should be installed in a Colnbrookbuilt chassis, de Adamich being assigned to drive this Italo-New Zealand cocktail. In addition to all this, Graham Hill left Lotus for Rob Walker, though it was thought that he would not have recovered from his Watkins Glen accident until at least half-way through the season, and Henri Pescarolo was chosen by Matra as driver number two to Jean-Pierre Beltoise. A total of twenty-five cars could be reckoned on; it was a lot and too many for the organizers of the Spanish (at Jarama) and Monaco Grands Prix who would allow only sixteen runners on their mini-tracks.

The touchpaper between the organizers and constructors was in any case already alight. The former were determined to get rid of the old system of starting-money and make everyone subject to the practice qualification rule, while the latter did not want to lose their guaranteed entries and asked that the prize-money be revalued. Following painful negotiations, a compromise was reached in March, after the South African Grand Prix and a month before the Spanish: known as the Geneva Agreement, it com-

pletely revised the financial organization of Grands Prix.

The main provisions were as follows: first, the organizers undertook to supply a budget of 350,000 Swiss francs per Grand Prix. However, the largest part of this was not to be reserved as in the past to provide the competitors with starting-money; from now on it was prize-money. The budget was to be divided into four unequal parts and distributed as follows: three parts were set aside as prizes, the largest to be allocated according to the final classification, the next largest according to the classification at two-thirds distance and the smallest according to the classification at one-third distance; the remaining fourth part to be used to defray the competitors' travelling expenses.

In accepting this scheme, the teams were obviously taking a certain financial risk. The era of the

Bruce McLaren.

provisional budget was over and a persistent lack of success could entail much more serious consequences than hitherto. However, in the final analysis it was simply a matter of financial adjustment and in any case did not concern anyone but the interested parties. The same, however, could not be said for the second part of the agreement: this directly involved the concept of sportsmanship and subjected it to a thorough mauling. To safeguard their interests with the firms that sponsored them—oil companies, tire manufacturers, non-motoring concerns like Gold Leaf and Yardley (whose colors were worn by Lotus and B.R.M. respectively)—the constructors got the organizers to agree that they should be allotted ten guaranteed entries. The list that was drawn up included all the names of the number one drivers of works or "established" teams—Rindt (Lotus), Rodriguez (B.R.M.), Ickx (Ferrari), Brabham, Hulme (McLaren), Beltoise (Matra) and Amon (March)—to which were added those of the three World Champions still racing, i.e. Stewart, Hill and Surtees. Elevated to the rank of drivers by divine right, they would all be entitled to compete in Grands Prix irrespective of their practice performance, while everybody else would have to qualify by virtue of their practice times for however many places were still available. At Jarama and Monaco this would be six, and only six. That these two criteria should exist side by side was a gross insult to the idea of fair play and it was easy to forecast what would happen: fantastic confusion (there were to be some fairly far-fetched interpretations of how the rule should be applied) and a shameful lack of justice since the haves could push the have-nots off the grid even though the latter had better practice times. This mess was still being concocted at the time of the South African Grand Prix, run under the old system. In the Kyalami sunshine sport and technical achievement resumed their rightful place and everyone was bustling round the new machines: fifteen out of twenty-three.

The Marches, of course, stole the limelight. They had been announced as conventional machines and conventional they were, apart from the nose with incorporated fins and the lateral streamlined fuel tanks in particular where special attention had been paid to the aerodynamics in order to create a negative lift effect. With the exception of these features, the cars looked heavy and the scales confirmed the impression, reading 1276 lb (580 kg), i.e. 110 lb (50 kg) over the limit. They also had a large overhang at the front made up of the radiator and the fire extinguisher. They were all there except Peterson's.

Another cause for excitement were the new Brabhams. This time, that was it: Ron Tauranac had been converted to the monocoque. Eight years after the

arrival of the Lotus 25, which had appeared at a time when the multitubular chassis was universal, there was not one Formula 1 machine left using this method of construction. What was more, the very small, fine BT33s (which weighed no more than 1188 lb (540 kg)) of Brabham and Stommelen had front suspension with inboard-mounted springs. Tauranac the traditionalist really had turned his back on the past.

The Ferrari 312B of Jacky Ickx was far and away the most sophisticated of the Formula 1 cars at Kyalami: because of its flat 12 engine, of course, for which 450 bhp at 11,500 rev/min was claimed. Also because of the form of its monocoque which recalled the 1968 air-cooled Honda by extending behind the cockpit under the engine. This very attractive Ferrari was no heavier than the Brabhams though it looked less compact.

The Matras were completely new. The rule which enforced the use of flexible tanks had obliged Bernard Boyer to abandon his familiar structure with transverse members and he had built a labored-looking monocoque which was sharply angular and very wide. It stopped at the back of the cockpit because the new V12 engine produced by the engineer Martin, was a stressed member. It was said to give 425 bhp at 10,800 rev/min; the MS120s weighed 1232 lb (560 kg).

They were, on paper at any rate, a little less brilliant than the very pretty, little B.R.M. 153s designed by Tony Southgate; at 1166 lb (530 kg) they were the lightest of the lot. The V12 engine, greatly revised by Aubrey Woods, was now semi-stressed with central intake and lateral exhausts; it was said to have 425 bhp and was coupled to a new B.R.M. five-speed gear-box.

Bruce McLaren and Denis Hulme both had a completely new car, the M14, very similar to the M7 from which it was derived. One of these, a type C, had been sold to John Surtees and slightly modified, principally to take Firestone tires.

The de Tomaso was also making its first public appearance. It was the work of engineer Dallara, a deserter from Maserati and Lamborghini, and had distinctive trapezoid sides. It was also noticeable for its weight which at 1287 lb (585 kg) was the heaviest car in the field.

Only Lotus were without a new car. It was a surprising situation but the project Chapman was working on was so unconventional (the 72) that it was not ready in time for Kyalami. All he had done therefore was modify the front suspension of his faithful 49s, now given the type number C, so that like everyone else, except McLaren, he could fit 13 in (330 mm) instead of 15 in (381 mm) wheels.

Owing to its good winter climate, Kyalami had become the constructors' chosen testing ground,

Compare them in action at
Kyalami:
Brabham (Brabham BT33).
Siffert (March 701).
Beltoise (Matra MS120).
Ickx (Ferrari 312B).
Rodriguez (B.R.M. P153)
and Hulme (McLaren M14).

particularly for tires. There they were sure of finding the fair weather they needed for carrying out the serious timed exercises from which they were able to measure the progress made by their machines. At the same time they were putting in some valuable practice for the first event of the season. Nearly all of them had therefore covered a great number of laps before official practice began, and it transpired that Stewart, at the wheel of the Matra, had recorded the best time: 1 min 19·6 s. So it seemed that the World Champion's choice of machine was justified and a glance at the starting grid as it was finally established confirmed this impression: Stewart and Amon were equal first on the front row with 1 min 19·3 s, March had indeed made a good entrance. However, alongside them was Brabham, beaten by 0·3 s. Another point to emerge from a look at the grid was that the race promised to be a close one since nine drivers were covered by 0·9 s. Graham Hill was not one of the nine, but nevertheless he took the start much to everyone's admiring amazement; after a fantastic program of rehabilitation, attacked with great verve and an iron will, he had kept his appointment with the beginning of the season. He was limping and suffering visibly, but he was happy to be there.

As the starter gave his signal, Stewart and Brabham sprang forward, followed by Ickx and Rindt. Amon stayed where he was. But Jack Brabham missed a gear-change and was overtaken by the Ferrari and the Lotus. Then they came up to the first corner: Stewart went into it first but chaos reigned behind. In trying to slip in between Ickx and Rindt, Brabham had bumped the Lotus which literally came unstuck and rose in the air above the still tightly bunched pack. Fortunately it fell back on to its wheels undamaged, but Amon had a spin as he took avoiding action. All this, of course, was to Stewart's advantage and he immediately increased his lead. Brabham, sixth at the end of the first lap, did not leave him his illusions for long, however. After swallowing up the four cars (of McLaren, Oliver, Beltoise and Ickx) that stood between him and the blue March, he bore down on Stewart and took over the lead on the twentieth lap. Brabham won the race without further trouble, 8 s ahead of Hulme who, running on Goodyears like the winner, had also caught and passed Stewart. Fourth, a little more than a minute behind Brabham, came Beltoise, the only other driver on the same lap and also equipped with Goodyears. At the end of it all it was hard to know whether to attribute the result to the tires or to the cars. In any case, it was pretty obvious that the Ford engines were still dictating terms.

Back to Europe and back to the political-financial problems. With the Geneva Agreement signed, it was assumed that everything was settled, but when the circus arrived in Madrid for the Spanish Grand Prix, they found themselves in the middle of a fantastic row. The organizers, constructors and drivers had all interpreted the terms for applying the agreement in their own separate ways. The results of the first practice session were declared null and void, there was a storm of protests, and every five minutes the list of those who had qualified was changed. On Friday evening Siffert and de Adamich were down as starters, but on Saturday afternoon they were eliminated in favour of Andretti and Servoz-Gavin. All the competitors signed a petition asking the organizers to accept (at no extra cost) twenty starters instead of the sixteen for whom provision had been made. Everyone

thought the request as good as granted but in fact it was turned down (reason—the circuit's insurance policy could not be changed). As a result four squatters (Siffert, de Adamich, Miles and local hero Soler-Roig) appeared on the track and were escorted off by the police.

All these quarrels had pushed something of great significance right into the background—the Lotus 72. Radically new, in looks it broke completely with its rivals which suddenly seemed old-fashioned even though most of them had first seen the light of day at Kyalami. In fact, the 72 embodied an astonishing number of completely new features: taking inspiration from the four-wheel-drive 63, its shape was a delicate, long and narrow wedge. It had front and rear inboard-mounted brakes, torsion-bar suspension and radiators on both sides and behind the cockpit. Colin Chapman and his designer, Maurice Philippe, had not hesitated to face originality. They had turned the page firmly and the result was refreshing. Rindt went out on to the track and was immediately beset by a swarm of problems. His thoughts on the matter were concisely but clearly summed up in his look of intense dissatisfaction.

They had also been hard at work at March, trying to improve the roadholding and reduce the weight of the cars. The whole rear end had been changed and now had the brakes coupled to the gear-box and two pairs of parallel arms instead of lower wishbones.

The BT33s on the other hand did not appear to have undergone any modification. No doubt Jack Brabham was quite happy with his car, as well he might be since he recorded the best time (1 min 23·9 s) with a 0·2 s lead on Hulme, 0·3 s on Stewart, 0·56 s on Beltoise and 0·6 s on Rodriguez. Rindt was eighth fastest with 1 min 24·8 s, and was preceded by Amon and Ickx.

The race started most dramatically; a stub axle on Oliver's car broke and the uncontrollable B.R.M. ripped open the side of Ickx's Ferrari, causing a huge fire to break out. The Englishman miraculously escaped unharmed but Ickx still bears the scars of this accident. The firemen poured thousands of gallons of water over the blazing cars, but all to no avail since they could not get the fire under control. The only result of their enthusiasm was a flooded track and a number of spins, two of which were notched up to Brabham alone.

As at Kyalami, Stewart pranced away in the lead, followed by Hulme, Brabham, Beltoise and Pescarolo —in short, the Goodyear pack were snapping at his heels. But this time things turned out very differently; first Hulme's ignition gave up; then Beltoise, taking advantage of Brabham's second spin, moved into second place with the idea of catching up with Stewart, but his engine did not last that long; neither did Pescarolo's (rev limit set too high); Brabham then caught Stewart, was right up behind him and expected to overtake and leave him behind when it was the turn of his engine to blow up. Behind Stewart they were dropping out like flies. At the end of the race there were only five survivors left; it was a Grand Prix that everyone endeavored to forget quickly. Bruce McLaren finished second, a lap in arrears, ahead of Andretti, Hill and Servoz.

On the cause-and-effect principle, the rigmarole over practice qualification inevitably cropped up again at Monaco. Fortunately this race, unlike the one at Jarama, was exciting and ended in a way that was so extraordinary no script-writer would have dared propose it.

Once again the arguments about qualifying caused an uproar and when it was all over Stommelen and de Adamich (1 min 26·3 s), Servoz (1 min 26·9 s), Eaton (1 min 27 s) and Miles (1 min 27·4 s) had been thrown out while Hill (1 min 26·8 s), Surtees (1 min 27·4 s) and Rodriguez (1 min 27·8 s) were included among the starters.

The Marches continued to show up well. After winning the Spanish Grand Prix on what was only their second time out, they made their presence very much felt in practice, Stewart (1 min 24 s) and Amon (1 min 24·6 s) occupying the front row of the grid ahead of Hulme (1 min 25·1 s) and Brabham (1 min 25·4 s). Next came the three twelve-cylinder cars of Ickx (who had recovered in record time from his burns), Beltoise and Pescarolo with whom Rindt shared the front row. Lotus had put the as yet far from perfect 72 to one side and Rindt was back in his 49C. This did not hold the road very well in practice so when the sessions were finished Rindt changed all the adjustments, taking a risk on making the situation worse.

At the beginning of the race he also experienced brake trouble. Since he was lying eighth in the early stages it seemed that all hope was closed to him, especially at a place like Monaco where overtaking is so difficult.

First of all Stewart took the lead and disappeared in vintage Stewart style. It must be added, though, that it appeared he was unwittingly abetted in his escape by Amon who was slightly blocking Brabham. At least that was the message Brabham put across as he furiously shook his fist. On the twenty-second lap Black Jack finally overtook him on the inside of the Gasworks corner; at the same time Jackie Stewart's engine started to splutter. The 12 s gap melted away and five laps later Brabham took the lead as Stewart came to rest. Beltoise retired with a worn-out crown wheel and pinion while Amon hung on in Brabham's wake with the energy born of despair, but yard by yard he was losing ground. Meanwhile Rindt had passed Pescarolo, so there he was, fourth at half-distance, hard on the heels of Hulme. Immediately he launched a successful attack on Hulme, who no longer had the·use of first gear and had slowed down. Rindt was now some 15 s behind the leader.

They were hardly into the final third of the race when Amon had to retire with broken rear suspension. So Rindt was second but the gap between him and Brabham remained the same. As there were only twenty laps left, it all seemed settled. Jack Brabham even started to slow down because he was having a bit of brake trouble and did not want to take any risks. But fate then played him a nasty trick: there ahead was Siffert, virtually out of oil and zigzagging from one side of the road to the other on the long climb up to the Casino, in an effort to make use of the last drops of fuel he had got left. Seppi Siffert was so totally absorbed in his own problem that he failed to see Brabham arrive and he had to ease off and wait for an opportunity to get past. This did not arise until they reached the Hotel de Paris by which time the operation had cost Brabham 3 s. Rindt's pit had let him know what was going on and off he flew to mount a devilish attack. But Brabham had only to hold out for two more laps and he had 2 s in hand. On the seventy-ninth lap he lost but a fraction of this. Then Rindt went

all out and during the course of a fantastic final lap, on which he established a new record, he had got to within about 1 s of Brabham when they came out of the Tobacconist's corner, four wheels adrift, one behind the other. For the informed spectator, one glance·was enough: Brabham would win, no problem. In front of him lay the Gasworks hairpin and savage braking in the bend. Well over to the right, with his hand raised to let him know he had seen him and wave him on his way was Courage, finishing gently. It was than that Jack Brabham, the most experienced, the shrewdest driver of them all, made an enormous, an incredible mistake. In order to put paid to any hopes Rindt might have of trying to slip in between Courage and himself, an impossibility given the Austrian's time deficit, he decided to change his line and instead of getting well over to the outside in the usual way, he braked in the middle of the track where the road surface was dusty and slippery. His front wheels locked immediately. In vain he pulled the wheel over to the right and, in a state of total understeer, went beyond the turning-point of the corner and finished up in the barriers on the outside of the track. Utterly amazed, Rindt took the bend and saw his rival entangled in the straw. He had scarcely time to realize that he had won before he was across the line where the Clerk of the Course, equally astounded, stood like a statue and forgot to drop his flag. No one would have imagined such an end; things like that can only happen in real life.

The picture of disappointment. In his garage after the Monaco G.P., a solitary Jack Brabham gets changed by the side of his car, its nose showing the scars of the accident which cost him certain victory.

With the aid of several marshals, a deeply disgusted Brabham disentangled himself and went on to finish second; he was still 30 s ahead of Pescarolo who had given a remarkable performance in view of the unsuitable size (13 in (330 mm)) of his Matra's rear tires. In spite of everything, it all turned out well for Jack Brabham as far as the Championship was concerned, since Stewart did not score a single point.

The outgoing World Champion was no luckier at Francorchamps where, following bitter arguments between the drivers and the organizers, the Belgian Grand Prix took place after a year's break. The drivers had obtained satisfaction over their principal demand: it was agreed that in the event of rain, the start of the race would be put back or the race itself suspended until the weather improved. It is clear that the Belgian Royal Automobile Club had taken a considerable risk

The Spanish Grand Prix was the only success of the season for Stewart and March.

Dispute before the start at Jarama: the Clerk of the Course makes it plain to the drivers that sixteen of them will start and not one more.

At Spa, Rodriguez and the B.R.M., which had changed its dark green coat for the Yardley products livery of white, maroon and black, were reunited with victory in spite of the stubborn resistance of Chris Amon.

as far as their public was concerned in accepting this proviso. Fortunately, the sun shone throughout the weekend and practice, like the race itself, was able to go ahead normally. The circuit, moreover, had been modified by the erection of a chicane intended to reduce the speed of the cars on the long downhill swoop at Malmédy.

The most intransigent of the drivers on the subject of Spa was Jackie Stewart but he was determined to make everyone realize that while he might be concerned about safety, he was not lacking in courage. In practice he recorded by far the best time (3 min 28 s), beating Rindt (still driving the 49C) and Amon by more than 2 s. The twelve-cylinder cars again seemed to be outclassed by the Ford V8 machines; their fastest driver was Jacky Ickx with 3 min 30·7 s, Rodriguez managing only 3 min 31·6 s and Beltoise 3 min 32.9 s. The race, however, turned in their favor, the first time this had happened since the Ickx/Ferrari victory in the 1968 French Grand Prix. By winning this race, Pedro Rodriguez, too, was reunited with success after a lapse of more than three seasons (1967 South African Grand Prix). Finally, B.R.M. put an end to the long period of failure which had started after Stewart's victory on behalf of the Bourne concern in the 1966 Monaco G.P.

Once Stewart had blown his engine up half-way through the race and Brabham had broken his clutch, there seemed to be only two likely winners left: Rodriguez, who had taken the lead on the fifteenth of the twenty-eight laps of the race, and Chris Amon, who was following close behind. The struggle between these two men was fierce and it lasted right to the finishing line which the B.R.M. crossed only 1 s before the March. As Rindt had also been forced to retire, the positions at the top of the Championship table were not modified in any way, except that the Austrian was joined in third place by Rodriguez. A blank round in short; it was still an open situation when the circus moved on to the Dutch Grand Prix. But this event was a decisive turning-point: Jochen Rindt, driving his now perfectly tuned 72, took the first of a series of four consecutive victories which were to put him out of reach of his opponents, particularly as Stewart, like Brabham, had a run of misfortune.

There has already been occasion to realize that the very special surface of the Zandvoort track puts particular emphasis on the part played by tires. A look at the starting grid makes this point quite clear: the fastest of the drivers using Goodyears, Beltoise, was in tenth place, while Brabham was in twelfth, more than 2 s behind Rindt in pole position. After Rindt came Stewart and Ickx. The list of starters on this grid included three names new to Formula 1: Clay Regazzoni, a Swiss driver who had Formula 3 and Formula 2 connections with the Italian concern Tecno and had been engaged by Ferrari to back up Jacky Ickx; François Cevert, a young Frenchman who had had a meteoric rise to the top—he had started in Formula 3 in 1967 after winning a beginners' competition, Volant Shell—and had been chosen by Elf and Ken Tyrrell to replace Servoz-Gavin; and Peter Gethin, who was already a successful and established driver in Formula 5000 and was now part of the McLaren team, making their reappearance after withdrawing from Spa because of Bruce McLaren's death. In addition to all this, Denny Hulme had suffered severe burns to his hands when his car caught fire at Indianapolis and he

was not fit enough to compete in the Belgian Grand Prix, so Dan Gurney was making an unexpected return to Formula 1.

Rindt's victory took shape on the third of the eighty laps of the race when, with ridiculous ease, he overtook Ickx in braking for Tarzan corner and disappeared unopposed. Smoothly and calmly driving the revised and corrected 72 (strengthened monocoque, suspension modified to suppress the anti-dive and anti-squat geometry which had hitherto made driving the car a matter of too much delicacy) he was regularly gaining 0·5 s a lap on his most effective pursuers, Ickx and Stewart. By the end of the race only the Scotsman had avoided the humiliation of being lapped by the Austrian; Ickx lost his second place when he had to have a punctured rear tire changed. Brabham twice experienced this trouble, but in any case he was a long way back and finished eleventh, four laps in arrears, failing once again to score Championship points. So Regazzoni who, on his first appearance in the big league, took fourth place at the end of a well-judged race, clearly beating Beltoise, and leading the Goodyear users as he had in practice.

As well as being the turning-point in the 1970 Championship, this Dutch Grand Prix will be remembered for Piers Courage's fatal accident. For some reason that was never discovered, the young Englishman lost control of his de Tomaso on a sweeping bend which is usually taken flat out. The car was thrown against a fence; it then turned over and caught fire when it crashed into the bank which clearly should have been protected by a barrier. Courage was a very close friend of Stewart and Rindt and they were particularly stricken by his death. This was very noticeable at the end of the race when Rindt took his place on the rostrum, because in spite of his victory his face was frozen; it was impossible to get a smile out of him.

This explains the intransigent attitude adopted by the G.P.D.A. who, after a meeting held just after this accident, announced that their members had decided to boycott the Nurburgring for the forthcoming German Grand Prix. The news of this radical stand broke like a bombshell: it was the first time in the history of racing that the drivers had refused to compete in a Grand Prix for reasons of safety. The G.P.D.A., although controversial, had certainly gained some weight. In practice it had become an official body and its claim to represent the drivers had been recognised, de facto, if not de jure, by the C.S.I. since 1968. It was then that they had set up a safety subcommittee and the G.P.D.A. President, Joakim Bonnier, had been co-opted on to it. The principal task of this committee, which had no executive power, was to inspect the various circuits, draw up a list of items that needed attention and see that the work was carried out. Its establishment was a victory for the drivers, but it was rather ponderous in the way it went about its business and was subject to internal strife. In addition, it was of fairly recent creation and had not yet made its authority felt. This is why the drivers bypassed the committee when they decided to object to the Nurburgring only a month and a half before the event was due to take place.

Immediately two sides lined up. There were the conservatives who considered the disputatious drivers discredited by their refusal to accept the risks which, according to them, was precisely the element that gave the profession its grandeur. They pointed out that the

G.P.D.A. decision had not been a unanimous one, as was proved by the subsequent resignation of Jacky Ickx and Pedro Rodriguez. Denis Jenkinson, the authoritative and talented high priest of the international sporting journalists, became the leader of this party and launched a virulent attack on the "milk-sops" of the G.P.D.A. The reply to this conception of motor racing, described by some as romantic and by others as out of date, came from those who agreed with the G.P.D.A.'s aims if not with their methods. They considered that by moving towards a more professional and efficient level of organization the sport was developing in a practical and natural way, and they regarded increased safety in the same light. To them this did not imply the removal or weakening of the essential nature of motor racing, but quite simply a step forward. Of course the public admire the drivers for their courage quite apart from their skill, but they do not demand that they should be careless of their safety. A brave man does not cease to be brave because he refuses to play Russian roulette, and nobody accuses contemporary mountaineers of cowardice because they make use of equipment and techniques that are more highly developed and more reliable than they used to be. In the case of motor racing the efficiency of the cars had progressed considerably, and it was therefore unthinkable that the appointment of the circuits should remain immutable. In these conditions, clearly the risks increase proportionately as the gap between the development of these two factors widens. To deny it is absurd. It is to ignore the fact that, to use the happy expression dreamed up by Jenkinson himself, driving a Formula 1 car at 10/10 (i.e. to the limit of its abilities) in 1970 necessarily represents a much greater risk, should a car go off the road, than it did ten years ago, since braking areas are shorter and cornering speeds are higher owing to the development of chassis, suspension and particularly tires—all elementary physical reasons. That is why, at the very least, something must be done to ensure that the risks faced by Formula 1 drivers do not become so high as to make their profession appear literally suicidal. What is more, the great majority of the public understood the G.P.D.A.'s attitude over the business of the Nurburgring and it in no way affected the personal popularity of the drivers or the popularity of motor racing—as was proved by the large crowds who turned up to watch subsequent Grands Prix.

The scene of the 1970 French Grand Prix, the mountainous Charade circuit at Clermont-Ferrand, rightly has the reputation for being a miniature Nurburgring. However, the safety problems posed by this track, which is only about one-third the length of the famous German track, are consequently three times less troublesome and difficult to resolve and on the whole they had been suitably if not completely dealt with.

This race was dominated by the same two drivers who had given the spectators a good show the year before: Jacky Ickx and Jean-Pierre Beltoise. But this time their duel was staked on victory and not on second place behind an inaccessible Stewart. At the end of practice, an important fact emerged: for the first time since its appearance in the 1967 Dutch Grand Prix, the Ford V8 had failed to qualify for a place on the front row of the grid. This was occupied by a Ferrari (in pole position) and a Matra. In spite of his enormous talent, Stewart had had to give way and was sharing the second row with Amon, while Rindt (who

was suffering from car sickness because of the switchback nature of the circuit) and Brabham (who was running here for the very first time in his long career) were relegated to the third row.

At the start, the Ferrari followed by the Matra set a ruinous pace; only Stewart managed to keep in touch but was shaken off after three laps, and it was not long before he was eliminated by ignition failure. Losing nearly 1 s a lap, Rindt and Amon led the rest of the field—Brabham, Hulme, Pescarolo, Peterson, Gurney, etc.—and seemed irretrievably beaten.

On the fifteenth lap, however, Jacky Ickx lost the lead to Beltoise. His engine had started to splutter, a broken valve was diagnosed and he retired. In fact it was discovered later that the circuit-breaker was the cause of the trouble: it would have been enough simply to disconnect it for Ickx to rejoin the race. Beltoise, an absolutely remarkable performer on this circuit he likes so much, found himself firmly installed in first place with a 13 s lead over Rindt who was cautiously holding back, apparently content with second place.

Suddenly, eight laps later, the gap that had re-

Piers Courage.

mained constant fell to 10 s. The Matra was seen to be pitching under braking and going sideways as it accelerated and its punctured left rear tire was slowly going down. Beltoise tried to continue in this state, but naturally the handling progressively deteriorated and one by one Rindt and Amon went by when, admitting defeat, Jean-Pierre Beltoise stopped at his pit. All Rindt had to do was hold Amon at bay, a task that was made easier for him by the fact that the latter's tires only just lasted out until the finish. At the end of a fierce and at times nearly ill-mannered struggle, Brabham, Hulme, Pescarolo and Gurney crossed the line in that order to fill the remaining points-scoring places. So Rindt pulled ahead in the

Championship stakes but neither Stewart nor Brabham was yet beaten.

At Charade Rindt had been fortunate and he was to be luckier still at Brands Hatch while Brabham again experienced the bitter disappointment he had already tasted at Monaco. The main feature of the British Grand Prix was the hard fight between these two men, a struggle which seemed to have turned definitely in the Australian's favor until, when leading his rival by 13 s, he ran out of fuel nearly at the end of the last lap of the race. His BT33 came coasting round Clearways bend a few hundred yards before the finishing line. At the same time the Lotus 72 surged out of the corner, passed the Brabham and went on to be greeted by the flag; the unlucky Jack Brabham could only coast to the line which he crossed in second place. It was the most improbable of repeat performances, but Brabham hid his feelings behind the impassive mask of a great Champion in spite of the fact that the lead taken by Rindt in the Championship was now more than merely worrying.

However, Rindt's third consecutive victory was not yet settled. While the crowd were applauding him, the scrutineers were checking the 72 in minute detail. Very minute detail, in fact, because the chief scrutineer had been involved in a lively dispute with Chapman during the pre-race scrutiny when his men had arrived late and been harshly ticked off for it by the Lotus constructor. It so happened that during the lap of honor, conducted in the usual Brands Hatch manner (the winner's car was put on a trailer and the driver, constructor, mechanics, etc. huddled round it as it was towed along by a tractor) one of the supports of the Lotus's rear wing had been bent. As they wished to check its height (i.e. that it was no more than 31·2 in (80 cm) above the lowest suspended part of the car), the scrutineers demanded that the Lotus mechanics straighten it out. In a fit of pique they refused to do so unless Chapman were present. Piqued themselves, the scrutineers proceeded to take an estimated measurement; the result was 31·7 in (81·5 cm) and they decided immediately to disqualify Rindt. In the whole history of World Championship Grands Prix this was the first time such a scandalous thing had happened.

Chapman, of course, reacted at once. With the support duly straightened and the wing in place, the height was found to be 31 in (79·8 cm) and by the end of the evening Rindt was re-established as the winner.

Rindt and Brabham had largely dominated this Grand Prix. Only one of their opponents, Jacky Ickx, seemed up to challenging their superiority but after taking the lead he had to stop on the seventh lap when his transmission failed. It was another brief but brilliant exhibition from the boxer-engined Ferrari which both at Clermont-Ferrand and at Brands Hatch was never anything but first while it was in proper working order. The progress made by the Italian machine contrasted sharply with the collapse of the Marches. They suffered in any case from too much unsprung weight and this trouble proved fatal on the bumpy Brands Hatch track: Stewart started from the third row, Andretti from the fourth, Peterson from the fifth, Cevert from the sixth, Amon from the seventh and Siffert from the eighth. The race was a wholesale disaster for them, a fact that was emphasized by two breakages (Andretti and Siffert) to the hastily modified rear suspension. What the talent and hard work of Stewart and Amon had managed to hide until then

suddenly became obvious: the 701Bs were outdated cars. Robin Herd was already working on a radically different model for 1971.

A marque new to Formula 1 made its début at Brands Hatch with the first track appearance of the Surtees TS7, a very attractive car in its simplicity and delicacy. It was powered, of course, by a Ford V8. This was the component that caused Big John's retirement when, after a cautious start and a splendid climb, he was in tenth place and magnificently resisting Brabham and Rindt who were trying to lap him.

Finally, this race provided the occasion for the first Grand Prix outing of the young Brazilian prodigy Emerson Fittipaldi. The term "meteoric rise" has already been mentioned in relation to Cevert's career and it could equally be applied to that of the young Swede Ronnie Peterson. But how is Fittipaldi's career to be described? He made his start in Formula Ford in 1969 and went on to Formula 3 at the end of that season; he moved up to Formula 2 at the beginning of 1970 and by the end of July 1970 here he was driving a works Lotus 49C. He undoubtedly holds the outright record for the fastest climb to the top.

By way of a contrast, an old Grand Prix regular announced at Brands Hatch that they would retire at the end of 1970; it was Dunlop, a company that had been identified with Formula 1 for nearly two decades. Indeed, they had been the only source of supply for all the competitors in this formula before Goodyear and then Firestone came along to dispute their monopoly. The most significant developments in the roadholding of Formula 1 machines during this period probably owed more to the technical and financial support of Dunlop than to any other factor.

As the Nurburgring had been boycotted by the G.P.D.A., the German Automobile Club fell back on the Hockenheim circuit as the venue for their 1970 Grand Prix. This flat and artificial track is to some extent the complete opposite of the Ring and as a race the event certainly lost a lot from the change. On the other hand, although this track had also been harshly criticized from the safety point of view following Jim Clark's fatal accident in 1968, it now offered all the right guarantees, with two chicanes breaking up the straights, wide verges and the proper equipment. There remained the question of whether it was a selective enough circuit to sort out the best drivers in the world piloting the most efficient cars in the world.

As it happened, while it was an extremely close race at the front between Rindt, Ickx, Regazzoni and Amon, Hockenheim turned out to be a better judge of these matters than Monza, for example. Suspense about who would win was maintained right to the end by Rindt and Ickx who were separated by only 0·7 s at the finish. This fourth consecutive victory (and his fifth of the season) meant that Rindt was virtually certain of the world title, particularly as neither Brabham nor Stewart figured in the final classification of this Grand Prix. Ferrari at last had confirmation that their cars were reliable as well as fast, a point that was again noticeable in the Austrian Grand Prix (revived for the first time since 1964 and held on the new Zeltweg circuit called the Osterreichring) when the Italian cars displayed a superiority that was to continue almost without flagging until the end of the season.

As at Clermont-Ferrand, the twelve-cylinder cars were dominant at Zeltweg. In front of his home crowd,

who had turned out in droves to cheer on the World Championship leader, Rindt recorded the best practice time ahead of Regazzoni, Stewart, Ickx, Amon and Giunti (driving a third Ferrari). However, in the race the local hero was unable to get higher than third before his engine gave up. Beltoise then assumed the role of hunter, and his Matra V12 was the only car to keep the prancing Ferraris in its sights before it had to make a brief pit stop towards the end of the race to take on more fuel. The race ended in triumph for the machines from Maranello. Right on the tail of Ickx was an astonishing Regazzoni, confirming that he was

The Surtees-Ford TS7: the elegance of simplicity.

Emerson Fittipaldi on his way to winning the U.S. Grand Prix.

Enzo Ferrari a man who has become a legend. In the eyes of his enthusiastic supporters and the public at large, he is the personification of motor racing.

Ickx-Regazzoni at Zeltweg, followed
by Beltoise: when the twelve-cylinder
machines dictated terms.

The four musketeers of the 1970 season:
Regazzoni.

Cevert.

First championship outing for the Tyrrell-Ford. In the lead, Stewart retires and Ickx goes past.

Peterson.

Emerson Fittipaldi.

indeed a star performer of exceptional ability; he lapped all his opponents except Stommelen and Brabham. The 1970 season had started to turn.

It was pushed a bit further round by the Italian Grand Prix, again won by a Ferrari but this time the one driven by Regazzoni (Ickx had trouble with his clutch), and marked by two significant events: Rindt's death during practice and Ken Tyrrell's unveiling of the car that bore his name. It had been built in the greatest secrecy under the direction of Derek Gardner, an engineer who came from Ferguson and whom Tyrrell had got to know the previous year at the time of the four-wheel-drive Matra MS84. With its thick-waisted monocoque and almost identical suspension geometry, the Tyrrell-Ford bore a very close resemblance to the Matra MS80, the 1969 World Champion car. However it was still in need of development and at Monza was seen only in practice. It was with this March that Stewart took second place in the Italian Grand Prix, but this was the last occasion on which the Scotsman would race the car that had been the cause of such severe disillusion.

In the Canadian Grand Prix, where the Tyrrell-Ford had its first championship outing, it showed that it had the sort of potential to help Stewart regain his rightful place at the top. After recording the best time in practice, beating Ickx by 0·1 s and Regazzoni by 0·4 s, Jackie Stewart went straight into the lead at the start of the race and left all his pursuers behind with astonishing ease, just as he used to in 1969. By the end of the first third of the event, he was already 17 s ahead of Ickx when a stub axle broke on the Tyrrell. Fortunately he managed to keep the car under control, but for him the race had ended and on a disagreeable note. Nevertheless, Jackie was smiling: it was clear that once his new mount was sorted out, he would have a Ferrari-beater. The race finished with another Ickx-Regazzoni double but it was no longer possible, as it had been in Austria, to talk of a triumph because the 312Bs had played a largely subordinate role until Stewart's retirement.

Jackie Stewart was therefore the favorite for the U.S. Grand Prix, the race with the $250,000 purse, which, being a good Scotsman, he viewed with a very beady eye. As for Jacky Ickx, with sixteen points fewer than Rindt and two events to go, he still had a hope of becoming World Champion.

This time Stewart had to give way to Ickx in the battle for the best practice performance, but in the event he made as decisive a start as he had done in Canada and by the 40th of the 108 laps that constituted the race had already lapped everyone except Ickx, Rodriguez (whose B.R.M. at last seemed to have regained the sort of competitiveness that had brought it victory at Spa), Amon and Fittipaldi (driving a 72) whose team-mate was the Swede Reine Wisell, replacing Miles and racing for Lotus for the first time. Chapman's team had withdrawn from the Italian Grand Prix after Rindt's death, and had not entered for the Canadian as they were still trying to establish what it was that had caused Rindt to go off the road. It was generally presumed that because of what had happened to Miles in Austria a drive shaft had broken, but Colin Chapman denied this and officially attributed the accident to the fact that Rindt was trying the car for the first time with the wing and fins removed and that in this condition the 72 became extremely difficult to drive.

Now back to a Grand Prix that was to prove full of surprises and changes of fortune before it had run its course. A little after half-distance a fuel line broke on Ickx's Ferrari while he was still in second place. A pause for repairs and Jacky Ickx rejoined the race in twelfth position. It seemed that he had lost all hope of winning the Championship but he set to and, given a hand by the retirements that occurred, made an exciting come-back to reach fourth place. It was not enough though: to keep his championship hopes alive he needed to have finished second. So the title remained the property of Jochen Rindt and Jacky Ickx had the grace to declare that that was how it should be.

As the eightieth lap came up, Stewart seemed to have the race more or less won when the Tyrrell started to emit a wisp of blue smoke: a badly placed oil line had chafed through and started to split. When it gave way completely he lost all his oil and on the eighty-second lap came to a halt. So Rodriguez found himself in the lead with a 17 s advantage over Fittipaldi and only twenty-six laps to go. This time it seemed all over. However, seven laps from the end the B.R.M. rushed into its pit to the amazement of the spectators. It was out of fuel. By the time it was refuelled, Emerson Fittipaldi had gone by and on the occasion of his fourth race in Formula 1 he won the U.S. Grand Prix.

This put him one step higher than Regazzoni who had won the Italian Grand Prix on his fifth time out: the discoveries of 1970 had fulfilled their promise before the year was out.

The season came to an end with the Mexican Grand Prix, fantastic confusion and a third double for Ferrari. It was on a track literally invaded by floods of spectators flowing over virtually non-existent crowd barriers that Jacky Ickx and Clay Regazzoni resumed their momentarily interrupted act as an unbeatable duo and added the finishing and triumphant touch to their series of thirteen World Championship Grands Prix in 1970 (this is still a record). Stewart, the only driver to constitute a threat to the Italian cars, was forced to retire when he hit a dog that was crossing the track (a number of spectators took the same short cut) and damaged his monocoque. In any case, the Tyrrell driver was already beaten because he had to stop to have a loose steering column fixed and this incident had cost him a lap. Ickx, therefore, won without any trouble, and although Regazzoni experienced some carburation difficulties, he none the less retained sufficient power to make sure of second place.

At Mexico Jack Brabham made his farewell appearance on the track. The three times World Champion who, according to rumor, had been on the point of retirement since 1962, had officially announced that he would give up racing at the close of the 1970 season. It was the end of a marvellous career: World Champion in 1959 and still in the running for the title in 1970, eleven years later. He had won the South African Grand Prix and missed the Monaco and British events by a hairsbreadth. Jack Brabham was taking his bow in full and double glory as a constructor and as a driver; his powers were in no way diminished as he had proved during his last season of racing when he had shown himself to be as good as the best. His departure seen against the arrival of the new wave was a telling symbol of the significance of the year 1970 in the history of Formula 1: a period of great transition.

1971

stewart in the style of clark

That the 1971 season developed as it did is explained by the interaction of two factors. The first of these was the unexpected and persistent failure of Ferrari. This was rather disconcerting as they were considered the favorites before the season began and not unreasonably in view of their dominant position at the end of the previous Championship. The second factor was the brilliant way in which Stewart's Tyrrell-Ford made good the promise it had shown briefly during the early stages of the 1970 Canadian and U.S. Grands Prix.

The Scuderia's chief engineer, Mauro Forghieri, had taken the hint of things to come very seriously indeed. After Stewart's two unopposed romps, he came to the conclusion that he would have to make some real improvements to his obviously no longer unbeatable 312Bs, and this is why he spent the winter of 1970–71 designing a new chassis for the flat 12 engine. The principal change was to the rear suspension system which had inboard-mounted springs acting through articulated arms. Unhappily for Ferrari, the B2 (as this model was called), which had its first championship outing at Monaco, proved very tricky to set up because the characteristics of the redesigned rear suspension conflicted with those of the car's new ultra-low-profile Firestone tires. The result was a serious vibration problem that they never managed to solve and matters were not improved by the fact that Ferrari and Firestone blamed one another for the trouble. Their row eventually came to a head at Monza, when, during the course of a sensational press conference, the Commendatore angrily accused his supplier of being the cause of his failure and ordered his mechanics to fit a set of Goodyears to a hack 312B. Jacky Ickx recorded the second-best practice time with this machine, but because they failed to do any directly comparative tests between the

two makes of tires, the protest was robbed of some of its value. With this controversial episode a climax was reached in the cut-throat competition that had gone on throughout the season between Firestone (supplying Ferrari, B.R.M., Lotus, Surtees and March) and Goodyear (as usual supplying Brabham and McLaren as well as Matra and especially Tyrrell). Following Dunlop's retirement, Stewart had signed up with Goodyear, and the traditional three-cornered fight turned into a duel, but though it lost one of its combatants, the battle lost none of its heat. On the contrary. Compared with the tires both companies had produced in 1970, their 1971 covers differed in that their circumference was smaller still. The diameter generally adopted for rear wheels tended to be 13 in (330 mm) while a truce was observed over the matter of contact width. Despite the disaster they had suffered at Zandvoort, Goodyear emerged the winner of this fierce duel with seven victories to four.

It became apparent during the second part of the 1970 season that the Ferrari twelve-cylinder engine—and perhaps even the B.R.M.—now had the edge on the Ford V8. The Anglo-American unit, unyielding World Champion since 1968, seemed to have reached the end of its development. There was a rumor that Duckworth was at work on a flat 12 for 1971, but this turned out to be nothing more than speculation. As it happened, this extraordinary British engine specialist still had potential to realise in the V8; he produced yet another new version (the series 11) and thus provided Stewart with a competitive weapon. And although Duckworth, who always reckoned to maintain an attitude of strict neutrality towards his customers, denied it, it seemed that the Scots driver, and during the second part of the season his team-mate Cevert, had the best of the series 11 engines for which their

constructor claimed 440–445 bhp. It is likely that the fundamental reason why Cosworth were able to rise successfully to the Ferrari-B.R.M. challenge was that the Northampton firm changed their policy. They rid themselves completely of the crushing task of maintenance, guaranteed in 1970, so that they could concentrate on developing and tuning the few series 11 engines they built. These were the only units that Duckworth was now personally concerned with, all the others were looked after by approved "preparers" like John Wyer and Brian Hart. Although it made its first appearance in August 1970, the Tyrrell was intended from the start for the 1971 season. Once its teething troubles had been cured as a result of running in the final rounds of a Championship that was already lost and a few minor finishing touches added during the winter, the team had a machine that was sufficiently well built and prepared to be just what Jackie Stewart needed to regain the title. Yet it could not have been more conventional in design, it was not the lightest of the 1971 Formula 1 cars (that honor fell to the Surtees and the B.R.M.s) and initially Stewart had great trouble asserting his authority before he reached the stage where, by virtue of three consecutive victories, he was almost unbeatable. In the final analysis the Scotsman's success was due to a remarkably well-arranged and organized team capable of exploiting a set of major tools on behalf of an exceptional driver, rather than to an overwhelming technical superiority. Taking the main components of a Formula 1 car—chassis, engine and tires in particular —there was nothing about the Tyrrell to suggest that it conferred on its driver any outstanding or lasting advantage. However, the fact that these components were well matched was undeniably an asset except on All Fools' Day at Zandvoort. That occasion apart, the car (later two cars) that the Tyrrell team lined up for the start of each Grand Prix was always prepared to the limit of its possibilities and that is where their strength lay. Their opponents, on the other hand, were all more or less seriously in trouble at one time or another. Indeed, everything suggests that the Tyrrell-Stewart duo had reached such an unrivalled level of maturity, cohesion and performance that they would have dictated terms no matter which of the 1971 Formula 1 machines they had used, provided they had been given complete responsibility for running it.

It is therefore worth stopping for a moment to consider Ken Tyrrell's personality. A legend has grown up round this man, yet no one could be further from being a legendary personage. His chief characteristic is in fact his fundamentally practical nature, which in no way implies that he does not have a brain, but it means that he is completely open-minded, with no preconceived ideas about anything. To say that Tyrrell is "a manager of genius" or "another Neubauer" is nothing but a superficial convention which bears no relation to the reality. In fact, his touch of genius is that he is on his guard against certain of the attributes that are said to accompany genius—impulsiveness, improvisation, rashness and inconsistency. With him it is a matter of sureness, coolness, reliability and determination, and while he might possess the virtues of courage he knows how to shield himself against its drawbacks.

A countryman, originally a timber man, Tyrrell has a common-sense approach. He tries hard to leave nothing to chance, to make use of all his experience— good and bad, and to surround himself with people who are reliable as well as talented. There is nothing of

the tyrant in him; he does not regard his mechanics, drivers and associates as a paramilitary organization, but his authority is such that he quite naturally gets the best out of everybody, and all in an atmosphere of typically British calm. Tyrrell also has a reputation for cunning; however, he is no Machiavelli, his reasoning is never devious. He is certainly a perfectionist but not to the point of mania, and this is reflected in the way his cars are turned out: perfect in the sense of functional. Immaculate because this is the best way of making sure that nothing has been done wrong or forgotten, but totally devoid of superfluous ornament. In short, Ken Tyrrell can be described as an intelligent, well-balanced and determined man. His particular genius is the way he combines these three qualities and uses them to satisfy his great motor racing passion.

The financial provisions of the Geneva Agreement were renewed (in principle if not in detail), but fortunately the disgraceful discriminatory clauses about practice qualification, which caused so many rows and controversies at the beginning of 1970, were abandoned. There were thirteen events listed in the calendar but two of them were cancelled for safety reasons. In fact, because of the disastrous way it had been organized in 1970, the C.S.I. refused to include the Mexican Grand Prix as a qualifying event for the 1971 World Championship, but under pressure from the organizers strangely (given the circumstances) supported by the G.P.D.A., they went back on their decision. Such forbearance on the part of the drivers, so different from their firmness on other occasions, caused no little surprise since it seemed so illogical. In fact, it was just as hard to follow the reasoning that led them to boycott the Nurburgring while they still consented to run at Oulton Park. Although it is fair to criticize them when opportunism seems to get the better of their great principles, it should nevertheless be recognized that despite a few blots of this nature the action of the G.P.D.A., and of Jackie Stewart in particular, must be regarded as positive taking the question of safety as a whole. Indeed, such action is even courageous since it is neither pleasant nor easy to risk seeing one's image tarnished in the eyes of the public; not to mention the strong resentment harbored by organizers and officials. Although the Mexican Grand Prix was reinstated, it was not held in the end as a sign of mourning for Pedro Rodriguez.

Some nine years after the death of his brother Ricardo, Pedro died at the wheel of a Ferrari 512S while competing in a second-class race on the German Norisring circuit; the cause of the accident was never established. He was a proud man and an individualist (he was certainly no G.P.D.A. activist) and though his enthusiasm on the track, which led him to disregard the risks he took, was a very Latin characteristic, he was almost Anglo-Saxon in the quiet and even shy demeanour he brought to everyday life. With his undiminished courage and wide experience he became a star performer in Formula 1 when he at last found himself driving a competitive car (the B.R.M.). In the rain his bravery and completely natural talent, expressed in a totally non-classical style, found their match only in the courage and subtlety of Jacky Ickx. It was particularly sad that Pedro's great rival and team-mate at B.R.M. and Porsche, Jo Siffert, should have disappeared from the scene during the same season. He was killed at Brands Hatch driving a Formula 1 car, but in a race where again there was nothing at stake—it was an event organized to fill the gap left by the Mexican Grand Prix and honor

Stewart's title. This dreadful coincidence deprived Formula 1 forever of two great drivers who were so very different in character but so much alike on the track where they both displayed great daring and extravagant generosity of spirit. Moreover, their sporting careers had followed more or less the same pattern. While they both rose to the top fairly quickly as drivers of the very fast sports prototype machines, they had had to wait many long years before they got a mount worthy of their talent in Formula 1. Here they were handicapped by the language barrier as neither of them spoke English fluently, an almost essential accomplishment in the world of Formula 1. Also, of course, neither of them, one Mexican and the other Swiss, had the opportunity of racing for a constructor of his own nationality.

The other Grand Prix that was cancelled was the Belgian, this time because the C.S.I., not just the G.P.D.A., objected to the Spa-Francorchamps circuit. So there were eleven official events in the calendar for the 1971 season; a season that confirmed the supremacy both of Jackie Stewart and of the Elf-Tyrrell team and witnessed the success of the attack mounted by a new generation of first-class, ambitious and talented drivers, the most outstanding of whom were Ronnie Peterson and François Cevert. The Swede collected a convincing series of good results to finish second to Stewart in the Championship, while the Frenchman, who established a new lap record at the Nurburgring and won the U.S. Grand Prix, was right on his heels in third place.

The principal transfer of the 1970–71 close season involved Chris Amon who left March for Matra. On top of this, the young Bicester firm lost Siffert to B.R.M. Neither of them was replaced so Peterson became the number one March driver. They also sold a car to Frank Williams (for Pescarolo who had left Matra) and made an arrangement with Alfa Romeo, similar to the one the Milanese firm had had with McLaren in 1970, whereby de Adamich and Nanni Galli would drive a March fitted with the Alfa V8 engine. Rob Walker decided not to enter cars of his own and joined forces with Team Surtees. As a result Graham Hill was appointed to the Brabham team to fill the vacancy left by Jack Brabham's retirement. Ron Tauranac chose the Australian hope, Tim Schenken, as his number two, whereupon Rolf Stommelen turned to Surtees. The Elf-Tyrrell, Lotus, Ferrari and McLaren teams remained unchanged.

The first meeting-place of the season was Kyalami where there was no shortage of interesting things to be seen in the paddock. Undoubtedly the prize for the most radically new car went to March for their 711, in appearance a most original device with its ultra-streamlined body and front wing in the form of a wide, elevated blade. It bore the stamp of British aerodynamicist Frank Costin whose other notable work included the 1957–58 Vanwalls, a certain number of Lotuses and the Le Mans D-type Jaguars. Robin Herd was very anxious to have his over-conventional 701 of the previous year forgotten and he had shown no hesitation about designing a very sophisticated car, which had lateral radiators and inboard front brakes like the Lotus 72. On the scales, however, this new March revealed a weight problem; at 1276 lb (580 kg) it was the heaviest Formula 1 machine in the field.

The new Ferrari, the 312 B2, was seen only during a preliminary test session which came to an end when Regazzoni lost control and the car was destroyed. Built on the same principle as the B1, the B2 mono-

coque was deeper and less wide with less rounded but higher sides. The chief modification lay in the completely revised rear suspension with brakes flanking the final drive and inboard spring/damper units working at an unusually small angle to the horizontal through a system of levers.

The main feature of Hulme's McLaren M19 was also an original suspension system. Ralph Bellamy, the designer, had given it a variable rate by operating the springs, mounted on sliding rods, through a varying leverage. The monocoque was very thick-waisted and low, unlike the old M14 chassis which was outstanding for the delicacy of its lines.

Rodriguez's B.R.M. P160 was a splendid machine. It was even lower than the 153, to which it nevertheless bore a close resemblance, with wider sides but a slightly narrower track front and rear. The rear brakes were now outboard and at 1166 lb (530 kg), the B.R.M. was down to the lowest legal limit. Similarly the Surtees TS9 seemed to be a development of the TS7 rather than a completely new model. It was still extremely elegant as a result of its simplicity (Mauro Forghieri confined that it was the Formula 1 car he admired the most) but it had a sturdier monocoque and a wheelbase longer by some 4·75 in (120·6 mm). The Matra, now called the MS120B, still had the 1970 angular monocoque but it was reinforced by tubes round the cockpit. The most obvious modification was the very wide, flat front hood with large aerodynamic fins ahead of the wheels on each side. The 1971 version of the Tyrrell was almost identical to the car that had run at the end of 1970, the only recognition feature being the inverted position of the roll-

First Grand Prix victory for the American champion, Mario Andretti. Surtees, here challenging him on the inside, could have won if his gear-box had not had lubrication troubles; he was never to be as competitive again.

over bar supports. Finally, the Ferrari 312Bs, the Lotus 72s and the Brabham BT33s were 1970 models pure and simple.

The very lively South African Grand Prix was won by a Ferrari—the one driven by Mario Andretti. Thus he claimed his first victory in an event counting towards the World Championship and in so doing went to the top of the table. Of course, this was a far from surprising result since the Ferraris were generally considered as favorites, only Stewart being regarded as capable of measuring up to them. Although he clearly outpaced the Italian cars in practice, when he was the sole driver to get below 1 min 18 s (1 min 17·8 s to be precise, against the 1 min 19·3 s best of the previous year, also recorded by Jackie Stewart), he just could not reproduce this superiority in the race, in spite of the fact that he was using the one and only Ford-Cosworth series 11 delivered so far. In fact, Jackie Stewart's relatively poor performance was explained by the problem of the choice of tires, a problem that to a large extent affected all the other competitors, too.

It very soon became clear at Kyalami that the new Goodyear G24s outclassed the Firestones, and it was with G24s that Stewart recorded the best practice time and Amon, appearing behind the wheel of a Matra for the first time, the second best ahead of Regazzoni. However, because of the extreme heat, the Scotsman (like the New Zealander) had to give up the idea of using them in the race; instead he ran with his left wheels fitted with G20s, appreciably less effective but more wear-resistant tires. The change affected the Tyrrell's performance which suffered in any case

because the engine did not come up to expectations.

It was the situation in reverse for the McLaren M19. In practice it was only seventh fastest but it used G24s in the race; apparently its new suspension caused less tire wear than its rivals' systems. After Regazzoni had held a secure lead for the first sixteen laps, taking advantage of the fact that both Stewart and Amon had made a complete mess of starting, Hulme challenged the Ferrari, which did not hold the road all that well, and went ahead. Only Surtees and Andretti managed to keep pace with him (Clay's engine was losing power). Then, a little before half-distance, Big John had to let himself slip back; he was in trouble with his gear-box which eventually broke down because of an oil leak. Andretti was now in second place and he started to pile on the pressure in an attempt to catch up with Hulme who was only about 4 s ahead of him during the battle of the last ten laps. The gap was closing but by mere tenths of a second; there was no longer any doubt that Hulme would win when, three laps from home, a bolt holding a rear strut sheared. Immediately Andretti overtook poor Denny Hulme who finished slowly in sixth place, while Stewart crossed the line a distant second, more than 20 s after the victorious Ferrari. The other two Ferraris also made it to the finish, Regazzoni's in third place and Ickx's in tenth after a puncture. Although he had worked very hard, Stewart had not been able to do a thing about Hulme, Surtees and Andretti; his teammate Cevert had gone off the road when lying seventh. Very much in evidence in practice, Amon's Matra was far from repeating this performance in the race when it was handicapped not only by the tires it wore but

also by an unwilling engine. This incidentally was the only Matra entered for Kyalami as Jean-Pierre Beltoise had had his licence suspended following Ignazio Giunti's fatal accident in the Buenos Aires 1000 km Race in January, an accident for which Beltoise was alleged to have had some responsibility. As for the new cars, the March 711s seemed very short of development, unlike the McLaren which just missed a win on its first outing. The B.R.M. P160, driven by Rodriguez, had been troublesome in practice, but in the race it performed in a much more convincing manner (it was in third place) before the cowling on the radiator became detached and the driver had to retire because his feet were getting burnt by the excessive heat from the engine. Finally, the performance of the Surtees TS9 had shown great promise.

The Tyrrell-Ford's first Grand Prix victory came at Barcelona in the second round of the Championship. On this extremely difficult circuit, which demands above all great subtlety from the driver, Stewart's class and his car took command, but Jacky Ickx responded fiercely to the challenge, as was proved by the very small gap that separated the two men at the end: 3·2 s. Following his second place at Kyalami, Stewart's Barcelona victory, of course, put him at the top of the Championship table, but in spite of appearances his position there was in fact very precarious.

It was felt after this race that Stewart's success had been a purely personal one, that he had won almost despite his car which, driven by anyone else, would probably have been forced to give way under the attack from Ickx. Although its weight had been reduced by about 44 lb (20 kg) since Kyalami, the Tyrrell did not hold the road well and its braking was poor. It was only due to the mastery of Stewart, who finished the race in a state of almost total exhaustion, that it scored its first nine points in the Constructors'

Cup competition. Because of these circumstances the struggle for victory was quite magnificent: a breathtaking spectacle right to the end thanks to a fantastic come-back from Ickx, whipping his car into second place after overcoming a slight fault. He might even have managed to win had it not been for a last-minute mistake which he made braking for the hairpin before the downhill swoop. This cost him 1·5 s and all hope of catching the leader who was then only about 2 s ahead with two laps left to go. This superb duel overshadowed everything else and Amon's third place in particular which he took with nearly 1 min delay. Hulme's performance was disappointing. He was one of the favorites after his exhibition at Kyalami, but he could not reproduce anything like this form and finished an unspectacular fifth behind Rodriguez and ahead of Beltoise who was racing again. What is more, the rest of the season did not hold much in store for the 1967 Champion who constantly suffered engine trouble. The M19 did not become competitive again until the very last Grand Prix of the year after its rear suspension had been changed back to a conventional layout and geometry.

Finally, the new Brabham BT34, whose strange appearance immediately earned it the nickname of "lobster claw", made its Grand Prix start at Barcelona. The cowlings of its two lateral water radiators were positioned not by the cockpit like those of the Lotus and March, but right at the front where they were connected by a wing, and it was this layout that recalled the claw of a lobster. Apart from the originality of its shape, the BT34 was otherwise very classical. Indeed Tauranac had even gone back to outboard-mounted front springs which he had abandoned with the BT33. The first championship outing of this car was very brief since Graham Hill had the steering knocked out of true when he bumped the rear wheel of Peterson's March at the beginning of the second lap. Unfortunately, its subsequent performance proved as disappointing as that of the McLaren, never giving any sign that it was superior to the 1970 model which, driven by Schenken, seemed on the whole a more competitive machine. In any case, the Brabham team appeared to be in constant trouble and Ron Tauranac rather overworked as he tried to do everything himself; he had a very small budget to play with and was forced to apply himself to running the business as well as the team (he had bought up Brabham's shares) and to looking after the design, construction and preparation of the cars both in the workshop and on the track. It was, of course, too much for one man to cope with on his own, even a man as capable as this excellent Australian engineer. Moreover it soon became clear that what had hitherto constituted the great strength of the Brabham team—a close partnership between a driver and an engineer who understood one another instinctively—no longer existed. There was no sympathetic spark between Hill and Tauranac and the BT34 never managed to reach a satisfactory stage of development.

The original rear quarters of the new Ferrari 312 B2 which caused a lot of difficulties for the Scuderia.

At Barcelona the race between Stewart and Ickx (in the background) reached a rare level of intensity.

The Brabham BT34, after a promising start in a non-championship event at Silverstone, experienced nothing but trouble thereafter.

Wearing a crown of glory after his victory at Barcelona, Stewart was the big favorite for Monaco (a fairly similar circuit to the one in Montjuich Park) in spite of the entry of the Ferrari 312 B2s. In fact the new Ferrari had already made its début in the non-championship Race of Champions which had just taken place at Brands Hatch where, driven by Regazzoni, it had beaten Stewart's Tyrrell. Theoretically, therefore, this victory should have inspired confidence in the B2s. In reality, however, it was due to the right choice of tires for the bad track conditions rather than to a well-sorted-out chassis. They never managed to make the chassis work properly and this was why the Scuderia failed.

Stewart now had a machine that, although it was not yet totally satisfying, had made some progress since Barcelona and this time there was nobody capable of challenging his superiority; this applied particularly to the man lying second to him in the Championship, Mario Andretti, who failed to qualify. He was unlucky enough to have a breakage during the practice session that took place in the dry, so the only

The McLaren M19 variable-rate front suspension.

There was a lot of preoccupation with aerodynamics in 1971. This early season B.R.M. front end is classical. . . .

. . the Tyrrell on the other hand is more original. . . .

Ronnie Peterson,
the discovery of the year.

. . . after the March 711 "cake scoop" . . .

. . . Matra developed the MS120B.

Black day at Zandvoort in the rain for Stewart who at this very moment is being lapped by Ickx.

timed laps he did were on a wet track. In spite of tremendous determination, his task was impossible in such conditions even though, as a result of pressure from the C.S.I. and the constructors, eighteen drivers were allowed to start instead of the usual sixteen.

The confusion at the start was appalling. Stewart immediately went to the front followed by Siffert and Ickx while Graham Hill left the track at the Tobacconist's corner and retired on the first lap. Inexorably the Tyrrell left the B.R.M. behind and Jackie Stewart went on to win without any trouble despite problems with his brakes. Attention was therefore centred on Peterson's magnificent drive. At first he was blocked behind Rodriguez, but once the Mexican had been forced to give way to him by a punctured tire, he closed on Ickx and Siffert in the most astonishing manner. The young Swedish driver, taking advantage of the fact that his tires had more grip than those of the opposition, shot up behind them, overtook them one after the other and seized second place; at the same time he confirmed his growing stature. His car, the March 711, had already been considerably modified. The front brakes, which had originally been mounted inboard, were now back in the wheels following a half-shaft failure which had sent Ronnie Peterson off into the scenery during the Race of Champions and the rear suspension had also been revised. The car seemed to work in this form, even though the rear and lateral streamlining fitted to the car when it first appeared, had had to be abandoned.

As the Belgian Grand Prix had been cancelled, everyone was getting ready to take the road to Zandvoort when it was learnt that this circuit, too, had its

safety problems and that as a result the Dutch Grand Prix was in jeopardy. Various jobs prescribed by the C.S.I. subcommittee had not been done, the G.P.D.A. made a fuss and threatened to boycott the race.

Jackie Stewart was the least conciliatory of the drivers in this affair, almost as though he had a foreboding that no good would come of his racing on the circuit of the dunes. As in 1968, the rain determined the pattern of the race. Three years earlier the bad weather had helped Stewart, but this time it let him down completely. Like all the others who were using Goodyear tires, Jackie Stewart failed even to figure in the event, finishing eleventh, five laps in arrears after one of the very rare spins of his career.

The two great rain specialists, on the other hand, Jacky Ickx and Pedro Rodriguez, were both running on Firestones, and they engaged in a magnificent duel, totally dominating all their rivals, the best of whom, Regazzoni, finished a lap behind.

The number of times people went off the road was quite fantastic. At Tarzan corner alone there were fourteen such incidents, as many as in the course of a whole season normally. The track was turned into a skating-rink by the mixture of rain-water, salt and sand that covered its surface and only Ickx and Rodriguez had sufficient mastery in these exceptionally difficult conditions to avoid making the slightest mistake.

The road was wet for the whole race, but it was worse at the beginning than it was at the end. This explains why Rodriguez, who at first had the decided edge on Ickx, was eventually caught, passed and forced to admit defeat. The B.R.M. engine proved to be less flexible than the Ferrari unit and Pedro Rodriguez had to use first gear coming out of the Hunzerug hairpin which meant that his speed fell considerably. While the track was awash Ickx had to do the same, but once it started to recover its grip he was able to stay in second by taking the corner more quickly. The Mexican, however, could not do this and he was overtaken a little before half-distance at the exit to this bend.

Behind these two there was total disorder; yet again

The French Grand Prix was the last for Pedro Rodriguez, the spirited Mexican seen below, one wheel locked in braking for the chicane at the Ricard circuit. He never had the success he deserved in Formula 1.

the unluckiest driver was Mario Andretti, forced to retire right at the start by fuel-pump failure. Suddenly Jacky Ickx, who had finished third at Monaco, moved up to within five points of Stewart and took second place in the Championship table, ahead of his team-mate Andretti, Peterson and Rodriguez all with the same score. So the two logical favorites for the title stakes found themselves neck to neck at the end of the first third of the season. However, from then on

fate carried them in completely different directions; while Stewart flitted from success to success, Ickx suffered one disaster after another.

In fact the next three Grands Prix—the French, the British and the German—proved to be the exclusive preserve not only of Stewart but of the whole Elf-Tyrrell team who twice succeeded in achieving the double. First on the new Paul Ricard circuit, the most up to date in the world from the point of view of safety, where Cevert took second place ahead of Fittipaldi. Then on a completely renovated Nurburgring, where the German G.P. was held once again after the rapid completion of a colossal improvement program. Here the young French driver obtained the same result, on this occasion getting the better of Regazzoni at the end of a very fierce struggle, in the course of which he established a new lap record of 7 min 20·1 s (116·07 mile/h (185·7 km/h)) even though it was only the second time in his career that he had raced on this circuit where experience is generally recognized as one of the essential and decisive ingredients of success. Meanwhile the British Grand Prix had been pocketed by Stewart who was so overwhelmingly superior that his victory was almost offhand. Since the French G.P., the Tyrrell, now fitted with a wide new streamlined nose section in the form of a shield designed to improve the adhesion of the front part of the car, had reached the peak of its development and this, combined with the spirit of its driver and the series 11 Ford-Cosworth engine, served to outclass the disordered opposition. Jacky Ickx failed to finish any one of these three Grands Prix and thus lost—from a realistic if not mathematical point of view—all hope of the Championship. It was a period when young talent came to the fore: in addition to Cevert, Peterson and Fittipaldi took more than their share of the high-points-scoring places. On the twelve-cylinder front, Ferrari and Matra collapsed while B.R.M., though obviously competitive and often well up with the leaders thanks to a very determined Siffert (he took

over as number one driver in the B.R.M. team when Rodriguez's accident deprived them of their leader), never managed to achieve any solid results.

This situation changed, however, with the next two Grands Prix. In Austria Siffert led from start to finish although he was forced to slow down during the last laps by a puncture, which allowed Fittipaldi to close up and he failed to catch him by only 4 s. For Tyrrell this race represented the only total failure of the season: neither Stewart (who lost a wheel) nor Cevert (who broke his engine) reached the finish. There was not a Ferrari at the finish either, while Matra, who had reached the depths of despair at the Nurburgring, had decided to withdraw from Zeltweg in order to devote themselves to a program of systematic testing.

At the end of practice at Monza it seemed that the French firm's decision had paid off. Chris Amon had recorded the fastest lap and had a place on the front row of the grid for the first time since the Spanish Grand Prix. Alongside him was another driver making a come-back—Jacky Ickx. He had achieved his result at the wheel of a hack B1 fitted with Goodyear tires instead of the usual Firestones. A comparison between Ickx's performance with this machine and Regazzoni's with the B2—he was relegated to the fourth row—gives some idea of the failure that the B2 represented for Ferrari. It reacted with too much sensitivity to the vibrations set up by the Firestone tires and it was an extremely delicate, if not impossible, task to adjust it in a way that was entirely satisfactory.

The race turned into the usual slipstreaming affair,

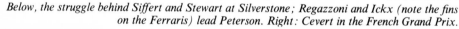

Below, the struggle behind Siffert and Stewart at Silverstone; Regazzoni and Ickx (note the fins on the Ferraris) lead Peterson. Right: Cevert in the French Grand Prix.

Driven by Wisell at Silverstone, the Pratt and Whitney turbine-engined Lotus 56B. A failure but the formula cannot be regarded as finally doomed.

Stewart goes off the road in the Austrian Grand Prix and brings his race to an end. The car has lost its left rear wheel.

The second great Champion lost to racing this season, Joseph Siffert who had the great satisfaction of taking his B.R.M. to victory at Zeltweg. Like Rodriguez, this marvellous driver, who had few equals for tenacity, will-power and skill, was not often as successful as he deserved.

Peter Gethin, surprise winner of the Italian G.P. Right until the last lap it was uncertain whether Hailwood (No. 9), Cevert (No. 2), Peterson, Amon (No. 12) or Ganley would win. It was Gethin (in the background) who caught up with the group at the front and beat the lot of them to the post.

The decisive phase of the Canadian Grand Prix: Peterson loses the lead, allowing Stewart to win.

utterly monotonous and, given the speeds reached by the tightly bunched cars, terrifying at the same time. The Ferraris were soon eliminated, Stewart broke his engine (but he was already World Champion) and Amon inadvertently tore his visor and then fell prey to carburation troubles, so four men arrived in a closely packed group at the final and decisive braking point for the Parabolica. Peterson locked a wheel and slid to the outside, Cevert hesitated and let himself be boxed in, Hailwood (making his return to Formula 1 in the Surtees team) was content to wait on events, and it was B.R.M.s new recruit, Peter Gethin, who with as much skill as determination, blasted straight through to take his first Grand Prix victory on the line.

In eighth place was Emerson Fittipaldi driving the Pratt and Whitney turbine-engined Lotus 56B. This modest result, a lap in arrears of the leading group, was undeniably a disappointment. The car had had its first outing in the Dutch Grand Prix where it had been assigned to the Australian hope Dave Walker. In view of the state of the track, the four-wheel-drive transmission gave it a real advantage, but Walker was not experienced enough to know how to make the best use of it and, like a lot of others that day, he finished up off the road after a spectacular straight on at Tarzan bend. Then the 56B was entered for Silverstone, driven this time by Wisell; but on this circuit it seemed outclassed in terms of handling and braking and was more than 1540 lb (700 kg) overweight. In fact, the 56B was nothing more than the 56 that had been built

for the Indianapolis 500-Mile Race three years earlier. The only modification was to the turbine to make it conform to the C.S.I. equivalent formula so that it could compete in Formula 1 events. In relation to the 1971 chassis it was therefore out of date and it was not at all surprising that it made no impression at Silverstone in spite of its 500 bhp.

At Monza, however, a good chassis is a lot less important than elsewhere, and the Lotus was expected to put in an honorable if not fantastic performance. That it did not was due to the very hot weather which had a marked effect on the power output of the turbine. Its best practice lap of 1 min 25·18 s was a long way from the 1 min 22·4 s achieved by Amon's Matra. Of course the turbine could not be objectively condemned out of hand as a result of this disappointing exhibition, but there is no doubt that it delivered a harsh blow to any interest such an engine might have aroused.

Stewart's poor showing in the two previous Grands Prix was a reminder of the mediocre results he had achieved at the end of 1969, the year in which he first won the title. This gave rise to the fear that he would not show himself in the best light in the two North American events that would bring the season to its close. Happily for him, history does not always repeat itself and Goodyear had pulled themselves together after their collapse at Zandvoort. In spite of the rain and the fog which prompted the organizers to bring the race to an end before it had covered the scheduled distance, Jackie Stewart won the Canadian Grand

Prix, held this time at Mosport. It was a far from easy victory, however. He was made to work for it by a very spirited, daring Peterson, justifying—if he had to —the position he definitely held in the Championship. It was a long, harsh and well-matched duel, and it did not swing in the Champion's favour until the Swede had an overtaking bump with George Eaton who had not seen him. This incident happened exactly half-way through the race and from then on Ronnie Peterson was unable to stop Stewart pulling away as his front wing had been damaged. He did, however, manage to contain the attack launched against him by a new-comer to Formula 1, American driver Mark Donohue, who gave a dashing performance in a McLaren bearing the colours of his manager Roger Penske, "the American Tyrrell".

One of the principal features of the 1971 season had been the way in which a new generation of drivers had proved themselves, and it would not have been complete without one of the new boys receiving the official sanction of a Grand Prix victory. It did not really come as much of a surprise that this seal of approval should be awarded by the U.S. Grand Prix, a singularly propitious event in the circumstances, having already provided the setting for the first G.P. victories of Rindt (in 1969) and Emerson Fittipaldi (in 1970).

The last time a French driver had won a Grand Prix was in 1958 when Maurice Tringtignant claimed victory at Monaco. Since then Jean-Pierre Beltoise had seemed all set to follow suit but luck was never on his side. So the privilege of adding another link to the chain fell to his brother-in-law, François Cevert, whose career in Formula 1 dated only from June 1970. This young driver had made a very rapid advance and already had two second places (in the French and German Grands Prix) to his credit when he scooped the pool at Watkins Glen where Stewart, handicapped by tire troubles that upset the handling of his car, had to slow down after taking the lead at the start of the race. It so happened that the driver who was following him most closely was his team-mate, and once he had taken over as front runner he managed to maintain the position. Not without difficulty, however, since Ickx, back at the wheel of his old B1, closed up on him in the most alarming manner. Ickx was badly placed at the start and had to overtake a number of competitors before slotting into second spot. At this point he was more than 6 s behind Cevert. Then he let fly and was only 2 s away from the Tyrrell when his alternator tore away from its mounting and brought his superb drive to an end. As he was less experienced than Ickx in the art of lapping back-markers, Cevert had let his lead get nibbled away but it was very much to his credit that he did not get rattled and make the mistake that such a relatively unseasoned driver might well have made under that sort of pressure.

Thus the 1971 season ended in glory for the Tyrrell team: the title for Stewart and the Formula 1 Constructors' Cup for a marque that had come into being scarcely a year before. They collected seven victories from eleven Grands Prix, one of them taken by the team's second driver who, in addition, finished third in the World Championship. It was an ascendancy reminiscent of that of Cooper and Brabham in 1959 and of Lotus and Clark in 1965. In short, it was a vintage year, with one of those rare peaks where the combined efforts of a team of men approach so near to perfection.

François Cevert is overjoyed—he has won the U.S. Grand Prix. It was indeed a victory for him but also for Derek Gardner (left) who designed the car and for Ken Tyrrell, the greatest team manager of the period. Unfortunately it was in practice for the 1973 U.S. Grand Prix that Cevert was killed on October 6th at Watkins Glen.

1972

the rise of emerson fittipaldi

The most remarkable feature of the 1972 season was Emerson Fittipaldi's rise to the top. In 1971 the young Brazilian, still trailing the glory of his surprise win in the 1970 U.S. Grand Prix, had slipped back a bit into the ranks. But after a season lurking in the shadows, he was destined to show that the days of his apprenticeship were over and to make his mark as a rival worthy of Stewart. Even though he had the advantage of a very efficient car, magnificently prepared by a Team Lotus restored to all their old brilliance after exchanging their red and white livery for an elegant uniform of black and gold, Fittipaldi's climb to the top demonstrated that in him motor sport had a perfect champion, a driver whose skill was combined with a rare judgment, coolness, and imperturbability.

If Stewart had to yield, then at least he could say that luck was against him and that he was handicapped by ill health: he had developed a stomach ulcer which prevented him from running at all in the Belgian Grand Prix. However, the decisive factor tipping the scale in favor of the Lotus driver was the difficulty the Tyrrell team experienced in bringing their new model, the 005, up to the required standard. The car made its first appearance in practice for the French Grand Prix at the beginning of July, but it wasn't performing satisfactorily until October, when it ran in the last two events of the season and won them easily. In the meantime Fittipaldi had made the most of his opportunity, and Stewart's American victories could not affect the outcome of the championship, which had been settled by the result of the Italian Grand Prix.

During the 1971-1972 close season the various teams underwent a fair number of changes. Principal among them was the arrival of Beltoise at BRM and Revson at McLaren. Surtees retired and established an entirely new team with Mike (The Bike) Hailwood and the Australian hope Tim Schenken. Another Australian, Dave Walker, took Wisell's place at Lotus. The South American contingent in Formula 1 was considerably reinforced by the entry on stage of Emerson Fittipaldi's brother, Wilson, and the Argentinian Carlos Reutemann at Brabham, while another Brazilian, Carlos Pace, found a drive with Frank Williams-Politoys. But the most significant event was the appearance on the Formula 1 market of a huge nonsporting concern. This was Marlboro. Using BRM as a medium they launched an ambitious publicity campaign based on motor racing and taking the form of a five-car team painted in Marlboro colors. As a sporting venture, however, the enterprise was accounted a failure; only the courage and talent of an inspired Beltoise

driving the race of his life in the pouring rain at Monaco saved the whole affair from ridicule.

The 1972 season saw the return of the calendar of the Argentine Grand Prix, held at the beginning of January on the Buenos Aires autodrome circuit. This event finished in victory for Stewart, who thus took the lead in the championship. Fittipaldi, however, had already given notice that he was a competitive force: before he abandoned the race with suspension failure he had been the only driver to keep up with the pace set by the world champion. Practice was a dramatic affair, with Carlos Reutemann, competing for the first time in a Grand Prix, recording the fastest lap. Unfortunately the wrong choice of tires ruined his chances of doing well in the race itself.

After Hulme's win in the South African Grand Prix, where Stewart was let down by his transmission when in the lead, Fittipaldi embarked on his series of four victories by taking the Spanish Grand Prix ahead of Ickx. The outcome of the race was decided just before the start when the choice of tires had to be made. The weather was unsettled, and while Ickx forecast rain, Fittipaldi predicted a dry period ahead. He was the better prophet. Stewart went off the track and the Brazilian established himself at the head of the championship table.

When you consider this season as a whole, Monaco appears as a strange interlude, an event quite outside the pattern set by the rest. Indeed the torrential rain upset the formbook completely. In normal conditions the BRM of Beltoise was in no way competitive, but at Monaco its lack of power was no handicap and the French driver took advantage of the circumstances to take the first Grand Prix victory of his long but hitherto not very lucky career. As he sailed through the flooded streets of the principality with an extraordinary sureness of touch, he outclassed all his rivals except Ickx, who was the only driver to finish on the same lap as the winner. Even Stewart was caught out and spun twice, a feat unique in his career.

But the maestro was now suffering the first symptoms of a stomach ulcer. It forced him to withdraw from the Belgian Grand Prix, held on the Nivelles circuit near Brussels. With Stewart out of the way, Fittipaldi performed a great solo recital, thus increasing his lead in the championship. Stewart soon put a curb on this by winning the French Grand Prix on his return to racing. However, the second place at Charade went to Emerson and he ended the first part of the season excellently placed with a seven-point lead over the outgoing champion. The pattern of this race was distorted by the numerous punctures caused by the stones that littered the track; they also cost the unfortunate Austrian driver, Helmut Marko, the sight of one eye.

The best race of the year was the British Grand Prix, held at Brands Hatch. It developed into an extraordinarily intense battle for victory between Fittipaldi, Stewart, and Ickx. Just as the Belgian seemed likely to emerge the winner, he was put out of the race by an oil leak. Now the sole contenders, Fittipaldi and Stewart, took turns as the leader, until in the end the Lotus led the Tyrrell across the finishing line by 4.1s. It was on this day that the Brazilian proved himself worthy of wearing the world champion's crown for there are few drivers who can boast of having beaten Jackie Stewart, if not on exactly equal terms (the Tyrrell appeared to be a less effective weapon than the Lotus) then at least in a perfectly systematic way.

Jacky Ickx is always a strong contestant at the Nur-

240

burgring, and it was there, a fortnight later, that he took his revenge for Brands Hatch. It was to be his only win of the season. Though neither Fittipaldi nor Stewart finished the Nurburgring race, by way of contrast they were the chief protagonists in the Austrian Grand Prix, where Jackie was trying out the new 005 which until then had been run only in practice sessions. Like the Lotus, this machine had been designed to have suspended front brakes, but they were abandoned at Zeltweg because they were still not working properly. Stewart went into the lead but the handling of his car deteriorated rapidly, and Fittipaldi eventually won after a hard struggle with Hulme. At this stage in the proceedings all the Brazilian needed to secure the title was a fourth place in one of the three remaining championship rounds.

He did much better than this: immediately after the Austrian victory he took first place in the Italian Grand Prix. Stewart, alongside him, had clutch failure on the starting line. So it was all over. At the age of 25 1/2, Emerson Fittipaldi took his place as Juan Manuel Fangio's successor in South American hearts. It was in vain that the end of the season was characterized by the complete resurrection of Stewart, the overwhelming victor both in Canada and the U.S. The title had changed hands.

1973

stewart's final triumph

During the close season a significant move was made when Team Lotus-JPS passed into the Goodyear camp alongside Tyrrell. This restored the effectiveness of Colin Chapman's cars which, at the end of 1972, had seemed to be outclassed by the Tyrrell 005. It was only a temporary handicap, however, caused by the defection of their tire contractor, whose directors had suddenly cut off supplies to the competition department.

Besides this change, Lotus had successfully negotiated a most important transfer in securing the services of the great Swedish hope, Ronnie Peterson, to run as Fittipaldi's teammate. Peterson hadn't yet managed to achieve the results in Formula 1 that his talents deserved, but everyone knew that all he needed for success was a very competitive car. Now he had one.

Nevertheless, the fight for the title in 1973 was, as it had been in 1972, essentially an affair between Fittipaldi and Stewart, and also of course between Elf-Tyrrell and Team Lotus-JPS. Still, the Yardley-McLaren team and their drivers, Hulme, Revson, and Jody Scheckter, the discovery of the year, succeeded in putting themselves on a level with the two leading teams.

This season was the longest in the whole history of Formula 1, with an unprecedented calendar of 15 events. It fell into four distinct phases. First, Fittipaldi built up a considerable lead and seemed well on his way to retaining the title after scoring three victories in the first four rounds. He won by a whisker in the Argentine at the end of a thrilling scrap which saw him pitted against Stewart and Cevert; majestically in Brazil before the admiring eyes of his tens of thousands of fans; with great application in Spain, where he was far from being the fastest on the track (beset as he was by insoluble tuning problems), but where he profited from his opponents' difficulties and had a rare stroke of luck in being able to run for nearly one-third of the distance with a punctured tire without losing his place as leader.

At this stage, however, Team Lotus experienced a noticeable falling off in the effectiveness of their performance, and Stewart, capitalizing on their misfortune, caught up with his rival. Jackie had already won the South African Grand Prix and went on to victory in the Belgian (which was the first of the three doubles that the Elf-Tyrrell team was to achieve in the 1973 season) and Monaco events. Then, following a period in which neither of the unlucky pair succeeded in making a decisive move forward, a period turned to good account by Hulme in Sweden, Peterson in France (his first Grand Prix victory), and Revson in England, the stalemate ended during practice for the Dutch Grand Prix, when Fittipaldi had an accident and injured his ankle. Despite his brave efforts, he was unable to defend his position in the race. Stewart won, ahead of Cevert, and confirmed his success a week later at the Nurburgring, again ahead of his teammate, where the Brazilian fell victim to fuel injection failure.

After that, victory eluded both Fittipaldi and Stewart. But the decisive moment for the championship came, as in the previous year, with the Italian Grand Prix. The Scot, thanks to a fourth place taken in heroic style, despite a stop for a puncture, and following a thrilling climb through the field, put himself out of reach in the table. So he won his third world title. Before this, his success in the German Grand prix had given him his 27th Grand Prix win, making him the driver with the greatest number of victories to his credit in the history of Formula 1, Clark having scored 25 and Fangio 24. As it turned out, Jackie Stewart had made up his mind as early as April to retire at the end of the 1973 season-whatever the outcome. It is a matter for rejoicing that this great champion, whose influence dominated the whole of the period following Jim Clark's death, should have achieved this final triumph, set this prodigious record, and retired from racing in full glory, still at the peak of his form and the master of his art.

The last part of the 1973 season belonged to Ronnie Peterson, who made his mark as the quickest driver of the year (he recorded fastest practice lap no fewer than nine times). Already overshadowed by the fatal accident to the young English hope, Williamson, at Zandvoort, the season had a tragic epilogue when François Cevert was killed in practice for the U.S. Grand Prix. The French driver had taken second place six times in

1973, and there was every indication that he was ready to take his place as Stewart's successor at the head of the Elf-Tyrrell team.

This very handsome young man, known as Prince Charming, had that rare quality of arousing spontaneous affection and understanding, which he never subsequently betrayed. He was the last person one might have expected to die on the track; he was so skillful and assured, so much the personification of well-being and zest for life.

The U.S. event should have been the 100th Grand Prix of Jackie Stewart's career but, overcome by their misfortune, the Elf-Tyrrell team withdrew from the race. Jackie, in civvies, accompanied by his wife, Helen, appeared on the starting grid where those who had been his rivals were getting ready to slide into their single-seaters. He greeted them all. A fortnight later the world was told that his greeting had in fact been a farewell.

So the Stewart era came to its close and another age began. Already we wonder who will be the new enchanter and what the future will hold for Formula 1. All one can say is that beyond the controversies and jealousies inseparable from human affairs, and therefore from motor racing as well, that in spite of the tragedies that shock and appal, there exists in these young men an enthusiasm too powerful to be destroyed. They are not simply driven by ambition or a lively competitive spirit, nor compelled to such a way of life by aggressive and suicidal tendencies, though they are all well aware of the risks involved; no, they are motivated by a conscious desire to live faster, more fully and — why not? — more dangerously than the common run of men. There is nothing arrogant or futile in this philosophy. Indeed, it embodies the most perfect assertion of a man's freedom to choose his own destiny, without doubt an increasingly challenged freedom. But strip a man of this freedom and what is he?

épilogue

This book has taken the technical revolution of 1959-1960 as its starting point. In 1974 the conception of the Formula 1 car is still fundamentally a legacy from the Coopers of that era. We have passed through a highly productive development period and we have witnessed the appearance of many great improvements on the technical side. The monocoque or semi-monocoque chassis has taken over from the multitubular space frame. The specific power of the engine has gone up from little more than 100 to nearly 150 (bhp/litre) with increased speed ranges, the general adoption of four valves per cylinder, and the widespread use of fuel injection and transistorized ignition systems. Tire technology has made lightning progress and has led to important modifications in suspension layout. These days, tires no longer have tubes, they are run at very low pressures, as a rule they are made of synthetic compounds rather than rubber, and their shape has changed completely, their width now being much greater than their radial depth. The main reason why the four-wheel drive experiment has been shelved for the time being is the increased efficiency of tires; another reason is the advance made in the aerodynamic field with the use of wings and fins. There has been a tendency to move such essential components as the radiator and front brakes from their usual positions in an effort to reduce as far as possible all excess overhang and unsprung weight. In terms of performance on the track, the effect of these changes is as follows: the average speed of the Italian Grand Prix at Monza increased from 124.4 mph in 1959 to more than 151 mph in 1970; at the Nurburgring it went up from about 80 mph in 1959 to over 117 mph in 1973, in spite of the chicane constructed in front of the stands. This represents an improvement of 40 % plus in ten years. The above examples substantiate the fact that not only the engine has progressed (though it takes most

of the credit on the fast Italian circuit), but an advance has been made with the car as a whole. These examples provide a spectacular illustration of how much the overall performance of the Formula 1 car has improved in fifteen years.

So, what would be a reasonable forecast for the not too distant future? A revolution comparable to the one that occurred in 1959-1960? Probably not, unless they decide to change the current regulations completely. However, a new factor outside racing threatens to cause an upheaval sooner or later, and that is antipollution legislation. These measures are expected to become ever more stringent and may well end in revolutionizing the type of engine used in mass-production cars. If, as some envisage, the piston engine (alternating and rotary as well) is condemned to an early death in consequence, then it is likely that competition engineering will have to fall into line. As for what could take the place of the conventional engine, one answer at the moment is the turbine, since it can be made to comply with governmental antipollution demands.

The turbine has already been seen at work on the racetrack-installed in the Lotus 56 and the Paxton Turbo, and it only just missed winning the Indianapolis 500-mile race. In addition there have been the Rovers at Le Mans, and in Formula 1 Lotus entered their modified Pratt and Whitney turbine-engined 56 for various of the 1971 Grands Prix. It was unsuccessful but there were several reasons for this. The main reason was that the engine had been in no way prepared for racing because its manufacturers were not interested in competition. But we cannot discount the possibility that before the seventies are out the whistle of the turbine will be heard on the track instead of that old familiar throb.

The energy crisis also threatens to have consequences for the future of Formula 1. The wish to economize on fuel, which will affect the design of production cars in the years to come, will perhaps have repercussions on the choice of the next formula. With this in mind, what are the chances of having a lower capacity limit as in 1961? Not very great while racing cars and production machines follow increasingly divergent paths, but nevertheless it is still possible.

We have already seen, in the way Grands Prix are now organized, the acceptance of a trend to promote racing as a spectacle. The most notable effect of this is a considerable reduction in the length of events. Because of safety requirements, a factor that effectively entered the picture toward the end of the sixties, many far-reaching alterations have been made to the circuits, and there are more to come.

Judging by past experience, this is bound to give rise to serious problems. At the moment, because Formula 1 is dithering between the spectacular and the traditional (i.e., a supreme sporting/technical exercise linked to the concept of progress as applied to automotive engineering in general), there is a danger that the situation will end in deadlock. In fact, the safety imperative and the idea of a road circuit pull in opposite directions. Undoubtedly it is the enormous increase in tire adhesion, resulting from recent technological developments, that has made it necessary to provide very wide verges at corners and to push the public well back from the edge of the track, sometimes to a point that is barely acceptable. The use of these tires has also modified driving technique in that they facilitate greater accuracy of line, thus making the spectacle less satisfying in the eyes of the public at large. From this point of view, a reduction in tire width would be nothing if not beneficial. The consequent reduction in adhesion would affect the handling of the cars, and drivers would have to approach and cope with difficulties more slowly so that the results of going off the road would therefore become less serious. And the public, watching from closer at hand and able to judge more easily what sort of effort the drivers were making, would get more pleasure out of the racing. But to put a brake on progress is to give Formula 1 a sideshow element, far removed from the European conception of the sport, and perhaps turn it in the direction of an Indianapolis-type formula, which holds few charms for the engineers, specialists, and informed public in Europe. Nevertheless a choice must be made and soon.

And what of the drivers? Have they changed since the days of Fangio, Hawthorn, Collins and Ascari, the champions of the fifties? Undoubtedly their job has changed. First it has become essential for them to understand the art of chassis tuning; these days not even the most gifted and daring of drivers has a chance of winning a Grand Prix if he can't define the perfect setup for his car for each circuit. Then there are more members of the elite than there used to be, a natural enough development considering the way motor sport as a whole has grown. This has had two main consequences: it has lowered the average age of the Formula 1 drivers and increased competitiveness. The dilettante driver has disappeared from the sport at this level and the exception that those first super-professionals, Fangio and Moss, represented has now become the rule for any candidate for the post of second or third driver in a Formula 1 team.

Finally, the almost total domination that English-speaking drivers exercised with Formula 1 from the beginning of the sixties has, since 1970, been widely challenged, if not in quality then at least in quantity. It was then that Rindt put an end to their uninterrupted (since 1959) series of victories in the world championship. Moreover, second place that year went to a Belgian and third place to a Swiss, and during the whole season only Stewart and Brabham of the En-glish speakers managed to take a Grand Prix. By contrast, no non-English speaker was listed in the first ten in the championship in 1962 for example, while in the following year the ten Grands Prix that made up the season belonged exclusively to the British: Clark, Hill, and Surtees.

Further proof of this phenomenal change lies in the fact since 1971 Team Lotus has called on the services of one Brazilian driver, two Swedes, and a Belgian (for 1974) while employing only one Anglo-Saxon (Dave Walker in 1972). Equally striking in this respect is the composition, since 1971, of the hitherto indelibly British team of BRM. Although they may have had two English-speaking drivers on their books during this period, they have also had a Mexican, two Swiss, a Frenchman, and an Austrian — and for 1974 all their three drivers are French.

There seems to be no stopping the trend. Now that Jackie Stewart has retired, the established stars, apart from Hulme, are either Scandinavians, continental Europeans or South Americans. However, two serious contenders might, given their performance in 1973, be equal to the task relinquished by Jackie Stewart: they are James Hunt, an Englishman, and Jody Scheckter, a South African.

On the other hand, Formula 1 remains undeniably dominated by the British as constructors, whether of engines (the Cosworth-Ford took the first three places in all the 1973 Grands Prix) or of chassis. Lotus have more than 50 Grand Prix victories to their credit, a record that no one else comes near to beating.

The most profound change that has overtaken Formula 1, however, probably lies in the realm of finance, a change characterized by the increasingly obvious and spectacular hold that nonsporting concerns have on teams and even organizing bodies. The epic era of cars bearing their national colors has almost run its course. Now the multinational corporations hold the purse strings and they call the tune. After having the cars painted in their proprietary colors, they are now baptizing them in the name of their company, an ancient custom in the United States but a revolutionary concept in Europe. As a result money has flowed into the coffers and the level of competition has been given a boost. Consequently it is a turn of events to be welcomed, and though it may have gone against tradition, upset certain purists, and been accompanied by some measure of regrettable excess, it has nevertheless been to the advantage of Formula 1, which emerges from this 15-year period in a stronger position than ever.

Of course, like any organism forced into rapid growth, Formula 1 is subject to crises that are sometimes violent, and the disputes between the ruling bodies, the constructors, and the drivers are tending to get sharper. A situation of semi-permanent conflict exists between the directors of the sport, who realize that they are openly challenged and who try to adapt to the modern way of life, and the competitors, who are mindful of safety and profitability and who demand that the business be directed with a professionalism equal to their own. Are we moving towards a breakdown in relations? A rupture of this kind could be very serious. If Formula 1 wishes to preserve its magic quality, it must retain a balance between its value both as a sport and as an entertainment. Obviously, though it may no longer be a hobby it must not turn into a circus. There are no regrets in closing the chapter on modern Formula 1 at this point. The Formula 1 of the future will be even more exciting than it has been in the past.

Year	Argentina	Brazil	South Africa	Spain	Monaco	Belgium	Holland
1959					Brabham (Cooper-Climax) 66.7 mile/h		Bonnier (B.R.M.) 93.5 mile/h Zandvoort
1960					Moss (Lotus-Climax) 67.4 mile/h	Brabham (Cooper-Climax) 133.6 mile/h Spa-Francorchamps	Brabham (Cooper-Climax) 96.3 mile/h Zandvoort
1961			Clark (Lotus-Climax) 92.1 mile/h East London		Moss (Lotus-Climax) 70.7 mile/h	Phil Hill (Ferrari) 128.1 mile/h Spa-Francorchamps	Von Trips (Ferrari) 96.2 mile/h Zandvoort
1962			G. Hill (B.R.M.) 93.6 mile/h East London		McLaren (Cooper-Climax) 70.4 mile/h	Clark (Lotus-Climax) 131.9 mile/h Spa-Francorchamps	G. Hill (B.R.M.) 95.4 mile/h Zandvoort
1963			Clark (Lotus-Climax) 95.1 mile/h East London		G. Hill (B.R.M.) 72.4 mile/h	Clark (Lotus-Climax) 114.1 mile/h Spa-Francorchamps	Clark (Lotus-Climax) 97.5 mile/h Zandvoort
1964					G. Hill (B.R.M.) 72.6 mile/h	Clark (Lotus-Climax) 132.8 mile/h Spa-Francorchamps	Clark (Lotus-Climax) 98.0 mile/h Zandvoort
1965			Clark (Lotus-Climax) 97.9 mile/h East London		G. Hill (B.R.M.) 74.3 mile/h	Clark (Lotus-Climax) 117.2 mile/h Spa-Francorchamps	Clark (Lotus-Climax) 100.8 mile/h Zandvoort
1966					Stewart (B.R.M.) 76.5 mile/h		Brabham (Brabham-Repco) 100.0 mile/h Zandvoort
1967			Rodriguez (Cooper-Maserati) 97.1 mile/h Kyalami		Hulme (Brabham-Repco) 75.9 mile/h	Gurney (Eagle-Weslake) 145.9 mile/h Spa-Francorchamps	Clark (Lotus-Ford) 103.4 mile/h Zandvoort
1968			Clark (Lotus-Ford) 107.4 mile/h Kyalami	G. Hill (Lotus-Ford) 84.4 mile/h Jarama	G. Hill (Lotus-Ford) 77.8 mile/h	McLaren (McLaren-Ford) 147.1 mile/h Spa-Francorchamps	Stewart (Matra-Ford) 84.6 mile/h Zandvoort
1969			Stewart (Matra-Ford) 110.6 mile/h Kyalami	Stewart (Matra-Ford) 92.9 mile/h Montjuich	G. Hill (Lotus-Ford) 80.1 mile/h		Stewart (Matra-Ford) 111.0 mile/h Zandvoort
1970			Brabham (Brabham-Ford) 111.7 mile/h Kyalami	Stewart (March-Ford) 87.2 mile/h Jarama	Rindt (Lotus-Ford) 81.8 mile/h	Rodriguez (B.R.M.) 149.9 mile/h Spa-Francorchamps	Rindt (Lotus-Ford) 112.9 mile/h Zandvoort
1971			Andretti (Ferrari) 112.4 mile/h Kyalami	Stewart (Tyrrell-Ford) 97.2 mile/h Montjuich	Stewart (Tyrrell-Ford) 83.5 mile/h		Ickx (Ferrari) 94.0 mile/h Zandvoort
1972	Stewart (Tyrrell-Ford) 100.325 mile/h Buenos Aires		Hulme (McLaren-Ford) 114.23 mile/h Kyalami	Fittipaldi (J.P.S. Ford 72D) 92.35 mile/h Jarama	Beltoise (B.R.M. P 160B) 63.85 mile/h	Fittipaldi (J.P.S. Ford 72D) 113.35 mile/h Nivelles	
1973	Fittipaldi (J.P.S. Ford 72D) 102.94 mile/h Buenos Aires	Fittipaldi (J.P.S. Ford 72D) 114.25 mile/h São Paulo	Stewart (Tyrrell-Ford) 117.145 mile/h Kyalami	Fittipaldi (J.P.S. Ford 72D 97.86 mile/h Montjuich	Stewart (Tyrrell-Ford) 80.966 mile/h	Stewart (Tyrrell-Ford) 107.74 mile/h Zolder	Stewart (Tyrrell-Ford) 114.36 mile/h Zandvoort

(Sweden)	France	Britain	Germany	Austria	Italy	Canada	U.S.A.	Mexico	Portugal
	Brooks (Ferrari) 127.5 mile/h Reims	Brabham (Cooper-Climax) 89.80 mile/h Aintree			Moss (Cooper-Climax) 124.4 mile/h Monza		McLaren (Cooper-Climax) 98.8 mile/h Sebring		Moss (Cooper-Climax) 95.2 mile/h
	Brabham (Cooper-Climax) 131.8 mile/h Reims	Brabham (Cooper-Climax) 108.6 mile/h Silverstone			Phil Hill (Ferrari) 132.1 mile/h Monza		Moss (Lotus-Climax) 99.0 mile/h Riverside		Brabham (Cooper-Climax) 109.2 mile/h
	Baghetti (Ferrari) 119.8 mile/h Reims	Von Trips (Ferrari) 83.9 mile/h Aintree	Moss (Lotus-Climax) 92.3 mile/h Nurburgring		Phil Hill (Ferrari) 130.0 mile/h Monza		Ireland (Lotus-Climax) 103.1 mile/h Watkins Glen		
	Gurney (Porsche) 101.9 mile/h Rouen	Clark (Lotus-Climax) 92.2 mile/h Aintree	G. Hill (B.R.M.) 80.7 mile/h Nurburgring		G. Hill B.R.M. 123.6 mile/h Monza		Clark (Lotus-Climax) 108.6 mile/h Watkins Glen		
	Clark (Lotus-Climax) 125.3 mile/h Reims	Clark (Lotus-Climax) 107.1 mile/h Silverstone	Surtees (Ferrari) 95.8 mile/h Nurburgring		Clark (Lotus-Climax) 127.7 mile/h Monza		G. Hill (B.R.M.) 109.9 mile/h Watkins Glen	Clark (Lotus-Climax) 93.3 mile/h	
	Gurney (Brabham-Climax) 108.7 mile/h Rouen	Clark (Lotus-Climax) 94.1 mile/h Brands Hatch	Surtees (Ferrari) 96.6 mile/h Nurburgring	Bandini (Ferrari) 99.2 mile/h Zeltweg	Surtees (Ferrari) 127.8 mile/h Monza		G. Hill (B.R.M.) 111.1 mile/h Watkins Glen	Gurney (Brabham-Climax) 93.3 mile/h	
	Clark (Lotus-Climax) 89.2 mile/h Charade	Clark (Lotus-Climax) 112.0 mile/h Silverstone	Clark (Lotus-Climax) 99.8 mile/h Nurburgring		Stewart (B.R.M.) 130.4 mile/h Monza		G. Hill (B.R.M.) 107.9 mile/h Watkins Glen	Ginther (Honda) 94.3 mile/h	
	Brabham (Brabham-Repco) 136.9 mile/h Reims	Brabham (Brabham-Repco) 95.4 mile/h Brands Hatch	Brabham (Brabham-Repco) 86.7 mile/h Nurburgring		Scarfiotti (Ferrari) 135.9 mile/h Monza		Clark (Lotus-B.R.M.) 114.9 mile/h Watkins Glen	Surtees (Cooper-Maserati) 95.7 mile/h	
	Brabham (Brabham-Repco) 98.9 mile/h Bugatti-Le Mans	Clark (Lotus-Ford) 117.6 mile/h Silverstone	Hulme (Brabham-Repco) 101.4 mile/h Nurburgring		Surtees (Honda) 140.5 mile/h Monza	Brabham (Brabham-Repco) 82.6 mile/h Mosport	Clark (Lotus-Ford) 120.9 mile/h Watkins Glen	Clark (Lotus-Ford) 101.4 mile/h	
	Ickx (Ferrari) 100.4 mile/h Rouen	Siffert (Lotus-Ford) 104.8 mile/h Brands Hatch	Stewart (Matra-Ford) 86.8 mile/h Nurburgring		Hulme (McLaren-Ford) 145.4 mile/h Monza	Hulme (McLaren-Ford) 97.2 mile/h Mont Tremblant	Stewart (Matra-Ford) 124.8 mile/h Watkins Glen	G. Hill (Lotus-Ford) 103.8 mile/h	
	Stewart (Matra-Ford) 99.50 mile/h Charade	Stewart (Matra-Ford) 127.2 mile/h Silverstone	Ickx (Brabham-Ford) 108.4 mile/h Nurburgring		Stewart (Matra-Ford) 146.9 mile/h Monza	Ickx (Brabham-Ford) 112.7 mile/h Mosport	Rindt (Lotus-Ford) 126.3 mile/h Watkins Glen	Hulme (McLaren-Ford) 106.6 mile/h	
	Rindt (Lotus-Ford) 98.4 mile/h Charade	Rindt (Lotus-Ford) 108.6 mile/h Brands Hatch	Rindt (Lotus-Ford) 123.9 mile/h Nurburgring	Ickx (Ferrari) 129.27 mile/h Österreichring	Regazzoni (Ferrari) 150.8 mile/h Monza	Ickx (Ferrari) 101.2 mile/h Mont Tremblant	Fittipaldi (Lotus-Ford) 126.0 mile/h Watkins Glen	Ickx (Ferrari) 106.7 mile/h	
	Stewart (Tyrrell-Ford) 111.6 mile/h Paul Ricard	Stewart (Tyrrell-Ford) 130.5 mile/h Silverstone	Stewart (Tyrrell-Ford) 114.4 mile/h Nurburgring	Siffert (B.R.M.) 132.3 mile/h Österreichring	Gethin (B.R.M.) 150.7 mile/h Monza	Stewart (Tyrrell-Ford) 81.9 mile/h Mosport	Cevert (Tyrrell-Ford) 115.1 mile/h New Layout		
	Stewart (Tyrrell-Ford) 101.56 mile/h Clermont Ferrand	Fittipaldi (J.P.S. Ford 72D) 112.06 mile/h Brands Hatch	Ickx (Ferrari 312-B2) 116.63 mile/h Nurburgring	Fittipaldi (J.P.S. Ford 72D) 113.32 mile/h Österreichring	Fittipaldi (J.P.S. Ford 72D) 131.61 mile/h Monza	Stewart (Tyrrell-Ford) 114.282 mile/h Mosport	Stewart (Tyrrell-Ford) 115.092 mile/h Watkins Glen		
Hulme (McLaren-Ford) 02.65 mile/h ...nderstorp	Peterson (J.P.S. Ford 72D) 115.117 mile/h Paul Ricard	Revson (McLaren-Ford) 131.75 mile/h Silverstone	Stewart (Tyrrell-Ford) 116.82 mile/h Nurburgring	Peterson (J.P.S. Ford 72D) 133.50 mile/h Österreichring	Peterson (J.P.S. Ford 72D) 132.631 mile/h Monza	Revson (McLaren-Ford) 99.130 mile/h	Peterson (J.P.S. Ford 72D) 118.00 mile/h approx.		

Results of the Drivers Worl[d]

	1959	1960	1961	1962	1963	1964	1965
1	Brabham Cooper-Climax	Brabham Cooper-Climax	Phil Hill Ferrari	G. Hill B.R.M.	Clark Lotus-Climax	Surtees Ferrari	Clark Lotus-Climax
2	Brooks Ferrari	McLaren Cooper-Climax	Von Trips Ferrari	Clark Lotus-Climax	G. Hill B.R.M.	G. Hill B.R.M.	G. Hill B.R.M.
3	Moss Cooper-Climax B.R.M.	Moss Lotus-Climax	Gurney Porsche Moss Lotus-Climax	McLaren Cooper-Climax	Ginther B.R.M.	Clark Lotus-Climax	Stewart B.R.M.
4	Phil Hill Ferrari	Ireland Lotus-Climax		Surtees Lola-Climax	Surtees Ferrari	Bandini Ferrari Ginther B.R.M.	Gurney Brabham-Clima[x]
5	Trintignant Cooper-Climax	Phil Hill Ferrari	Ginther Ferrari	Gurney Porsche	Gurney Brabham-Climax		Surtees Ferrari
6	McLaren Cooper-Climax	Von Trips Ferrari Gendebien Cooper	Ireland Lotus-Climax	Phil Hill Ferrari	McLaren Cooper-Climax	Gurney Brabham-Climax	Bandini Ferrari
7	Gurney Ferrari		Clark Lotus-Climax McLaren Cooper-Climax	Maggs Cooper-Climax	Brabham Brabham-Climax	McLaren Cooper-Climax	Ginther Honda
8	Bonnier B.R.M. Gregory Cooper-Climax	Ginther Ferrari Clark Lotus Rathmann Ken Paul		Ginther B.R.M.	Maggs Cooper-Climax	Arundell Lotus-Climax Brabham Brabham-Climax	Spence Lotus-Climax McLaren Cooper-Climax
9			Baghetti Ferrari	Brabham Lotus-Climax Brabham-Climax	Bonnier Cooper-Climax Ireland B.R.P.-B.R.M. Bandini B.R.M.		
10	Ward Leader Card 500		Brooks B.R.M.	T. Taylor Lotus-Climax		Siffert Brabham-B.R.M.	Brabham Brabham-Clima[x]

1966	1967	1968	1969	1970	1971	1972	1973
abham abham-Repco	Hulme Brabham-Repco	G. Hill Lotus-Ford	Stewart Matra-Ford	Rindt Lotus-Ford	Stewart Tyrrell-Ford	Fittipaldi J.P.S. Ford 72D	Stewart Tyrrell-Ford
rtees oper-Maserati	Brabham Brabham-Repco	Stewart Matra-Ford	Ickx Brabham-Ford	Ickx Ferrari	Peterson March-Ford	Stewart Tyrrell-Ford	Fittipaldi J.P.S. Ford 72D
ndt oper-Maserati	Clark Lotus-Ford	Hulme McLaren-Ford	McLaren McLaren-Ford	Regazzoni Ferrari	Cevert Tyrrell-Ford	Hulme McLaren-Ford	Peterson J.P.S. Ford 72
ulme abham-Repco	Amon Ferrari Surtees Honda	Ickx Ferrari	Rindt Lotus-Ford	Hulme McLaren-Ford	Ickx Ferrari Siffert B.R.M.	Ickx Ferrari 312-B2	Cevert Tyrrell-Ford
Hill R.M.		McLaren McLaren-Ford	Beltoise Matra-Ford Hulme McLaren-Ford	Brabham Brabham-Ford Stewart March-Ford		Revson McLaren-Ford	Revson McLaren-Ford
ark otus-Climax otus-B.R.M.	G. Hill Lotus-Ford Rodriguez Cooper-Maserati	Rodriguez B.R.M.			Fittipaldi Lotus-Ford	Ragazzoni Ferrari 312-B2 Cevert Tyrrell-Ford	Hulme McLaren-Ford
tewart R.M.		Siffert Lotus-Ford Surtees Honda	G. Hill Lotus-Ford	Amon March-Ford Rodriguez B.R.M.	Regazzoni Ferrari		Reutermann Brabham BT42
andini-Parkes errari	Gurney Eagle-Weslake		Courage Brabham-Ford		Andretti Ferrari	Hailwood Surtees-Ford	Hunt March-Ford 731G
	Stewart B.R.M.	Beltoise Matra-Simca Matra-Ford	Siffert Lotus-Ford	Beltoise Matra-Simca	Amon Matra-Simca Gethin B.R.M. Rodriguez B.R.M.	Amon Matra-Simca Peterson March-Ford 721	Ickx Ferrari 312-B2
carfiotti errari	Spence B.R.M.	Amon Ferrari	Brabham Brabham-Ford	Fittipaldi Lotus-Ford	Hulme McLaren-Ford Wisell Lotus-Ford		Beltoise B.R.M. P 160B

Information compiled by *Motoring News*